Rich Dad's

Retire Young Retire Rich

How to Get Rich and Stay Rich Forever

Rich Dad's™ *Classics*

#1 *New York Times,* #1 *Wall Street Journal,*
#1 *Business Week,* #1 *Publishers Weekly,* as well as a
San Francisco Chronicle and *USA Today* bestseller.
Also featured on the bestseller lists of
Amazon.com, Amazon.com UK and Germany,
E-trade.com, Sydney Morning Herald (Australia),
Sun Herald (Australia), *Business Review Weekly*
(Australia), *Borders Books and Music* (U.S. and
Singapore), *Barnes & Noble.com.*

Wall Street Journal, New York Times Business
and *Business Week* bestseller.
Also featured on the bestseller lists of the
Sydney Morning Herald (Australia), *Sun*
Herald (Australia), *Business Review Weekly*
(Australia), *Amazon.com, Barnes &*
Noble.com, Borders Books and Music
(U.S. and Singapore).

USA Today, Wall Street Journal, New York Times
Business, Business Week and *Publishers Weekly*
bestseller.

Wall Street Journal, New York Times,
and USA Today bestseller.

Rich Dad's Advisors™ Series

Rich Dad said,
"Business and Investing is a team sport."

Each of us has a million dollar idea in our head. The first step in turning your idea into millions, maybe even billions of dollars is to protect that idea. Michael Lechter is an internationally known Intellectual Property attorney who is Robert Kiyosaki's legal advisor on all his intellectual property matters. His book is simply written and is an important addition to any business person's library.

Loopholes of the Rich is for the aspiring as well as the advanced business owner who is looking for better and smarter ways to legally pay less tax and protect their assets. It gives real solutions that will be easy to apply for your unique situation. Diane Kennedy offers over 20 years in research, application and creation of innovative tax solutions and is Robert Kiyosaki's personal and corporate tax strategist.

Your most important skill in business is your ability to communicate and sell! *SalesDogs*™ is a highly educational, inspirational and somewhat "irreverent" look at the world of sales, communications and the different characters that occupy that world. All of us sell in one way or another. It is important for you to find your own unique style. Blair is respected internationally as an extraordinary trainer, speaker and consultant in the field of sales, communication and management.

Rich Dad's Advisors™ Series

Dolf de Roos is a real estate investor, who bought his first property as an undergraduate student. After completing eight years of university education and earning a Ph.D. in Electrical Engineering, he was offered a job at $32,000 per year. The week before, he had completed a real estate deal worth $35,000. Consequently, he didn't accept the job, and to this day, has never had one. Dolf willingly shares his enthusiasm for real estate, and has "rattled cages" in audiences in over 16 countries. He passionately believes that the "Deal of the Decade" comes along about once a week.

Own Your Own Corporation reveals the legal secrets and strategies that the rich have used for generations to run their businesses and protect their assets. Written in a clear and easily understandable style, *Own Your Own Corporation* provides the necessary knowledge to save thousands of dollars in taxes and protect your family assets from the attacks of creditors.

Rich Dad's

Retire Young Retire Rich

How to Get Rich and Stay Rich Forever

By Robert T. Kiyosaki with Sharon L. Lechter, C.P.A.

The Authors of *Rich Dad Poor Dad*

WARNER BUSINESS BOOKS™

Published by Warner Books

An AOL Time Warner Company

Although based on a true story, certain events in the book have been fictionalized for educational content and impact.

Warner Books Edition

Published by Warner Books in association with CASHFLOW Technologies, Inc.

Warner Business Books are published by Warner Books, Inc.,
1271 Avenue of the Americas, New York, NY 10020

Visit our Web site at www.twbookmark.com

An AOL Time Warner Company

Printed in the United States of America

First Printing: January 2002
10 9 8 7 6 5 4 3 2 1

Special Edition ISBN: 0-446-53083-2
Special Limited Edition ISBN: 0-446-53082-4

Designed by imagesupport.com, llc

Authors' Note

This book was completed six months before the tragic events of September 11, 2001. Nonetheless, the information in this book is more important *now* than ever before.

During these uncertain times, your financial education becomes even more valuable.

If you're tired of the same old investment advice—such as "be patient," "invest for the long term," and "diversify"—then this book is for you.

This book is dedicated to all people who have gone before us . . .
people who have made all of our lives better and more abundant today

Contents

Introduction:

Why David Met Goliath

David and Goliath was one of rich dad's favorite stories. I suspect he may have seen himself as David, a man who started with nothing, yet rose to compete against the giants of business. Rich dad said, "David could beat Goliath because David knew how to use the power of leverage. A young boy and a simple slingshot were far more powerful than the feared giant, Goliath. That is the power of leverage."

My previous books were on the power of cash flow. Rich dad said, "*Cash flow* is the most important word in the world of money. The second most important word is *leverage.*" He also said, "Leverage is the reason some people become rich and others do not become rich." Rich dad went on to explain that leverage was power and that power can work in your favor or against you. Because leverage is power, some use it, some abuse it, and others fear it. He said, "The reason less than 5 percent of all Americans are rich is because only 5 percent know how to *use* the power of leverage. Many who want to become rich, fail to become rich because they *abuse* the power. And most people do not become rich because they *fear* the power of leverage."

There Are Many Forms of Leverage

Leverage comes in many forms. One of the recognized forms of leverage is the leverage of borrowing money. Today we are aware of the severe problem of people abusing this powerful form of leverage. Millions of people struggle financially because the power of debt leverage is used against them. Because of the consequences of the *abuse* of debt leverage, many people now *fear* this form of leverage, saying, "Cut up your credit cards, pay off your mortgage, and get out of debt." My rich dad would chuckle and say, "Cutting up your credit cards won't make you rich. Cutting up my credit cards only makes me miserable." Nonetheless, rich dad agreed that if you were abusive with the power of debt leverage, you definitely should cut up your credit cards, pay off your mortgage, and get out of debt. He said, "Giving a credit card to some people is like giving a loaded gun to a drunk. Anyone who is near the drunk is in danger, including the drunk." Instead of teaching us to fear the power of debt leverage, rich dad taught his son and me how to *use* the power of debt leverage in our favor. That is why he often said, "There is good debt and bad debt. Good debt makes you rich and bad debt makes you poor." Most people are loaded down with bad debt and many others live in fear of debt and are proud to be debt free . . . even to the point of being free of any good debt. In this book, you will find out how my wife, Kim, and I retired young and retired rich because we were deeply in debt, deeply in debt with good debt, debt that made us rich and financially free. In other words, we *used* the power of leverage, we did not *abuse* the power, nor do we live in *fear* of its power. Instead we *respect* the power of leverage and use it wisely and cautiously.

Can Everyone Be Rich?

During the hundreds of interviews I have given after the release of the first Rich Dad book I am asked this question: "Do you think everyone can be rich?"

I reply, "Yes. I believe everyone has the potential to be rich."

At that point, I am often asked, "If everyone has the potential to be rich, why do so few actually become rich?"

My usual reply is, "I don't have the time today to answer that question." If they insist, I may say, "Many of the answers are found in my first four books in the Rich Dad series."

If the interviewer is persistent they may ask something like, "When will you give us all the answers?"

I reply, "I don't know if anyone has all the answers."

Even though I do not have all the answers, I am very happy to be finally bringing this book, book number five in the Rich Dad series, to you. This book will definitely explain why I believe all of us already have the power and the potential to be very rich . . . and I do mean all of us, not just some of us. It will also explain how my wife, Kim, and I could retire young and retire rich, even though we started without any money. And it will also explain why some people are rich and why others are poor even though we all have the power and the potential to be very rich and retire young. It's all a matter of leverage.

The first four books in the Rich Dad series were primarily about the power of cash flow. This book is about leverage. Why one entire book? The reason is because leverage is a very big word, encompassing and touching virtually everything in our lives. This book will focus on three important forms of leverage. They are:

SECTION I: THE LEVERAGE OF YOUR MIND

This is the most important section of the book. In this section, you will find out why money does not make you rich. In this section, you will find out that the most powerful form of leverage in the world, your mind, has the power to make you rich or make you poor. Just as someone can use, abuse, or fear the power of debt leverage, the same is true when it comes to your brain, a very powerful form of leverage.

Words Are Leverage

You will find out the power of words. Rich dad always said, "Words are leverage. Words are powerful tools . . . tools for the brain. But just as you can use debt to make you rich or poor, words can be used to make you rich or poor. In this section, you will find out about the power of words and how rich people use rich words and poor people use poor words. Rich dad often said, "Your brain can be your most powerful asset or it can be your most powerful liability. If you use the right words in your brain you will become very rich. If you use the wrong words, your brain will make you poor." In this section you will find out about rich words and poor words . . . slow words and fast words.

You will find out why rich dad said, "It does not take money to make money." He said, "Getting rich begins with your words and words are free." In *Rich Dad Poor Dad*, you may have read that rich dad forbade his son and me from saying, "I can't afford it." Rich dad said, "The difference between rich people and poor people is that poor people say 'I can't afford it' more often than rich people. That is the primary difference."

Why Investing Is Not Risky

In this book, you will find out why people who say "Investing is risky" are some of the biggest losers in the investment markets. Again it goes back to words. You will find out that what you think is real becomes your reality. You will find out why people who think investing is risky invest in the riskiest of all investments. It's caused by their reality. In this book, you will find out why investing does not have to be risky. In order to find safer, higher yielding investments, people must first begin by changing their words.

As stated earlier, the power of leverage can be used, abused, or feared. In this section, you will find out how to use the leverage of your brain in your financial favor, rather than use it against you. Rich dad said, "Most people take the most powerful leverage in the world, their brain, and use that power to make them poor. That is not the use of that power. It's abuse. Every time you say, 'I can't afford it' or 'I can't do that' or 'Investing is risky' or 'I'll never be rich,' you are using the most powerful form of leverage you have . . . using it to abuse yourself."

If you want to retire young and retire rich, you will need to use your brain in your favor, not against you. If you cannot do that, the two other sections of this book will not be possible for you, even though they are easy to do. If you can gain control over your most powerful form of leverage, the next two sections will be easy because they are easy.

SECTION II: THE LEVERAGE OF YOUR PLAN

In book number three, *Rich Dad's Guide to Investing,* I wrote that "investing was a plan." In order for Kim and me to retire young, we had to have a plan . . . a plan that started with nothing, because we had nothing. The plan had an end or an exit and it also had a time limit. Our time limit was ten years or less. It took us nine years, retiring in 1994. I was forty-seven and Kim was thirty-seven. Although we started with nothing we exited with approximately $85,000 to $120,000 a year in income, depending upon the market, without working. Our income was now coming solely from our investments. Even though it may not have been a lot of money, we were financially free because our expenses were less than $50,000 a year.

We Retired Young in Order to Get Rich

One of the advantages of retiring young is that we now had the free time to get rich. By the way, *Forbes* magazine defines rich as $1 million or more a year in income. In other words, according to *Forbes*, we were not yet rich when we retired. Knowing that, one of the reasons for retiring young was so that we would have the time to get rich. After retiring, our plan was to spend time investing and building businesses. Today, not only do we have substantial real estate holdings, we have built a publishing company, a mining company, a technology company, and an oil company, as well as investments in the stock market. As rich dad often said, "The problem with having a job is that it gets in the way of getting rich." In other words, we retired young so that we would have the time to become rich. Today, our income per year from our investments and businesses is in the millions and is climbing steadily, even after the stock market crashed. Everything is going according to plan.

In book number three, *Rich Dad's Guide to Investing,* I wrote that most people have a plan to be poor. That is why so many people say, "When I retire, my income will go down." In other words, they are saying, "I plan on working hard all my life and then I will become poorer after I retire." That may have been an okay plan in the Industrial Age, but that is a very poor plan in the Information Age.

Millions of workers are now counting on their retirement plans, plans such as a 401k, IRA, Superannuation plans of Australia, RRSP plans of Canada, and other plans to be there when they retire. These plans are what I call Information Age retirement plans. I call them that because in the Information Age, employees are now responsible for their retirement. In the Industrial Age, it was the company or the government that would take care of your financial needs once your working days were over. There is one tragic flaw in these Information Age retirement plans. The flaw is that most of these plans are indexed to the stock market, and as you may have noticed, stock markets go up and stock markets go down. It shocks me to realize that millions and millions of hardworking people are now betting their financial future and their financial security on a stock market. What will happen to these workers if, for example, they are eighty-five years old, their retirement plan is wiped out, either by depletion, theft, or market crash? Are you going to say to them, "Get a job and begin saving for retirement?" That is why I am concerned and why I write and why I teach. I believe we need to better educate and better prepare people for the Information Age, the age where we all need to know a lot more about money. The age where we all need to be more financially responsible and depend less on a company or government to take care of us when our working days are over.

Just look at the numbers. By the year 2010 the first of 75 million baby boomers will begin to retire. Over the years, let's say that each of these 75 million begins to collect just $1,000 per month from the promised government retirement plan that they have contributed to, and another $1,000 per month from the financial markets. If my math is correct, 75 million × $1,000 comes to $75 billion per month from the government program and another $75 billion from the financial markets. Seventy-five billion dollars per month coming out of the government and from the financial markets will have a dramatic impact on both institutions. What will the government do? Increase taxes? What will the financial markets do when $75 billion comes out of the market instead of going in? Advise you to "Buy and hold, invest for the long term, and de-worsify your portfolio?" Will the financial advisors continue to say, "The stock market on average has always gone up?" I don't have a crystal ball and I do not pretend to predict the future. But I can say this much. A combined $150 billion coming out of these two large institutions instead of going in will cause a few ripples in the economy.

The old plans from the old economy will cause millions of people financial hardship once their working days are over. Millions in America do not have a company retirement plan or personal retirement plan. What will they do? Look for a job? Work all their lives? Move in with their kids or grandkids? Planning to work hard all your life is a poor plan. In spite of this plan being a poor plan, millions of people have this plan, even some people who are making a lot of money today. They are working hard today but have nothing set aside for tomorrow. For many baby boomers, time, our most important asset, is running out.

Then I hear people say, "I won't need much money after I retire. My house will be debt free and my living expenses will go down." While it is true that your living expenses may go down, what goes up are your medical expenses. Already medicine, health, and dental care are too expensive for many working people. What will happen when the medical industry is faced with millions of retirees who need health care to live, but have no money to pay? And if you believe in Medicare saving you, then you probably believe in the Easter Bunny also.

Maybe this is why Alan Greenspan, chairman of the Federal Reserve Board, recently said on television, "We need to start teaching financial literacy in our schools." We need to start teaching our kids to take care of themselves financially, rather than teaching them to expect the government or the company they work for to take care of them after they retire.

If you want to retire young and retire rich, you will need a better plan than most people have. Section 2 is about the very important leverage of having a plan on how to retire young and retire rich.

SECTION III: THE LEVERAGE OF YOUR ACTIONS

There is an overused story about three birds sitting on a fence. The question is, "If two birds decide to fly away, how many birds are left?" The answer is, "Three birds are left." The lesson is, just because you decide to do something does not mean you will do what you decide to do. In the real world less than 5 percent of the U.S. population is rich because 95 percent of the population may want to be rich but only 5 percent takes any action.

In book number four, *Rich Kid Smart Kid*, I write about how our school system punishes kids for making mistakes. Yet, if you look at how we learn, we learn from our mistakes. Most of us learn to ride a bicycle only by falling off a few times. We learn to walk by falling a few times. Then we get to school and we are taught not to fall. We are taught that people who fall are stupid people. We are taught that smart people are people who sit like the three birds on the fence and memorize the right answers. It's a small wonder why only 5 percent of America's people become rich. If you look at some of the richest people in the world, people such as Bill Gates, founder of Microsoft, Michael Dell, founder of Dell Computer Corporation, Ted Turner, founder of CNN, Henry Ford, founder of Ford Motor Company, and Thomas Edison, founder of General Electric, they all did not finish school.

I am not saying that school is bad. In the Information Age, school and education are more important than ever before. I am saying that sometimes to be successful we need to learn to *not do* what we have been taught *to do*. If you want to be more successful, simply watch how kids learn and copy them. One of the things I had to learn was how to overcome the fear of making mistakes, the fear of failing, and the fear of being embarrassed. Most young kids know how to do that naturally, but then we teach them not to do it in school. If I had not been able to learn how to make mistakes, learn how to fail, learn how to overcome my embarrassment, I would not have been able to retire young and retire rich.

Three Easy Things Everyone Can Do to Become Rich

I have always said that what you have to do to become rich is simple and easy. Almost everyone can do it. I am happy to share this book because Sections 1 and 2 prepare you to do the simple things you need to do, if you want to retire young and retire rich. In Section 3, I will go into simple and easy things most of us can do to become rich. I will go into the three main assets that make people rich and allow them to retire young. The three assets are:

1. Real estate
2. Paper assets
3. Businesses

In Section 3, you will find out what you can do to begin acquiring these three vitally important assets. *The reason Kim and I could retire young and retire rich is because we spent our time acquiring assets rather than working for money.*

If you can read this book, you can do the simple action steps to begin acquiring these three important assets, the assets that the rich 5 percent of the population acquires. I promise you that you can do the action steps, but you will need to read the first two sections of this book. If you do not read the first two sections, you may not be able to do the action steps, even if they are easy to do. As rich dad said to me years ago, "Getting rich begins with the right mind-set, the right words, the right plan. After you have that, the action steps are easy."

So why did David meet Goliath? Rich dad's answer to this was, "David met Goliath so he could meet the giant inside of himself." He also said, "Inside each of us is a David and a Goliath. Many people are unsuccessful in life because they run when they meet Goliath. Without Goliath, David would never have become a giant of a man." Rich dad used this story to inspire his son and me to become financial giants. In other words, instead of killing the giant, rich dad inspired us to become giants.

This book is about becoming financially free. Kim and I achieved that freedom by acquiring or building assets . . . assets that worked hard so we did not have to work. Once we were free, we simply continued to build our portfolio of the three asset classes, which are businesses, paper assets, and real estate, into giant portfolios. We retired young and became richer and richer by using all the leverage we could to build these assets. Today those assets produce more and more income while we work less and less. If you would like to do the same, this book is for you. This book is written to assist you in finding your own financial freedom . . . freedom from the drudgery of earning a living.

In closing, David became a giant by using all the leverage he could. You can do the same. This book is about bringing out the giant in you.

Section I

The Leverage of Your Mind

The most powerful form of leverage we have is found in the power of our minds. The problem with leverage is that leverage can work in your favor or against you. If you want to retire young and retire rich, the first thing you must do is use the power of your brain to make you rich. When it comes to money, too many people use the power of their brain to make themselves poor.

As rich dad said, "One big difference between the rich and the poor is that poor people say 'I can't afford it' more often than rich people." He also said, "In Sunday School I learned 'and the word became flesh.'" Continuing on, he said, "Poor people use poor words and poor words create poor people. Your words do become flesh." In this section you will learn the difference between rich words and poor words and fast words and slow words. You will find out how to change your financial future by changing the words you use and the way you think. If you can change your words and your thoughts to those of the rich, retiring young and retiring rich will be easy.

Chapter 1

How to Become Rich and Retire Young

The following is the story of how my wife, Kim, my best friend, Larry, and I began our journey from broke, to rich, to retired in less than ten years. I tell this story to encourage any of you who may be doubtful or in need of some self-confidence to begin the journey to retiring young. When Kim and I started, we were nearly out of money, low on confidence, and filled with doubt. We all have doubts. The difference is what we do with those doubts.

The Journey Begins

In December of 1984, Kim, my best friend, Larry Clark, and I were skiing in Vancouver, British Columbia, on Whistler Mountain. The snow was very deep, the runs were long, and the skiing was excellent, although very cold. At night, the three of us sat in a little cabin that was snuggled in between tall pines, barely visible because the snow was up to the roof.

Sitting around the fire every night, we would discuss our plans for the future. We had very high hopes but very little resources. Kim and I were on our last few dollars and Larry was in the process of building another business. Our discussions ran late into the night, every night. We discussed books we had recently read as well as movies we had seen. We listened to educational audiotapes we had brought along and then discussed the lessons on those tapes in depth.

On New Year's Day, we did what we do every year, we set our goals for the coming year. But this year our goal-setting session was different. Larry wanted to do more than just set goals for the coming year. Instead of discussing just our goals for the year, he wanted us to set goals that changed our lives by changing our realities. He said, "Why don't we write a plan on how we can all become financially free?"

I listened to his words and heard what he said. But I could not fit what he said into my reality. I had talked about it, dreamed about it, and knew that someday I would do it. But the idea of being financially free was always an idea in the future, not today . . . so the idea did not fit. "Financially free?" I said. The moment I heard my voice I knew how much of a wimp I had become. My voice did not sound like the old me.

"We've talked about it many times," Larry said. "But I think it is time to stop talking, stop dreaming, and start committing. Let's write it down. Once we write it down you know we have to do it. Once we write it down, we'll support each other on this journey."

Being almost out of money, Kim and I looked at each other. The glow from the fire illuminated the doubt and uncertainty on our faces. "It's a good idea but I think I would rather just focus on surviving for the next year." I had just left the nylon and Velcro wallet business. After it had crashed in 1979, I had spent the next five years rebuilding it and then walked away from it. I walked away early because the business had changed drastically. We were no longer manufacturing in the United States. In order to compete with increasing competition, we had moved our factories to China, Taiwan, and Korea. I left the business because I could no longer stand the idea of using sweatshop child labor to make me rich. The business was putting money in my pocket, but it was taking life out of my soul. I was also not getting along with my partners. We had grown apart and did not see eye to eye. I walked away with very little equity. I just could not continue to work in a business that violated my spirit and with partners I could not talk to. I am not proud of how I left, yet I knew it was time to leave. I had been there for eight years and I had learned a lot. I learned how to build a business, how to destroy a business, and then how to rebuild it. Although I walked away with very little money, I did walk away with priceless education and experience.

"Come on," said Larry. "You're being a wimp. Instead of setting simple one-year goals, let's go for it. Let's set a big multiyear goal. Let's go for freedom."

"But we don't have much money," I said, looking over at Kim, whose face reflected my concerns. "You know we're starting over again. All we want to do is survive for the next six months and maybe a year. How can we think about financial freedom when all I can think about right now is financial survival?" Again I was shocked at how wimpy I sounded. My self-confidence was really low. My energy was really low.

"Even better. Think of this as a fresh start," Larry was now on it. He would not stop.

"But how can we retire early when we don't have any money?" I protested. I could hear more and more of the wimp in me coming out. I felt weak inside and did not want to commit to something just yet. I did just want to survive for the financial short term and not think about the future.

"I did not say we were going to retire in a year," said Larry, now irritated with my wimpy responses. "All I am saying is let's plan on retiring now. Let's write down the goal, create a plan, and then focus on the idea. Most people do not think about retiring until it's too late . . . or they plan on retiring when they're sixty-five. I don't want to do that. I want a better plan. I don't want to spend my life working just to pay bills. I want to live. I want to be rich. I want to travel the world while I am young enough to enjoy it."

As I sat there listening to Larry sell me on the benefits of setting such a goal, I could hear the little voice inside of me telling me why setting a goal to be financially free and retiring early was unrealistic. It even sounded impossible.

Larry continued. He did not seem to care if Kim or I were listening so I tuned him out as I began to think about what he had said. Silently, I said to myself, "Setting a goal to retire early was a good idea . . . so why am I fighting it? It is not like me to fight a good idea."

Suddenly, in my silence, I began to hear my rich dad saying, "The biggest challenge you have is to challenge your own self-doubt and your laziness. It is your self-doubt and your laziness that define and limit who you are. If you want to change what you are you must take on your self-doubt and your laziness. It is your self-doubt and laziness that keep you small. It is your self-doubt and laziness that deny you the life you want." I could hear rich dad driving home his point, saying, "There is no one in your way except you and your doubts about you. It is easy to stay the same. It is easy not to change. Most people choose to stay the same all their lives. If you will take on your self-doubt and your laziness, you will find the door to your freedom."

Rich dad had had this talk with me just before I left Hawaii to come on this trip. He knew I was probably leaving Hawaii for good. He knew I was leaving my home and a place I felt very comfortable in. He knew I was venturing out into the world without any guarantees of security. Now just a month after my talk with rich dad, I found myself sitting on this tall snow-covered mountain, feeling weak, vulnerable, and insecure, listening to my best friend telling me the same things. I knew it was time to grow up or give up and go home. I realized that it was this moment of weakness on the mountains that I had come for. It was decision time once again. It was time to choose. I could let my self-doubt and laziness win or I could go on and change my perceptions about myself. It was time to move forward or to go backward.

As I tuned back into Larry talking about freedom I realized that he was not really talking about freedom. At that moment, I came to realize that taking on my self-doubt and my laziness was the most important thing I could do. If I did not take it on, my life would go backward.

"Okay, let's do it," I said. "Let's set the goal to be financially free."

That was New Year's Day 1985. In 1994 Kim and I were free. Larry went on to build his company, which became one of *Inc.* magazine's fastest-growing companies of the year in 1996. Larry retired in 1998 at the age of forty-six after selling his company and took a year off.

How Did You Do It?

Whenever I tell this story, the question I am asked is, "How? How did you do it?"

I then say, "It's not about *how*. It is about *why* Kim and I did it." I go on to say, "Without the *why*, the *how* would have been impossible."

I could go on to tell you *how* Kim, Larry, and I did it, but I won't. How we did it is not that important. When it comes to how we did it, all I will say is that from 1985 to 1994, Kim, Larry, and I focused on rich dad's three paths to great wealth, which are:

1. Increasing business skills
2. Increasing money management skills
3. Increasing investment skills

There are many books written on each of these paths, and if I did the same, this would be just another *how to* book. But what I think is more important than *how to*, is the *why* we did it, and the *why* is because I wanted to challenge my own self-doubts, my laziness, and my past. It was the *why* that gave us the power to do the *how.*

Rich dad often said, "Many people ask me *how to do something*. I used to tell them until I realized that even after I told them how I did something, they often did not do it. I then realized that it was not the *how to* but *why* I do something that is more important. It is the *why* that gives you the power to do the *how to*." He also said, "The reason most people do not do what they can do is because they do not have a strong enough *why*. Once you find the *why*, it is easy to find your own *how to* to wealth. Instead of *looking inside of themselves* to find their own *why* they want to become rich, most people *look for the easy road* to wealth, and the problem with the easy road is that the easy road usually ends in a dead end."

Arguing with Myself

That night, sitting in the cold mountain cabin, listening to Larry, I found myself silently arguing with him. Every time he said, "Let's set it as a goal, write it down, and create a plan," I could hear myself arguing in response, saying such things as:

1. "But we don't have any money."
2. "I can't do that."
3. "I'll think about it next year, or once Kim and I get settled."
4. "You don't understand our situation."
5. "I need more time."

Over the years, my rich dad had taught me many lessons. One of the lessons was, "If you find yourself arguing with a good idea, you may want to stop arguing."

That night as Larry went on and on about getting rich and retiring early, I again heard rich dad warning me about arguing against a good idea. Explaining further, rich dad said, "Whenever someone says something like 'I can't afford it' or 'I can't do it' to something they want, *they have a big problem.* Why in the world would someone say, 'I can't afford it' or 'I can't do it' to something they want? Why would someone deny themselves the things they want? It makes no logical sense."

As the fire crackled in the fireplace, I found myself arguing against something I wanted. "Why not retire rich and retire early?" I finally asked myself. "What would be wrong with that?" My mind began to open slowly and I repeated silently to myself, "Why am I arguing against the idea? Why am I arguing against myself? It is a good idea. I have talked about it for years. I did want to retire by thirty-five and now I'm soon to be thirty-seven years old and I'm not even close to retiring. In fact, I'm nearly broke. So why am I arguing?"

Once I said that to myself, I realized *why* I had been arguing against a good idea. At the age of twenty-five, I had planned on becoming rich and retiring between ages thirty to thirty-five. It was my dream. But after losing my Velcro wallet business the first time, my spirit was crushed and I had lost much self-confidence. That night sitting by the fire, I realized it was my lack of self-confidence that was doing the arguing. I was arguing against a dream I wanted. I was arguing because I did not want to feel disappointed again. I was arguing because I was protecting myself from the pain that dreaming big dreams can bring if that big dream does not become reality. I had dreamed and failed. That night I realized that I was arguing against failing again, not against the dream.

"Okay, let's set a big goal," I said quietly to Larry. I had finally stopped arguing against a good idea. The argument was still there but I was not going to let the argument stop me. After all, it is only an argument I was having with myself and no one else. The little person in me was arguing against the person that wanted to grow up and be bigger.

"Good," said Larry. "It's about time you stopped being such a wimp. I was really getting worried about you."

The reason I had decided to do it was because I had found my *why*. I knew *why* I was going to do it, even though at that moment I did not know *how* I was going to do it.

Why *I Decided to Retire Early*

How many of you have ever on occasion said to yourself, "I am sick and tired of myself"? Well that New Year's Eve, sitting around the fire with Kim and Larry, I got sick and tired of my old self and decided to change. It was not just a mental change; it was a change that came from deep inside. It was time for a big change and I knew I could change because I found out why I wanted to change. The following are some of my personal *whys* . . . *why* I decided to go for retiring young and retiring rich:

1. I was fed up with being broke and always struggling for money. I had been rich for a brief moment with my wallet business, but after the business crashed, I was back to struggling again. Although my rich dad had taught me well, I still only had his lessons. I had still not become rich and it was time for me to become rich.

2. I was tired of being average. Through school, teachers said, "Robert is a bright boy but he just does not apply himself." They also said, "He's bright but he'll never be as smart as the gifted kids. He is just above average." That night sitting on the mountain, I got sick and tired of being average. It was time for me to stop being average.

3. When I was eight years old, I came home and found my mom crying at the kitchen table. She was crying because we were buried under a mountain of bills. My dad was doing the best he could to earn more money, but as a schoolteacher, he wasn't doing so well financially. All he would say was, "Don't worry, I'll handle it." But he didn't. The way my dad handled it was by going back to school, working harder, and waiting for his annual pay raise. Meanwhile, the bills kept piling up and my mom felt more and more alone with no one to turn to. My dad did not like to discuss the subject of money, and if he did, he only got angry.

I remember deciding at the age of eight to find the answers that could help my mom. That night sitting on the mountain, I realized that I had found the answers I had searched for since the age of eight. It was now time to take those answers and turn them into reality.

4. The most painful *why* of all was the reality that I now had a beautiful young woman in my life, Kim. I had met my soul mate and she was in this financial mess because she loved me. That night on the mountain I realized that I was doing to Kim what my dad had done to my mom. I was repeating a family pattern. At that moment, I found my real *why*.

So those are my whys. I wrote them down that night and kept them in a secret place. For those of you who read my second book, *Rich Dad's CASH-*

FLOW Quadrant, you may recall that things got worse for us once we left the mountain. I started that book by telling the story of Kim and me living in a car for about three weeks after our money ran out. So things did not get better just because we made the decision to retire rich, but it was the reasons *why* that kept us going.

Things did not go well for Larry either after leaving the mountain. He too had substantial financial setbacks in the late 1980s, yet his *whys* kept him going.

> I found out as my rich dad did that I cannot tell anyone *how* to get rich. I now first ask people *why* they want to become rich. Without a strong enough *why,* even the easiest *how* to get rich will be too hard. There are many, many, ways to get rich . . . but there are only a few personal reasons why *you* want to get rich. Find your *why* and then you will find your *how*. As the old saying goes, "Where there is a will there is a way." For me, I would say finding my *will* made finding my *way* possible. Without the *will*, the *way* would have been *way* too hard.

A suggestion: I learned years ago that *passion* is a combination of *love* and *hate*. Unless someone has a passion for something, it is difficult to accomplish anything. Rich dad used to say, "If you want something, be passionate. Passion gives energy to your life. If you want something you do not have, find out *why you love what you want* and *why you hate not having what you want*. When you combine those two thoughts, you will find the energy to get off your seat and go get anything you want."

So you may want to start with a list comparing loves and hates. For example, I would create the following list:

Love	*Hate*
Being rich	Being poor
Being free	Being required to work
Buying anything I want	Not having what I want
Expensive things	Cheap things
Having other people do what I don't want to do	Doing things I don't want to do

My suggestion is, you may want to start your list of loves and hates in the space listed below. If you need more space, which I hope you do, find a much larger sheet of paper. May you live your life with more and more passion.

Your Loves	*Your Hates*

So sit quietly to find and define your loves and hates. Then write down your whys. Write down your dreams, goals, and plans on becoming financially free, retiring early, and retiring as young as possible. Once it is in writing, you may want to show it to a friend who will support you in achieving your dreams. Take a look at this paper with your dreams, goals, and plans on a regular basis, talk about it often, ask for support, be willing to continually learn, and before you know it, things will begin to happen.

As a final comment, I have heard many people say, "Money does not make you happy." That statement has some truth to it. But what money does do is buy me the time to do what I *love* and pay other people to do what I *hate* doing.

Chapter 2

Why Retire as Young as You Can?

After nearly ten years of hard work and struggle I had become financially free at the age of forty-seven. That year, in 1994, a friend called and said, "Be sure you take at least a year off after the business is sold."

"A year off?" I replied. "I'm going to retire and take the rest of my life off."

"No you won't," said my friend Nyhl. Nyhl had been a member of the team that started and built several major businesses, two of them being MTV and CMT, Country Music Television, back in the early 1980s. After having built and sold some of those businesses, he retired at age forty-one. We had become friends and he was now passing on his lessons from retirement to me. "In less than three months you'll be bored and you'll start another company," he said. "The hardest thing for you to do is to do nothing. That's why I recommend you set a goal to wait at least a year before even thinking about starting another business."

I laughed and tried to reassure him that I was retired for good. "I have no plans on starting another business," I said. "I'm retired. I'm not going back to work. The next time you'll see me you won't recognize me. I won't have a suit on nor will I have short hair. I'm going to look like a beach bum."

Nyhl heard my words, yet he was insistent. He wanted me to hear and understand what he was trying to tell me. It was important to him that I understand his message. After a very long conversation he was beginning to get through to me. Finally I heard him when he said, "Very few people have the opportunity you have. Not many people are financially able to stop working and do nothing. Not many people can truly retire in midlife . . . during your prime earning years. Most people can't afford to stop working, even if they want to . . . even if they hate their job . . . they can't stop working. So don't take this gift lightly. It is a gift few people will ever be presented with . . . so take it. Take a year to do nothing."

Nyhl went on to explain that most entrepreneurs sell their businesses and start another business right away. He said, "I used to build a business, sell it, and start immediately building another one. I had built and sold three businesses by the time I was thirty-five. I had a lot of money but I could not stop working. I did not know what stopping meant. If I was not working I felt useless and felt I was wasting time, so I would work harder. My hard work was robbing me of life and time with my family. Finally I realized what I was doing and decided to do something different. After I sold my last business and put the check for millions in the bank, I decided I would take a year off. Taking that year for my family and me was one of the best decisions I have ever made. That time alone with myself, having nothing to do, was priceless. Do you realize that since we are five years old, we are in school studying and once we are out of school, we are working? Very few people have the luxury of at least one year to sit and just think and be with yourself."

He told me that as soon as his affairs at home were tied up, he and his family moved to a remote island in Fiji and sat on the beach. He said, "For months, I just sat on the beach, gazed at the crystal blue ocean, and watched my kids enjoy a life we all dream about." Once they had had enough of Fiji, he moved his family to Italy and sat there for months doing nothing. "It was a full year before I became a sane human being again," he said. "I had no idea how hard it was to stop waking up and thinking I had something to do, a meeting to attend, a plane to catch, to make enough money to pay the bills. It took a full year for me to slow down and let the adrenaline leave my body. It took a full year of relaxing to slow down enough so I could think straight and become whole again. I was now forty-one years old. For thirty-six years I had been running to get somewhere, and now I was there."

The Hardest Thing I Had to Do

Nyhl was correct. The hardest thing about being retired was having nothing to do. After years of school, classrooms, tests, meetings, airplanes, and deadlines, I was truly conditioned to get up and rush off to do something. Just before retiring, I remembered hating the pressure and the worry of work. I remembered thinking, "Only six more months and I will be free. I can retire and do nothing. I can't wait till the business is sold and I can stop this madness."

In September of 1994, the sale and transfer of assets out of the business was complete. I put some money in the bank, invested in a few more apartment houses and warehouses, and formally retired. I was forty-seven and my wife, Kim, was thirty-seven. We were financially free with the rest of our lives yet to live and enjoy. And just as Nyhl warned, within weeks after selling the business I was restless. I continued to wake up early, only to realize that I had no plans for the day. I had no one to call and no one called me. I was alone in my house with nowhere to go. I was soon restless and irritable. I felt useless and unwanted. I felt my life was being wasted and I was unproductive. I wanted desperately to work on something but there was nothing to do. Nyhl was correct, in that for me, having nothing to do was the hardest thing for me to do.

Kim had her business of investing and managing her real estate portfolio. She enjoyed it and went about it at her own pace. She would find me in the kitchen bumping around trying to do nothing. "Are you looking for something to do?" she would ask.

"No," I replied. "I'm just looking for a way to do nothing."

"Well let me know when you find nothing to do and we can do it together," Kim said with a grin. "Why don't you call your friends and get together and do something?"

"I did," I replied. "But they're all busy at work. They don't have any free time."

After a few months of trying to do nothing, Kim and I decided to vacation in Fiji where Nyhl went for part of his year off. I was excited about just going somewhere, even if it was to just do nothing.

Within three weeks of deciding to go to Fiji, we arrived by seaplane and were greeted by smiling Fijians with flower leis and tropical drinks. As Kim and I walked down the long pier that jutted out over the crystal blue water, I thought I had arrived on Fantasy Island and was waiting to hear a short chubby guy saying, "Boss, de plane, de plane."

This island was more beautiful than Nyhl had described. I could not believe its beauty. Being raised in Hawaii, I could not help but say to myself, "This is the way Hawaii used to be and this is how Hawaii should be." Yet as fabulous as this secluded island was, it was too slow for me. I could not believe that paradise was making me crazy. I would get up, have a healthy breakfast of fruit, jog for a while, and then spend the day at the beach. After an hour I was stir-crazy. As beautiful as the beaches of this island were I was ready to get back to the States and start a new business. I did not know why I had promised Nyhl that I would take at least a year off. Two weeks was all that I could take of paradise. Kim could have stayed forever but I was ready to get home to Arizona. Why I needed to get home, I do not know . . . but we left paradise and headed home.

Sitting at home was not much better than sitting on the beach, but at least I had my car and familiar places to keep me distracted. A new neighbor came over to introduce himself one day. He too was retired but he was about twenty years older than I was. He was sixty-eight years old and had been a high-profile manager of a Fortune 500 company. Every day he would come over and talk about the news, weather, and sports. He was a nice guy but sitting around trying to do nothing with him was worse than the worst meetings I had ever been in. All he wanted to do was work in his backyard and play golf. To him, retirement was pure heaven. He did not miss the corporate world at all and just loved his free time doing nothing. I realized that I would wind up like him if I hung around him much longer. When he wanted me to join his men's card group at the country club, I realized that I had to find something else to do in order to do nothing.

Finally, I could take no more. One day I said to Kim, "I'm moving to Bisbee. I need to go somewhere that I can be busy doing nothing." In a few days, I moved to the small ranch that Kim and I owned. It is a beautiful yet secluded piece of land, hidden in a valley, covered with tall oak trees, an intermittent stream, with lots of deer and an occasional mountain lion, nestled high in the mountains on the Mexico, New Mexico, Arizona border. I had finally found my place to take my year off . . . a place where I could be busy doing nothing. After a few days of just sitting in the mountains, in my cabin without television or radio reception, I began to calm down and settle into my year off. My breathing slowed down and so did my pace. Peace and tranquillity became a part of everyday life, rather than the pressure of meetings and deadlines. My year off had finally begun and it was as Nyhl said, "A gift few people will ever be presented with . . . so take it." It had taken me nearly six months to slow down enough to begin my year off.

Starting Life Over Again

Sitting alone in my mountain cabin, I had the time to reflect on my life. I thought of all the stupid and impulsive things I had done in my youth. I thought about the choices I made and how each choice, even though not a brilliant choice, had been important in shaping who I eventually became in life. I had the time to sit and remember my high school days and the friends I grew up with . . . friends I rarely see today. I recalled my friends from college and wondered how they were doing. This time alone gave me the opportunity to reflect on how much the friends of my youth impacted the man I had become.

There were so many moments sitting in my cabin that I wished I could go back in time and be with my boyhood friends again. I wanted just to laugh and be young again . . . but now all I had were the precious memories. I wished I had taken more pictures and written more letters and kept in touch more . . . but we had all become busy with life and had gone our separate ways. Sitting in the mountains, in front of a roaring fire, playing back the memories of my youth was better than going to a movie theater. The time off gave me the time and the solitude to replay in vivid detail the memories of my past. It is interesting that even the bad times were not that bad. I came to appreciate my life, the people in my life, the good and the bad, and as messed up as my life was at times, I greatly appreciated my own unique life.

In those quiet moments, I realized that we all have the potential to be good and bad. We all have the potential to be great, but greatness was not to be a part of my youth. I was not a child genius, a musical prodigy, an athletic star, nor was I in the in crowd, or invited to many parties. In looking back upon my life, I realized my life was average . . . but sitting in the mountains made my average life very special to me.

I had time to think about my family, old friends, guys I played sports with, old girlfriends, and old business partners. I thought about choices I had made and wondered what would have happened if I had made different choices . . . choices such as, what would have happened if I had married my girlfriend from college, settled down, and had kids, as she wanted to do? What would have happened to my life if I had not decided to become a pilot and fly in Vietnam? What would have happened if I had avoided the war as most of my friends did? What would have happened if I had gone for my master's degree instead of starting my nylon and Velcro wallet business? What would have happened if I had not lost two businesses before finally having one work? What would have happened if I had not met Kim and gotten married? What if Kim had not stuck it out with me when times were really bad? And most importantly, what did I learn and who did I become because of the successes and failures my life had presented me?

It is true that you cannot change your past . . . but you can change your opinion of your past. Up until this time in the mountains, my past was just a blur. It was just a series of people and events that whirred by as I rushed through each day of my life. The solitude in the mountains gave me the opportunity to stop my life and take a look at it. There are also many things I have done in the past that I am not proud of and would not do again. There are many mistakes I wish I had not made and lies I wish I had not told. There are also many dear friends and loved ones that I hurt along the way. There are many people I love dearly but I do not talk to anymore because we disagreed on something silly. During this year off, I found out how important those events were in my life. Sitting alone in the quiet of the mountains, I reconnected with my past friends, family, and myself and thanked them all for being a part of my life. Sitting alone in the mountains, I had the time to say "thank you" to my past and prepare for the future.

Today when I speak to groups about taking a year off, I say, "The best thing about retiring early and taking that year off in midlife was that it gave me a chance to start life over again."

Eighteen months after selling my business and retiring, I finally drove out of the mountains of southern Arizona. As I drove out of the mountains, I really did not know what I was going to do next . . . I just knew that I wanted to do things differently. In my Apple Macintosh computer was the rough draft of *Rich Dad Poor Dad* and in my briefcase was a rough sketch of my game CASHFLOW® 101. The second half of my life had begun. This time it was *my* life. I was now older, wiser, smarter, less reckless, and a bit more trustworthy.

As I drove out of the mountains the second half of my life had begun. It was no longer a life dictated to by the wishes and dreams of my parents, teachers, or friends, or the dreams of a child. The second half of my life had begun and this time it was to be *my life* on *my terms.*

And that is the main reason I recommend retiring as young as possible. It will give you a chance to start your life over.

A suggestion: Regardless if you can retire early or not, I suggest taking at least an hour each month to reflect on your life. Taking the time to reflect on my life I found out:

1. What I thought was important was *not* that important.
2. What was important was where *I was at*, not where *I was going to*.
3. There is no one more important than the person in front of you at that moment. Take that moment to be with him or her.
4. Time is precious, don't waste it . . . appreciate it.
5. Sometimes stopping for a moment is harder than staying busy.

For me, the best thing about retiring early was learning to appreciate life, even if it was hectic, stressful, and filled with problems. When I had nothing to do, I found out that I did not know what to do if I had nothing to do. Today, I truly appreciate the hustle and bustle of life because I know what it is like to sit around doing nothing. So whatever state your life is in at present, take a moment to appreciate it . . . because tomorrow it will only be a memory.

A note from Mary Painter, Director of Operations at CASHFLOW® Technologies, Inc.

During my working career, I worked in the Disability and Death Benefits Division for the Pennsylvania State Retirement System. I recall very vividly, at the young age of nineteen or twenty, processing death benefits for survivors of retirees. As I sat there day in and day out reviewing death certificates, I was amazed at how many folks had died just a few short months after they retired due to illness or disease, and also from suicide. When I questioned several folks with whom I worked about why they thought people died so soon after retiring or why someone would commit suicide after working their entire life and finally being on easy street, I was told that for some people, working was their entire life. They had nothing else in their life. The second reason that was offered was that many people worked their whole life, relying on a pension when they retired, and found out that pension barely got them through month to month. They were at the point in their lives when they had all the time in the world to do whatever they wanted, but had no money with which do it.

In my naïveté, I thought that would not happen to me. Then I went about putting myself on the exact same path that many of these folks must have traveled. Nineteen years later, after many promotions and climbing the career ladder, I found myself realizing this just wasn't going to do it for my family and me. My husband and I both agreed we needed to make drastic changes in our lives. We moved to Arizona where we took a few months to collect our thoughts and interviewed for some jobs. One of those interviews just happened to be for a position with CASHFLOW Technologies. I was given a copy of *Rich Dad Poor Dad.* I went home and devoured the book in a day. While I consider myself extremely fortunate to have landed the job with CASHFLOW, more importantly, I understood what I needed to do so that I did not end up like one of those unfortunate folks I remembered from many years ago.

Chapter 3

How I Retired Early

In the spring of 1999, I was scheduled to give a talk to a group of approximately 250 bankers in Los Angeles. Since I was to be the first speaker in the morning, I flew in the night before from Phoenix, where I live. After having breakfast, I sat in my hotel room and scratched my head as to what I could say to this group of bankers. My standard talk about financial statements, financial literacy, and the differences between an asset and a liability seemed inadequate for this group. Since they were more than ordinary bankers, they were *mortgage* bankers, I assumed they would know the financial basics I most often talk about, or at least I hoped they did.

My talk was scheduled for 9:30 A.M., it was now 8:00 A.M., and I was at a loss for an angle or a new idea appropriate for the group. Sitting at the desk in my hotel room, I glanced at the complimentary morning newspaper the hotel had provided. On the front page was a photograph of a happy couple sitting in their golf cart. The bold headline over the picture read, "We Decided to Retire Early."

The article went on to explain that this couple's 401(k) retirement plan had done so well over the past ten years in this booming stock market that they decided to retire six years earlier than planned. He was fifty-nine years old and she was fifty-six. The article quoted them saying, "Our mutual funds have done so well that we realized one day we were millionaires. Instead of working for six more years, we scaled back, sold our home, bought a smaller home in this retirement village, put the extra money from the sale of our house in a high-yield certificate of deposit, reduced our expenses, and now we play golf every day."

I had found the subject for my talk. Finishing the article, I showered, dressed, and headed down to the waiting mortgage bankers. At exactly 9:30, I was introduced and brought up onstage. Lifting the newspaper up in the air, I opened my talk by pointing to the picture of the newly retired couple and repeating the headline, "We decided to retire early." I then stated the couple's ages, fifty-nine and fifty-six, and read a few comments from the article. Putting the paper down, I said, "My wife, Kim, and I also retired early. We retired in 1994. I was forty-seven and she was thirty-seven." I looked around the room and allowed the difference in ages and dates to sink in. After a silence of about ten seconds, I continued asking, "So let me ask you this . . . how is it that I could retire twelve years earlier than he could . . . and my wife nineteen years earlier? What made the difference?"

The silence was deafening. I was off to a bad start. I knew it was early and I knew that I was asking the audience to think instead of just listen. I knew that I probably sounded arrogant and cocky, comparing my early retirement to the couple in the newspaper. Yet I wanted to make a point to this group and it was too late to turn back. I felt like a stand-up comedian who had just told his best joke, and the audience was not laughing. Pushing on, I asked, "How many of you plan on retiring early?"

Again there was no response. No one raised a hand. The discomfort in the room was growing. I was dying onstage. I knew I had to do something quickly. Looking out on the group, I could see that most of the group was younger than me. The few that were my age were not impressed with my talking about retiring young. Quickly I said, "How many of you are under forty-five?"

Suddenly there was life. There was response. Slowly hands began to rise from all around the room. I estimated that it was about 60 percent of the group that raised their hands, indicating that they were younger than forty-five. It was a young crowd . . . relative to me at least. Changing my tactics, I then played to this group, asking, "How many of you would like to retire in your forties and be financially free for the rest of your life?"

Now the hands were shooting up with more enthusiasm. I was beginning to communicate a little better and the audience seemed to be coming to life. The participants of my age and older began to squirm as they looked around at their younger peers, many of whom had their hands in the air, indicating they did not want to grow old in the industry. Sensing the discomfort of those of my age and older, I realized that I needed to say something quickly to not alienate this group.

Smiling, I paused as the hands came down. Looking at those in the group who were of my age and older I said, "I want to thank the mortgage bankers of this world because you made it possible for me to retire early. Not my real estate broker or my stockbroker. Not my financial planner, and not my accountants. It was you, the mortgage bankers of the world, who made it possible for me to retire approximately twenty years earlier than my father."

Looking out at the audience, I could tell that some of the uneasiness was dissipating, and I could now continue on with my talk. My acknowledgment of their industry seemed to have helped. I estimated that I now had about 80 percent of the audience's attention. Continuing, I repeated the question I asked earlier, which was, "So how is it that I could retire earlier than the couple in the newspaper and how did you mortgage bankers help me retire early?"

Again there was silence. I began to realize that they did *not* know how they helped me. Even though there was that same dead silence, at least they seemed to be more awake than they were a few minutes earlier. Deciding to stop asking a question that they were hesitant to answer I continued. Turning to my flip chart on stage, I wrote in big bold letters,

DEBT **VS.** **EQUITY**

Returning to the audience, I pointed to the word *debt* and said, "I was able to retire early because I used *debt* to fund my retirement. And this couple in the newspaper, the people with the 401(k), used *equity* to fund their retirement. That is why they took longer to retire."

Pausing for a moment, I wanted to let what I had said sink in. Finally a hand popped up and asked, "You are saying that the guy in the newspaper used *his* money to retire and you used *our* money to retire."

"That is correct," I said. "I was using your money to get deeper in debt and he was trying to get out of debt."

"So that is why it took him longer," another person said. "Twelve years longer than you. It took him longer because he used his money, his own equity to retire."

Eighteen Years of Life

I smiled, nodded my head, and said, "And for me, retiring at age forty-seven gave me eighteen years of extra life when compared to someone who retires at age sixty-five. And how much is eighteen years of life worth to you . . . eighteen years of your youth? For my wife, it was twenty-eight years of extra time to enjoy her youth. How many of you would rather retire early so you can enjoy your youth, your vitality, and your freedom . . . the freedom to do whatever you want with all the money you need?"

Hands went up all over the room. There were now more smiles attached to those arms. People seemed to be coming to life. Yet, as expected, there were those sitting with their arms folded across their chests and legs crossed over their knees. My talk did not seem to be too well received by those individuals. The cynics and skeptics wanted to be cynics and skeptics. I did not seem to be reaching them. At least I was saving myself from a very bad start and some of the group was coming over to my side.

A young man in the front row raised his hand and asked, "Would you mind explaining a little more about how you retired early using debt and how he used equity?"

"Certainly," I said, happy to have the opportunity to explain further. Picking up the newspaper and pointing to the picture I said, "This person retired six years ahead of schedule, if age sixty-five is the benchmark for retirement, because the stock market did well. So he did well because he invested *his own money* into the market. How much better would he have done if he had borrowed *your* bank's money and invested *your* money into the same market?"

A rush of uneasiness went through the audience. What I had just said had disturbed many in the audience. The young man, now with a puzzled look on his face, then said, "But we would *not lend him our money* to invest in the stock market."

"Why?" I asked.

"Because it's too risky," he said.

Nodding, I said, "And because it's too risky this retiree had to use his own money . . . his equity. His retirement plan, his 401(k), did well and so did his own stock picking. He did well because the market did well. The stock market did well because millions of people, just like him, were doing the same thing at the same time . . . so he retired early. But he took longer because he basically used his own money, his *equity,* to buy *equity* in other investments. Interestingly, he invested in investments your industry generally does not lend money to invest in because of the risk factor. You bankers don't lend people money to speculate in the stock market, do you?"

Most in the room shook their heads.

"So are you saying he got lucky?" another person asked.

"Well, he was in the right place at the right age and in the right cycle of the market," I said. "If and when the trend reverses, he might wish he had not retired so early."

"And you used *our* money to invest in what?" asked another participant.

"Real estate," I said. "What else do you lend money on? You are mortgage bankers, aren't you? You're not investment bankers, are you?"

The young man nodded his head and said quietly, "We are mortgage bankers and we lend money for real estate, not stocks, bonds, and mutual funds."

"But didn't the stock market go up in value more than real estate in the last ten years?" asked a young woman sitting a few rows back from the front row. "My 401(k) did far better than most of the real estate investments I have seen."

"That may be true," I replied. "But your 401(k) increased in value because of market momentum and *capital appreciation.* Do you make it a policy to invest in market momentum or possible capital appreciation?"

"Not as a policy," said the young woman.

"Neither do I," I said. "I *do not* invest for *capital appreciation* only. The values of my properties do not need to appreciate in value for me to make money . . . although some have appreciated greatly in the same period of time and none have gone down in value like many stocks and mutual funds have."

"So if you do not invest for capital appreciation, what do you invest for?" asked the young woman.

"I invest for *cash flow,*" I said quietly. "How much cash flow per month does your 401(k) put into your pocket to spend each month?"

"Well nothing," said the young woman. "The purpose of my retirement plan is to have all the capital appreciation grow tax free so all my money stays in my retirement account. It is not designed to give me monthly cash flow."

"And do you own any investment real estate that gives you monthly cash flow plus tax breaks?" I asked.

"No," said the young woman. "All I have is an investment plan that invests in mutual funds."

"And you're a mortgage banker?" I asked with a teasing smile.

"Let me get this straight," said the young woman. "You borrowed *our* money to buy *your* real estate. Each month that real estate returns you cash flow. You and your wife were able to retire early because you have *cash flow* while the rest of us are hoping for the *capital appreciation* of our mutual funds and hoping to retire later in life . . . hoping the market does not crash when it is our turn to retire. In other words we helped you retire early but we do not help ourselves?"

"That may be one way of looking at it," I replied. "And that is why I am here to thank you and your industry for contributing to my retirement fund. You have contributed millions so I could retire early. I would like to have you think about doing the same for yourself."

My time was soon up and I received a courteous applause as I left the stage. The room was now awake and there seemed to be some excitement about what I had to say, especially from the young people. As I walked through the crowd shaking hands, I got a chance to listen to some of the comments about my talk. And even though they were mortgage bankers, I could still hear the usual comments I always hear from any crowd. Comments such as:

1. "What he says is far too risky."
2. "I would never lend him any money."
3. "He doesn't know what he is talking about."
4. "You can't do that today. The market is different."
5. "He got lucky. Just wait till the market crashes and he comes begging to us on his knees."

6. "I don't fix toilets. That is why I don't own any real estate."
7. "The real estate market is overbuilt. It will soon crash."
8. "You know how many guys like him have been wiped out in real estate?"
9. "If his debt is so high, I would not lend him any money."
10. "If he is retired, why is he talking to us?"

Poor Dad's Lessons

My poor dad often advised, "Go to school, get good grades, find a safe secure job, work hard, and save money." He would also quote other famous lines such as, "Neither a borrower nor lender be." And "A penny saved is a penny earned." Or "If you can't afford something don't buy it. Always pay cash."

My poor dad's life would have been pretty good if he followed his own advice, but like many people, he *said* what he thought were the right words but he *did not do* the right things. Instead he borrowed money to buy his house and his cars. He never invested because he always said, "Investing is risky." Instead he tried to save money . . . but each time there was an emergency, he would take the money out of his savings. He borrowed money for things that made him poor and he refused to borrow money for things that might have made him rich. It is these subtle differences that made a lot of difference in his life. It is because of these lifelong ways of thinking and handling his money that he could not afford to retire at age sixty-five. It also explains why he had to work up until the day he was too ill with cancer to work anymore. He worked hard all his life and for the last six months of his life, he fought for his life in a cancer ward. He was a good, hardworking man, who spent his life working hard, trying to avoid debt, and trying to save money. And those were the lessons about life and money he tried to pass on to me.

Rich Dad's Lessons

My rich dad, the man who was my best friend's father, offered different advice and different ways of thinking about money. He would say and ask such things as:

1. "How long would it take you to *save* $1 million?" He would then ask, "How long would it take you to *borrow* $1 million?"

2. "Who is going to get richer in the long run? Someone who works all their lives trying to save a million dollars? Or someone who knows how to borrow a million dollars at 10 percent interest and also knows how to invest it and receive a 25 percent per year return on that borrowed million dollars?"

3. "To whom would a banker rather lend money? Someone who works hard for money, or someone who knows how to borrow money and have that money safely and intelligently work hard for them?"

4. "Who would you have to be and what would you have to know in order to call your banker and say, 'I want to borrow a million dollars.' Then have the banker say, 'I will have the papers ready for you to sign in twenty minutes.'"

5. "Why does the government *tax your savings* but give you a *tax break for being in debt?*"

6. "Who *has* to be financially smarter and better financially educated? A person with a million dollars in savings or a person with a million dollars in debt?"

7. "Who has to be financially smarter with money? Someone who works hard for money or someone who has money work hard for him?"

8. "If you had a choice of education, would you choose to go to school to learn how *to work hard for money*, or would you rather go to school *to learn how to have money work hard for you?*"

9. "Why is it that a banker will *gladly lend you money* to speculate in real estate, but *will hesitate to lend you money* to speculate in the stock market?"

10. "Why do the people who work the hardest and save the most pay *more* in taxes than people who work less and borrow more?"

When it came to work, money, savings, and debt, it is obvious that my two dads had completely different points of view. But the biggest difference in points of view was this statement by my rich dad: "The poor and middle class have a hard time getting rich because they try to use their own money to get rich. If you want to get rich, you need to know how to use other people's money to get rich . . . not your own."

This Book Is *Not* About Debt

> **A word of caution and warning:** This book is *not* about borrowing money and getting into deep debt . . . although I will discuss the use of debt as a tool for retiring early and retiring rich. As I stated in the introduction to this book, leverage is power . . . and power can be used, abused, or feared. We should treat debt as we would a loaded gun, very carefully. Debt, like a loaded gun, can help you and it can kill you . . . regardless of who's handling it. Treat *all debt as dangerous* just as you should consider *all guns dangerous.*

I emphasize this because on my Web site, a young man wrote that he had just quit his job, taken out several credit cards, and gotten deeply in debt buying real estate. He said, "I am following Robert's advice and getting deeply in debt with good debt."

First of all, I would *never* advise anyone to use credit cards to buy real estate. If you know how to invest, you do not need to use such a risky scheme of financing your investing.

Although I know people who have invested in real estate using credit cards, I do not recommend this process, as it can be very dangerous. I do not recommend the process because I know many more people who have used credit cards to buy real estate who have gone broke. What I *do* advise is *to get educated and learn how to use debt wisely.*

While I started this chapter talking about the difference between debt vs. equity, this book is not just about debt. This book is about a more important subject for anyone who wants to retire young and retire rich.

The Second Most Important Word

In the introduction I wrote about rich dad saying, "The most important word in the world of money is *cash flow.* The *second most important word* is *leverage.*"

When I spoke to the mortgage bankers about using their money to retire early, I was really speaking about using their money as leverage. As a child learning from my rich dad, he spent much of his time teaching his son and me about the importance of leverage.

Earlier in the introduction, I wrote that rich dad's favorite story of leverage was the story of David and Goliath. Rich dad would tell this story to us as often as we would listen. He would say, "Always remember, boys, that David beat Goliath because David understood the principle of leverage."

"I thought he used a slingshot," I said.

"That is correct," said rich dad. "In the right hands, a slingshot is one form of leverage. Once you begin to understand the power of leverage, you will see it everywhere. If you want to be rich, you must learn to harness the power of leverage." Rich dad also drummed into our heads, "Even if you are just little guys in the world, you can beat the big guys if you understand the power of leverage."

As we got older, rich dad had to find other examples of leverage. In order to make his lessons about money interesting to his son, Mike, and me he would often use subjects that we were interested in to teach us his lessons. For example, when the Beatles first came to America, in the '60s, and the kids of my age were going wild, my rich dad was impressed at how much money they were making. During this lesson he said, "The reason the Beatles make more money is because they have more leverage." Rich dad went on to explain that the Beatles made more money than the president of the United States, medical doctors, lawyers, accountants, and even himself because of the financial principle of leverage. Rich dad said, "The Beatles use television, radio, and records as leverage. That is why they are rich."

It was his son, Mike, who asked, "Are television, radio, and records the only form of leverage?"

"Do we have to become rock stars to become rich?" I asked. I was sixteen at the time and I knew that singing was not my strong suit and the only instrument I could play was the radio.

Rich dad laughed and said, "No you don't have to become rock stars to be rich, and no, television, radio, and records are not the only forms of leverage. But if you want to become rich, you have to use some form of leverage. The difference between the rich, the poor, and the middle class is the different forms of leverage each class uses. The rich are richer simply because they use different forms of leverage and they use more of it."

This Book Is About Leverage

Rich dad would repeatedly say to his son and me, "Financial leverage is the advantage the rich have over the poor and the middle class." He would also say, "Financial leverage is how the rich get richer quicker." So the first books in the Rich Dad series focused on cash flow; this book will focus more closely on the word *leverage* because in order for you to retire young and retire rich, you will need to use some form of leverage. It was *leverage*, not *hard work,* that allowed Kim and me to retire early. In the next chapter, this book will go into a few more examples of leverage.

I started this chapter with the story of my talk to the mortgage bankers and how I used *their money* rather than *my own money* to retire early. That was an example of using debt as a form of leverage.

The problem with leverage is that leverage is like a two-edged sword, which can cut in either direction. In other words, a person can use leverage to get ahead financially, and that same form of leverage, if misused, can be used to have them fall behind financially.

One of the main reasons the middle class and the poor work harder, work years longer, struggle to pay off debt, and pay more in taxes is because they lack a very important form of leverage . . . and that is the leverage of *financial education.* So before you run out and borrow money to invest in assets, please know that debt is only one form of leverage and that all forms of leverage have a sharp edge on two sides. To repeat something my rich dad said:

> "Who *has* to be financially smarter and better financially educated? A person who has a million dollars in savings or a person who has a million dollars in debt?"

The most important point I want to make is that *this book is primarily about financial education,* and regardless of what form of leverage you use, I first recommend the education on how to use whatever form of leverage interests you.

A suggestion: Rich dad said, "If you want to be rich, you need to know the differences between good debt and bad debt; good expenses and bad expenses; good income and bad income; and good liabilities and bad liabilities."

Since this chapter is specifically about debt as a form of leverage, you may want to make a list of your good debt and bad debt. If you are not familiar with the distinctions between these concepts, simply put, good debt is debt that puts money in your pocket every month, and bad debt is debt that takes money from your pocket every month. For example, the debt on my apartment houses puts money in my pocket every month, and the debt on my residence (my mortgage) takes money from my pocket every month.

Good debt	*Bad debt*

After you inspect your list, you may want to think about what you want to do with your debt. You may want to reduce bad debt and think about increasing good debt. If you work on increasing good debt, your chances of retiring young and retiring rich are greatly improved. But always remember to treat *all* debt as you would treat a loaded gun, and that is very carefully.

Chapter 4

How You *Can* *Retire Early*

Having two dads allowed me to see two different worlds of leverage. My real dad was a highly educated, hardworking man. My rich dad was a highly leveraged man. That is why he worked less and earned far more than my poor dad. If you want to retire early and retire rich, it is very important to understand the principle of leverage.

In the broad definition of the word, the word *leverage* simply means *the ability to do more with less.* When it came to the subject of work, money, and leverage, rich dad would say, "If you want to become rich, you need to work less, and earn more. In order to do that, you employ some form of leverage." He contrasted that statement by saying, "People who only work hard have limited leverage. If you're working hard physically and not getting ahead financially, then you're probably someone else's leverage." He also said, "If you have money sitting in the bank in your savings account or retirement account, then others are using your money as their leverage."

Leverage Is Everywhere

As a young boy, my rich dad drew the following pictures to illustrate the principle of leverage.

Person without leverage:

Person using leverage:

Rich dad said, "Leverage is everywhere." He also said, "Humans have gained more of an advantage over animals simply because humans naturally seek more and more leverage. In the beginning, animals could run faster than humans, but today humans can travel faster and further than animals because they created tools of leverage, such as bicycles, cars, trucks, trains, and planes. In the beginning, birds could fly and humans could not. Today, humans fly higher, further, and faster than any bird.

Leverage Is Power

Animals tend to use only their God-given leverage and are generally not capable of gaining any more leverage. That is why animals eventually lost their natural advantages over humans and humans took over the planet. The same thing happens when some humans use more leverage than other humans. My rich dad said, "People with leverage have dominance over people with less leverage." In other words, just as humans gained advantages over animals by creating leveraged tools, similarly, humans who use these tools of leverage have more power over humans that do not. Saying it more simply, "Leverage is power."

Explaining how humans gained more and more leverage rich dad said, "A bird utilizes its God-given wings as its unique leverage. Humans observed birds in flight, then used their minds to discover how humans could also fly. A person who can fly from America to Europe has greater leverage over a human who only has a rowboat to get across the Atlantic." He also said, "Poor people use fewer leveraged tools than rich people. If you want to be rich and keep up with the rich, you need to understand the power of leverage."

The good news is that more and more leveraged tools are being created today, tools such as computers, the Internet, and more to come. The humans who can adapt to use these tools of leverage are the humans who are getting ahead. The people who are not learning to use more and more tools of leverage are falling behind financially or working harder and harder just to keep up. If you are getting up and going to work only to earn money, rather than working to gain some leveraged advantage in life, the chances are you are falling behind today. Never in the history of the world have so many tools of leverage been invented in such a short period of time. The people who use these tools get ahead and people who do not fall behind just as the animals did.

God-Given Leverage

While studying the history of international commerce in New York, I learned that 5,000 years ago, humans began utilizing sails and the power of the winds to propel their ships across vast expanses of water. In this case, the wind and the sails of the ship were the leverage, allowing humans to travel further and carry greater payloads, with less effort. The people who employed the power of large ships with large sails became far richer than people who did not. It dawned on me that the people who become rich are the people who create tools to use the God-given leverage in front of them. Today, we can move more *cargo* and more *wealth* with just the click of a mouse than any ship of the sea could ever move.

People Without Leverage Work for Those with Leverage

Throughout history, the people who have fallen behind are the people who fail to utilize the new tools of leverage created during their lifetime. And the people who fail to use these leveraged tools are the people who work for the people who do . . . and they physically work harder than the people who use the tools of leverage. My rich dad often said, "The people without leverage work for those that have leverage."

Obsolete Leverage

Because of the technology that came from human minds, we have different choices in *leveraged* transportation than our ancestors. Today, instead of just walking, we have the choice of riding a bicycle, driving a car, or flying a plane. Or we might choose to use the television, telephone, or e-mail to span the distances.

Just as we have more choices when it comes to types of transportation leverage, we have more choices when it comes to the types of financial leverage we can use. The people who utilize the more leveraged financial tools get ahead financially. People who use obsolete, out-of-date, or inadequate tools of financial leverage put their financial security and their financial future at risk. Today millions of people are utilizing the financial tool known as the mutual fund to prepare for their retirement. While mutual funds are by no means obsolete, they are not the leveraged financial tools of choice of the more educated investor. And that is what this book is about. If people want to retire young and retire rich, they may need to supplement their mutual funds with faster, safer, and more *information-rich* tools of financial leverage.

Why People Do Not Use the Tools of Financial Leverage

It is ironic that the poor and the middle class think of the financial tools of leverage as *too risky.* Because they think that financial leverage is too risky, most people do not utilize the faster tools of financial leverage. Rather than utilize the *financial leverage* the rich use, the poor and middle class tend to use *physical leverage* to try and get ahead. *Physical leverage* is also known as *hard work.* The rich get richer primarily because they use the financial tools of leverage and the poor and middle class do not . . . at least not in the same way the rich use the same tools.

Debt Can Be Winner's Leverage . . . It Can Also Be Loser's Leverage

In the previous chapter I talked about the use of *debt* to acquire income-producing real estate. In this example *debt* was my *leverage.* I can acquire much larger investments and get ahead faster than someone who simply works hard and tries to invest with their savings, otherwise known as *equity*. A person who knows how to use debt to acquire assets has superior financial leverage over someone who does not understand how to harness the power of debt. My rich dad said, "The rich use debt to *win* financially and the poor and middle class use debt to *lose* financially." But in order to use debt as a tool of leverage, a person needs to have more financial education. The following chapters of this book will explain how you can gain this financial education.

My poor dad often said, "Neither a borrower nor lender be." He also said, "Pay off your bills as soon as possible. Pay off your mortgage as soon as possible. Being in debt is risky." Those ideas and beliefs are some of the reasons why my poor dad worked very hard all his life and never got ahead financially. My rich dad worked less than my poor dad and yet he made more and more money the older he got. My rich dad's life was different because he knew how to harness the power of financial leverage and my poor dad didn't because he thought it was risky.

It is ironic that the poor and middle class think using debt for buying assets is risky yet they eagerly go out and use debt to buy liabilities. One reason the middle class and poor fall behind the rich is because they use the financial power of bad debt to fall *behind* in life. The rich use the financial power of good debt to *propel* them ahead. The person who works hard, saves money, and stays out of debt falls financially behind someone who has been trained to use debt as financial leverage. The average person thinks of debt as bad or they use debt badly. That is why most are trying to get out of debt and save money, in order to retire. To them, staying out of debt and saving money is a smart and safe way of living life . . . *And for them it is a smarter choice, given the average person's financial education* . . . or lack of it.

Other Forms of Leverage

There are other forms of leverage, other than debt, that Kim and I used to retire early on. In order to build a business with eleven offices, we had to use OPT (other people's time) to build another type of asset, an asset known as a business. In this example, the *leverage* was the *employment of people*, in order to create an asset faster and make the asset bigger and more valuable.

The reason most people *do not get richer quicker* is simply because it is their money (their savings held in a bank) and their time and labor (a safe secure job) that the rich are using as leverage to acquire and create the assets that make them rich. I could not have acquired so many assets in such a short period of time if I had not used those two different forms of financial leverage, which are OPM (other people's money) and OPT (other people's time).

The good news is that there are many forms of leverage, other than OPM and OPT, that you can use to acquire or create assets for yourself. Just as humans 5,000 years ago harnessed the wind to power the sails of their ships, you can find many different forms of leverage to help you. There are infinite forms of leverage once you understand the principles of leverage and begin to look for it. As my rich dad said to me years ago, "Humans have always sought new and higher forms of leverage, naturally." Consider the person who takes time to make a fishnet. A person with a net has more leverage over people who try to catch fish with their bare hands . . . of course that is only true *if* the person with the net knows how to use the net. A farmer with 1,000 acres of land to plant has more leverage than a farmer who has just 100 acres. Again, a lot still depends on the farmer's abilities to manage a larger farm. A computer is a tremendous tool of leverage, but then again, it depends on what the computer is used for.

The following are a few examples of other forms of leverage. Your health, your time, your education, and your relationships can all assist you or hinder you in your goal to retire young and retire rich.

HEALTH

Obviously, *health* is a very important form of leverage. All too often people do not appreciate the value of their health until they begin to lose it. What benefit will early retirement serve you if you are too ill to enjoy it?

TIME

Time is also an important leverage. Once people begin to fall behind financially, it is often difficult to find the time to get ahead in life. If a person is playing financial catch-up, it is difficult to be prepared to take advantage of opportunities that pop up in front of them. I often hear people say, "He got lucky because he was in the right place at the right time." I think a more accurate statement is, "He got lucky because he was educated, experienced, ready, and prepared to take advantage of the opportunity when the opportunity presented itself."

The extra time I enjoy from early retirement has helped me increase my wealth even more. I now have the time to look for and recognize opportunities.

EDUCATION

Education is an important form of leverage. The difference in earnings between someone who drops out of high school and a person who graduates from college can be measured in the millions of dollars, when measured over a lifetime. Yet a person who graduates from college but has little financial education will often fall far behind a person who is financially educated, with or without a college education. I have met so many college graduates who leave school deeply in debt from school loans. But worse than the school loans, many of these graduates are anxious to get a job so they can become deeper in consumer debt. That is the price of having a good education but a lack of basic financial education. A high-paying job without financial education often means the person gets deeper in debt faster than someone with a low-paying job. That is not too intelligent.

Not only will financial education help you retire young, it will help you keep your wealth for generations.

RELATIONSHIPS

Leverage can be found in your *relationships,* business and personal. The following are examples of the leverage found in relationships:

- I have seen many people suffer because they work for a business that is run by incompetent owners or management. I have also seen people do very well financially because they associate with financially knowledgeable people.
- A labor union, such as the teachers union or pilots union, is a form of relationship leverage. A professional organization such as the American Medical Association can be a form of relationship leverage. Unions and professional associations are people with *professional leverage* that often bind together to protect themselves from people with strong *financial leverage*.
- Many people do well financially because they have excellent *financial advisors.* There are also many people who suffer financially because they have incompetent financial advisors. As my rich dad said, "The reason so many financial advisors are called *brokers* is because they are often *broker* than you. So be careful from whom you take advice." Rich dad also said, "The most *expensive* advice is often *free* advice. It is the advice about money, investments, and business that you get from your poor friends and relatives."
- Most of us have heard about power marriages. A power marriage is the marriage of two strong people who come together to become even more powerful. We have also seen married couples suffer financially because their marriage is not a loving, harmonious, and prosperous one. I would not be rich today without my wife, Kim, as a best friend and business partner.
- Speaking of marriage, I once heard a speaker say, "It is almost impossible to become rich if your spouse does not want to become rich too." I do not know if that is 100 percent true but I am sure there is some truth to it.

So the people around you can be a great source of leverage, positive and negative. You may want to ask yourself how many people around you are holding you back financially and how many are pushing you ahead financially. When it comes to money, your relationships can be important sources of leverage. Rich dad used to say, "Being rich is not so much *what* you know but *who* you know."

TOOLS

A plumber finds leverage in using the right tools. A doctor uses medical tools in order to do his or her work. A car is a form of leverage for many of us. A computer now allows us to do business with the world, through the Web, so it is a very important tool of leverage.

SPARE TIME

Leverage can be found in your *spare time*. I know many people who spend their time watching TV or shopping. Many of the people I have met or read about became rich in their spare time, rather than at their job. Hewlett-Packard and Ford Motor Company were started in garages and Dell Computer was started in a dormitory room. A friend of mine was a lawyer by weekday and real estate investor on the weekends. Today he donates his legal services for free to charitable organizations and plays with his kids or plays golf full-time. He just turned thirty-nine.

Find the Leverage That Works Best for You

So I want to emphasize by repeating the message that there are many forms of leverage that you can use today to acquire and create assets to allow you to get ahead financially faster. You *do not* have to use OPM and OPT to get rich if you do not want to use those forms of leverage. Yet, if you want to retire young and retire rich, you need to find the leverage that works best for you.

Repeating once again, because it summarizes the theme of this book, rich dad said: "People who only work hard have limited leverage. If you're working hard physically and not getting ahead financially, then you're probably someone else's leverage." He also said, "If you have money sitting in the bank in your savings account or a retirement account, then others are using your money as their leverage."

The Importance of the Word And

One definition of leverage is *the ability to do more with less.* Rich dad added to that definition by saying, "Leverage is the ability to do *more and more* with *less and less.*" This idea of *more and more* with *less and less* is very important at this point. Rich dad said, "The difference between the rich, the poor, and the middle class is found *in between* the word *more* and the next word *more*. And the word in between these words is the word *and*."

Rich dad explained further by saying, "The rich keep adding more *and* more leverage, which is why they get richer *and* richer. The poor and middle class stop adding more leverage. The point at which you stop adding *more leverage* defines your financial station in life." In other words, a person becomes poor when they stop increasing their leverage. The same is true for the middle class. The truly rich never stop increasing their leverage.

An example of this idea is my poor dad saying, "Get a good education so you can get a good job." For many people in the middle class, their academic and professional education is where their education stopped. The rich do not stop there. They add more leverage by adding *financial education* to their list of *more and more* leverage.

The poor are different from the middle class because they generally have less education in their list of educational leverage. The poor often do not have even a basic education or they fail to add professional education to their list as the middle class does. The poor reach a certain level of education and the middle class add a little more education . . . but not enough education to make them rich.

In previous books I wrote that there were three different kinds of education. They are:

1. Academic or scholastic education
2. Professional education
3. Financial education

My poor dad stopped at professional education and was not interested in his financial education. That determined his financial station in life. My rich dad never stopped his financial education and that determined his financial station in life, rich. The poor are often poor because they often lack the basics of all three types of education.

The people falling behind today include those who have gained some form of leverage, but are failing to gain more leverage. Just because you graduated from college ten years ago does not mean you can stop working to gain more and more leverage. As rich dad used to say, "A college degree does not entitle you to stop learning or to stop increasing your leverage." He went on to say, "Neither does a million dollars in the bank entitle you to stop learning. In fact, if you stop learning, your money will soon go to someone who has continued to keep learning. Your money will go to the person who realizes that true leverage is the ability to constantly do more *and* more with less *and* less."

The Future of Leverage

Today we have high school kids who sell their businesses for millions of dollars and retire without ever having a job simply because they used a different form of leverage than their parents use. At the same time, we have baby boomers needing to go back to school in order to keep their jobs. The difference is found in the word *leverage* and the word *and.* Today your competition does not need to live in your city or even in your country. The people who will win financially are those willing to do more *and* more with less *and* less . . . not those who want to be paid more and more for doing less and less.

In the coming chapters, some of the dollar amounts I will talk about may not sound real to you. After all, it is often difficult to think about earning a million dollars a year *without* working when, at present, you may be *working very hard* just to make $50,000 a year. I emphasize the idea of *more and more* leverage because regardless of what you earn today, a million dollars a year without working is entirely possible, if you are willing to keep thinking about doing *more and more with less and less*. If you are *not* willing to think in those terms, then going from $50,000 to $1 million a year may be difficult.

The irony is, the people that are *unwilling* to think in terms of doing *more and more with less and less* are the people who often wind up *working more and more for less and less.* The good news is that as long as you are *willing* to think in terms of doing *more and more with less and less*, the *more and more you will earn* with *less and less work*. All you have to do is keep this idea in your head and it will be easier for you to retire young and retire rich.

A suggestion: Get a clean sheet of paper and begin to write your answers to this question. The question is:

How can I do what I do for *more* people with
less work and for a better price?

If you cannot think of anything, keep thinking. *This is a very important question.* It is the question, if answered and acted upon, that makes people millionaires, even billionaires. That is why rich dad called it "the million-dollar question."

In the next section, I will be going into the power of your mind as a tool of leverage. Being able to answer questions such as this one is vital to being able to retire young and retire rich.

Chapter 5

The Leverage of Your Mind

Why Some People Can and Some People Can't

In *Rich Dad's Guide to Investing,* I wrote of a lesson with rich dad that is worth repeating at this time.

The lesson begins with rich dad, his son, and me walking along a piece of beautiful beachfront property. Rich dad stopped, pointed, and said, "I just bought this piece of land."

I was surprised that he could afford to buy such an expensive piece of property. Although I was relatively young, I did know that oceanfront property in Hawaii was expensive. Since my rich dad was not yet rich, I wondered how he could afford such an investment. Rich dad was about to share with me a very big secret on how he could afford investments he *could not* afford. It was one of the secrets that made him rich.

A Different Reality

Simply said, my rich dad could afford an expensive piece of land, even though he did not have much money at the time, because he made "affording it" a part of *his reality.* My poor dad, although he earned more money at that time, would have said, "I can't afford it," because the idea of buying such an expensive piece of real estate was *outside his reality*.

A Most Important Lesson

Over the years, rich dad taught me many important lessons . . . lessons that radically affected the direction and outcome of my life. This lesson on the power of a person's reality is one of the most important. For those of you who read *Rich Dad Poor Dad*, you may recall that he forbade his son and me from saying the words "I can't afford it." Rich dad understood the power of a person's reality. His lesson behind his lesson was:

"What you think is *real* is your *reality*."

Being a religious man, rich dad often quoted the passage from the Old Testament, "and the word became flesh." He would put that passage into more everyday terms so we as young boys could understand it. He constantly said to Mike and me, "What 'and the word became flesh' means is that whatever you think and say is *real* becomes *your reality.*" When he came across that beautiful piece of oceanfront property, he refused to say, "I can't afford it," even though he did not have the money at that time. Instead he spent months coming up with a plan on *how he could afford it.* He worked hard at taking what was *outside his reality* and making it *a part of his reality*. It was not money that made my rich dad richer. *It was his ability to expand his **reality** that ultimately made him richer and richer*.

Is Investing Risky?

People often say, "Investing is risky." To them, that idea is real, and because they think it is *real,* it becomes their *reality,* even though investing *does not* have to be risky. While there is always *risk,* just as there is risk in crossing a street or riding a bicycle, the acts themselves *do not have to be risky*. So many people think investing is risky because they think their ideas are real.

A few months ago, a noted investment advisor from a famous bank and I were being interviewed on a radio program. The noted advisor was brought in to challenge the ideas I wrote about in *Rich Dad Poor Dad*. He started out, "Robert Kiyosaki states that people should start their own businesses if they want to be rich. What Mr. Kiyosaki fails to realize is that most people cannot start their own businesses. Starting a business is far too risky. Statistics show that nine out of ten businesses fail in their first five years. That is why Mr. Kiyosaki's ideas are risky. Ask him what he has to say about those facts."

The radio commentator, happy to have some controversy on his show, asked me in a gleeful tone, "Well what do you have to say about those facts, Mr. Kiyosaki?"

Having heard this many times before, I was ready to take on the verbal challenge, calmly. Pausing a moment, I cleared my throat and said, "I have seen and heard those same statistics quoted before . . . and from my experience, I would say those statistics are accurate. I have seen many businesses fail before their fifth anniversary."

"So how can you recommend people start their own businesses?" asked the noted advisor with a hint of anger in his voice.

"First of all," I replied, "I do not recommend people start their own businesses. I state that everyone should *mind their own business.* When I say 'mind their own business,' I mean they should mind their investment portfolio. That does not necessarily mean start their own business, although a well-run business is often the asset that makes the rich very rich."

"So what about the risk?" asked the noted financial advisor. "What do you think about the nine out of ten businesses that fail?"

"Yes. What about that?" asked the commentator a little less gleefully after realizing the discussion was not escalating into an on-air argument.

"First of all, while nine out of ten do not make it, notice that one out of the ten *does* make it. Once I realized that the odds were nine out of ten do not make it, I knew that I needed to be prepared to lose at least nine times."

"You were prepared to lose nine out of ten times?" asked the financial advisor with a sarcastic tone.

"Yes," I replied. "In fact, I have been part of the nine that did not survive. In fact I have been that nine out of ten that did not survive twice, but then I made it on my third try."

"So how did you feel when you failed?" asked the investment advisor, who was an employee of the bank and not an owner of a business. "Was it worth it?"

"I felt terrible the first time I failed. It felt even worse the second time. But yes, to me, it was worth it. If I had not failed twice, I would not have retired eighteen years early nor would I be financially free today," I replied. "It took me a while to recover each time. Yet even though I felt bad, I was mentally prepared to keep going ten times, even twenty times, if I had to. I did not want to fail that many times, but I was willing."

"It sounds too risky for me and it is too risky for most people," said the advisor.

"I agree," I replied. "It is especially risky if you are not willing to fail or fail only once before you quit. It's even worse if you think that failing is bad. I was taught by my rich dad to understand that failing is part of winning. Even though I was successful in the past, I still realize that the odds remain the same. Every time I start a business, I continue to be aware that nine out of ten do fail."

"Why do you say that?" asked the commentator.

"Because I always need to remain humble and respect the odds. I have seen too many people build a business, make a lot of money, get cocky, and start another business thinking the odds are now in their favor. While their odds may have improved a little because of their past experience and success, we all need to be humble enough to know that the odds remain nine out of ten for all start-up businesses."

"That makes sense," said the commentator. "So today when you start a new business you still remain cautious. You still respect the one-out-of-ten possibility for success."

"That is correct," I replied. "I have had several friends get cocky and put all the money from their last business into a new business and then lose it all. If you want to be successful in life, you need to always be respectful of the odds, regardless of how successful you were in the past. Every professional blackjack player knows that just because they drew an ace and a king their last hand, it does not change the odds for their next hand."

"I'll keep that in mind," said the commentator.

"I still think it is too risky," said the advisor. "You and your book are dangerous. Most people cannot do what you do. Most people are not prepared to run their own business."

"Do you agree?" asked the commentator.

"There is some truth in that statement also," I replied. "Our school system trains people to be employees rather than to be business owners and that is why most are not prepared to run their own businesses. So I would agree with our noted advisor."

Pausing, I let my comment of agreement settle in. I was doing my best to not get into an argument, even though I felt provoked by the investment advisor. Continuing on I said, "Yet I will remind you that less than 100 years ago, most people were small independent businesspeople. Many of us had relatives who were farmers or owners of small businesses. They were all entrepreneurs. People 100 years ago were strong enough to run their own businesses in spite of the risks. It was only until people like Henry Ford began building mega-businesses that more and more people became employees. Yet even with the advent of mega-businesses like Ford or General Electric, small independent businesses continue to thrive.

"In fact, small businesses are responsible for almost all of the job growth and are responsible for a large portion of all taxes collected. So in spite of the risks, more and more people continue to start their own businesses. Without them, there would be much higher unemployment. Without these individuals willing to take risks, we would be a financially backward nation. Free enterprise gives us all the opportunity to take risks and grow. If these individuals did not take risks, our nation would not be as prosperous as it is today. People who take risks increase prosperity."

The interview went on for another ten minutes. There was no resolution and no agreement. It was obvious we came from different realities. As the conversation without agreement continued, I could hear rich dad saying, "Many arguments in real life are caused by differences in reality."

The Risk-Reward Ratios Are in Your Favor

One of the things I wanted to say to the advisor was that the *risk-reward ratio* was in my favor. But that would have certainly led to an argument . . . a test to see who was right and who was wrong. I did not make my point on the radio, but I want to explain my point to you . . . the point that there is risk in what I do but it does not have to be risky.

Years ago, rich dad explained to his son and me the importance of knowing the risks, the rewards, and having a winning strategy . . . a winning strategy that included losing. Rich dad was aware of the nine-out-of-ten failure rate of most start-up businesses. He was also aware that the reward for making it only one out of ten times far outweighed the risk of losing nine out of ten times. Rich dad further explained his position by saying, "Most people think only in the realm of what is *smart* and what is *risky*. Financially intelligent people think in terms of *risk* and *reward*. In other words, instead of immediately saying something is too risky, or right or wrong, good or bad, financially intelligent people weigh the *risks* and they weigh the *rewards*. If the rewards are great enough, they will come up with a strategy or a plan that will increase their chances of success regardless of how many times they will *lose* before they will *win*.

A Winner's Strategy

For example, I have a friend who uses his own simple risk-reward strategy for day-trading the stock market. He knows that chances are he will find a market move on one out of twenty trades. That is why he sets up what he calls a money management strategy. If he has $20,000 to play the market with, which is one tenth of the $200,000 in total cash he has, he will only risk $1,000 per trade. In other words, his strategy is to always have enough money to lose nineteen out of twenty times. I have seen him lose $14,000 on fourteen straight trades, and then suddenly make $50,000 on the next market move. His winning strategy took in the probability of losing nineteen out of twenty times although he has never lost that many times in a row . . . yet. Each time he wins, he immediately goes back to the same odds, which are one out of twenty. He knows the odds do not change regardless of how much money he has. He still plans on losing nineteen out of twenty times.

A Loser's Strategy

The average person who avoids losing and expects to win 100 percent of the time is the person who often has the loser's strategy. Expecting to win 100 percent of the time and never failing is a loser's reality. As rich dad said, "A winning strategy must include losing." Most people today have a retirement plan that does not include the possibility of losing. Most people today simply expect the stock market to always go up, and that when they retire, their nest egg will last them as long as they live. That is a plan that has no room for losing, and that is why it is a loser's plan. Winners know that losing should be a part of any plan. When I was in the Marine Corps, we always had *contingency plans,* which are plans for times when things do not go the way we expect them to go. Many people today do not have retirement contingency plans. Most people do not have retirement plans that include the possibility of a severe market crash after they retire, or outliving their retirement nest egg. In other words, when it comes to retirement planning, most people have a loser's strategy because it is a strategy that does not allow any room for error.

Losing 98 Percent of the Time

In direct response marketing, most marketers know that the chances are that 98 percent of the mailers they send out will *not* generate a sale. So professional marketers compute their marketing campaigns on a 2 percent return, some even lower. They know that the 2 percent return must cover the cost of mailing to the 98 percent that do not reply. Once direct marketers find the mailing that can return 2 percent or better, they simply increase the number of mailings, knowing that they will still lose 98 percent of the time. They know how to become very rich winning just 2 percent of the time and losing 98 percent of the time.

Losers Think Losing Is Bad

Rich dad said, "Losers are people who think that losing is bad. Losers cannot afford to lose and often avoid losing at all costs. Many losers bet only on sure things . . . sure things such as job security, a steady paycheck, a guaranteed pension, and interest from a bank account. Losers keep losing and winners keep winning simply because winners know that losing is part of winning."

As little boys, rich dad often asked us, "Are you willing to lose ninety-nine out of 100 times?"

The answer he was looking for from us was, "If the reward for winning outweighs the risks and costs of losing ninety-nine times." Asking us to explain further we would say, "If we knew we could win a million dollars, and the risk-reward ratio was 1:100 and the minimum bet was $1, we would get $100 dollars in single bills and work our strategy to bet $1 100 times. After we won once, we would go back to playing the same odds because the odds rarely change. We might increase our bets, but only if we could survive losing ninety-nine out of 100 times."

That was his simple way of training us to think in terms of *risk and reward* instead of *right and wrong, risky or safe.* Rich dad did not like gambling nor did he encourage us to gamble. He simply was training his son and me to think in terms of risk and rewards.

Why the Wright Brothers Were Right

Rich dad told his son and me about his trip to Kitty Hawk, North Carolina. He went there while on leave from the military in World War II. He said, "Boys, someday you need to go to Kitty Hawk and see just how smart Orville and Wilbur Wright were. The brothers knew there were *risks* in being the first to fly but they were not *risky*." Rich dad explained that the Wright brothers chose a large flat expanse of grassy sand to practice failing. He said, "Those young men knew they were going to fail so they found a very safe piece of ground to fail on. They did not jump off bridges or cliffs. They found a large flat piece of ground with a good strong wind, and practiced failing until the day they could fly.

"Because of their willingness to take risks wisely, those two young men changed the world forever. Someday, you two boys should go and see this piece of land where those two brave men chose to practice failing so one day we could fly. Most people will never fly financially simply because they choose to avoid failing." In August of 2000, I stood on that same wide piece of grassy sand and saw what my rich dad had seen some fifty years earlier. I saw a piece of land that was the perfect place to fail before flying.

I was transported back to rich dad's lesson about the Wright brothers. Rich dad would draw this diagram for his son and me:

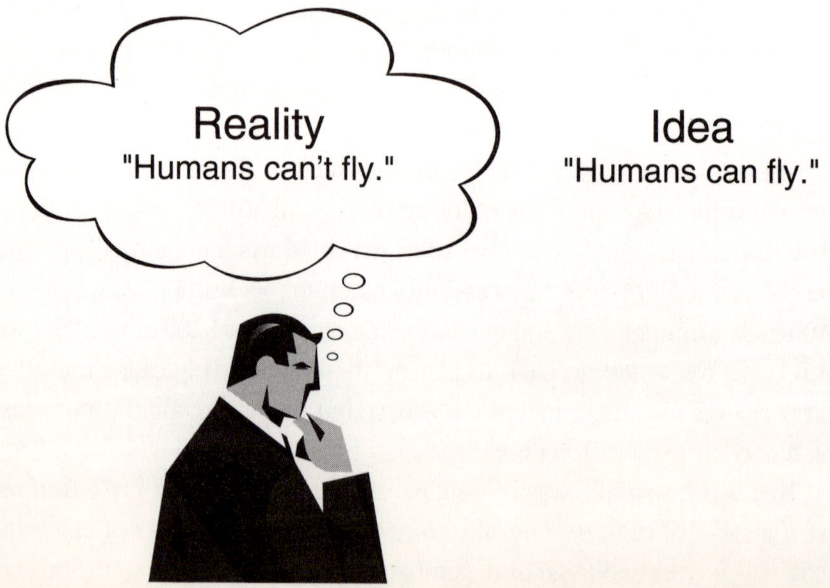

Explaining this diagram, rich dad said, "When a person says things such as:

1. "I can't afford it."
2. "You can't do that."
3. "I can't do that."
4. "That's impossible."

they are usually speaking from within their reality, making comments on ideas outside their reality."

He would continue, "When the Wright brothers announced that they were going to be the first humans to fly, many people said, 'Humans can never fly.' In fact, one of the people who said that was their own father, a respected man of the church."

So looking at rich dad's simple diagram, you can see that for most people the idea that humans could fly was outside their reality. So that comment came from within the border of their known reality.

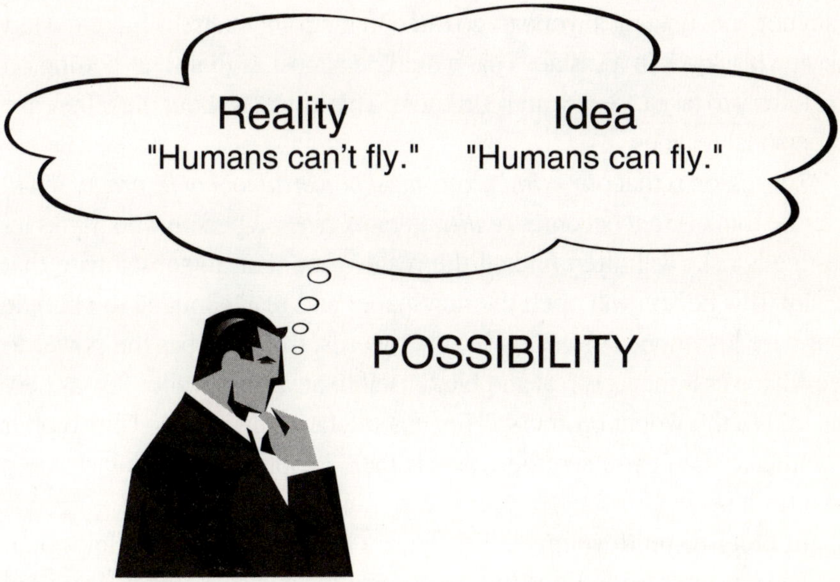

The reason so many people said "Humans will never fly" was because that idea was outside the *reality* of most people at that time. But that idea was not outside the realm of *possibility* for the Wright brothers . . . and they spent years working on making the possibility a reality. When it came to money, that is the same thing rich dad did and my poor dad did not. Today, the common phrase is "Be willing to think outside the box." Rich dad would say, "Everyone can think outside the box for a day. The question is, can you think outside the box for years? If you can, you will become richer and richer."

When later in my life I said to that financial advisor that I was willing to fail nine out of ten times in business just because the *rewards* far outweighed the *risks,* I doubted he heard me. He really did not hear me when I said, "I started the businesses knowing that I was probably going to fail. I did not think I would be successful yet I knew I had to start failing." That kind of thinking did not seem to be a part of his thinking. The point here is not who is right or who is wrong. The point to be made here is that our realities are different. And because our realities are different, we think differently and see the world differently.

The Leverage of Your Mind

I am not encouraging anyone to go out and randomly start losing or to start playing blackjack in a casino. That would be almost as foolish as betting on the lottery to take care of your retirement. This lesson is about the difference in personal realities.

The lesson is that *our mind is our most powerful tool of leverage.* Whatever we think is *real* becomes *reality,* in most cases. A person who thinks investing is risky will often find all the reality they want to substantiate that reality. This person will open the newspaper and read about all the people that have lost money investing. In other words, the mind has the power to see whatever it thinks is real and blind itself to any other reality. Just as people said to the Wright brothers, "Humans will never fly." And to Christopher Columbus, "Can't you see the world is flat?" People will always have their own realities.

In order to retire young and to retire rich, one of the most important things you can learn to do is to take control of your own reality. If you can learn to do that, making more and more money with less and less effort will become easier and easier. If you cannot control and change your reality, then getting richer and richer may take longer than you like. It was my rich dad's ability to continually change his reality that ultimately made him rich. It was *not* the beachfront property that made him rich. It was his ability to change his reality. After he bought that piece of property he was soon looking for even bigger pieces of property to test his reality on.

At the same time, it was my poor dad's *inability* to change his reality that caused him to work harder and not get ahead financially. It was his constant saying "I can't afford it" that shaped his reality. My poor dad was a very smart man. He could have afforded the same piece of land if he was willing to change his reality, but he did not know it was his reality that was in the way. He truly thought he could not afford a multimillion-dollar piece of real estate. His thoughts were his reality.

In the end, the primary difference between my rich dad and my poor dad was simply the difference in their realities. One chose to expand his reality by saying, "How can I afford that piece of beachfront property?" even though he could not afford it at the time. The other chose to say, "I can't afford it." As I said it was not the beachfront property that made one rich and one poor. It was their choice of realities.

The #1 Leverage

The number one leverage is the leverage found in your mind because it is where your realities are formed. For Kim and me to retire young and retire rich required us to constantly control, change, and expand our realities. Today I tell people, "The first step in going from $50,000 a year and a lot of hard work to $1 million a year with very little work begins with a change of reality."

Reality change does not necessarily mean bigger or better. A change of reality may simply be a shift in point of view. For example, instead of saying something is "too risky," as many unsophisticated investors say, ask instead, "What is the risk-reward ratio?" or "How many times will I lose before I win?" Instead of saying, "That piece of land is too expensive," read a book about a person who could afford that piece of land, or ask someone who could afford that piece of land and find out how they could afford it. The important thing is not the land but the changing of your reality.

Why One Dad Got Richer and Why One Dad Got Poorer

Rich dad had the ability to continually change, control, and expand his reality. And because he could continually expand his reality, he became richer and richer while working less and less. My poor dad, on the other hand, chose to live *within* his reality. My poor dad lived in a world of what he thought was real and it was the *only* reality possible for him. That is why he worked harder and harder and retired poor. He had one fixed reality and he did not know how to control, change, or expand it. Instead of changing his reality, he kept making statements such as, "I can't afford it." "I'll never be rich." "I'm not interested in money." "When I retire, my income will go down." His words became his life's reality.

If you want to retire young and retire rich, you may need to change and expand your reality and make expanding and changing your reality a habit. As my rich dad constantly reminded his son and me, "Your thoughts and words do become flesh."

Outside Our Reality for Years

Sitting on the cold Canadian mountain that New Year's Eve, I realized I needed to be willing to think thoughts outside my reality, and continue to think those thoughts until those *ideas from the realm of possibility* became my reality. Just as the Wright brothers spent years being willing to live outside the reality of most people, Kim, Larry, and I also had to live outside the reality of most people for years. In fact, we had to live outside our own reality for years. We often got into arguments with other people, and were occasionally criticized for being dreamers, foolish, reckless, or risky. Kim, Larry, and I had to live with the faith of our convictions for at least four years before we began to see any tangible results inside our reality. In other words, it took four to eight years to push our reality out to our goals that were found in the realm of possibility.

Today when people ask me what it takes to be rich, I say, "It takes the ability to expand your reality. If you are *not* willing to expand your reality, getting rich may take a very long time."

A suggestion: One way rich dad had his son and me expand our realities was through reading biographies of people who lived the lives we wanted to live. For example, rich dad had us read the biographies of John D. Rockefeller and Henry Ford. More recently, I have read books by or about Bill Gates, Richard Branson, George Soros, and others.

When I run into people who say, "I'm too old," I ask them if they would be willing to read the story of Colonel Sanders, a man who did not start becoming rich until he was in his sixties. When I hear a woman say, "I can't get ahead because it's a man's world," I ask her if she has read the story of Anita Roddick, founder of the Body Shop, or Muriel Schiefer, the first woman to have a seat on the New York Stock Exchange. When people say they are too young, I ask them to read about Bill Gates, a person who became the richest man in the world in his early thirties. If those stories do not expand their realities, I doubt if anything will.

Another great book is *Body for Life* by Bill Phillips. A friend recommended I read it because he saw my waistline growing. I just finished reading it and I am now following the program explained in the book. Bill Phillips says much of the same things my rich dad taught me, but his subject is *physical health*, and rich dad's subject is *fiscal wealth*.

Regardless of the subject, I found the process to be the same. For example, Bill Phillips writes about finding the reasons for losing weight before beginning to lose weight. Rich dad called it the *why*. Bill Phillips has an excellent section on dreams vs. goals and why both are important to the process. Yet the subjects in which I found the closest correlation between being healthy and being wealthy had to do with eating and going beyond your reality.

Bill Phillips encourages people to eat more, *not* less. He recommends eating six meals a day if you want to lose weight, gain strength, and get back your health. He says that many people who try to lose weight by starving themselves only starve for a short time; during that time they lose muscle, not fat, and then they come roaring back on a binge, which makes them fatter. They get fatter since they now have more calories and less muscle to burn off the added calories. I know that pattern well.

Rich dad said the same thing about people who try to become rich by being cheap, being frugal, not spending money, living below their means, and scrimping. Most people do not become financially strong with that type of behavior. A person needs to spend more if they want to become rich . . . but they must know *how to spend* and *what to spend on* in order to become rich. As my rich dad said, "There are good expenses and bad expenses." And most of us know that there is good food and bad food. Just as a person tries to lose weight by starving, a person who tries to get rich by being cheap only gets financially weaker, and then suddenly they too go on a binge, but it is not on an *eating binge,* it is a *spending binge*. And just as a binge eater will load up on junk food, the binge spender loads up on cheap junk.

Bill Phillips also suggests that "maximum intensity occurs after you have 'perceived' failure." I believe what Bill Phillips is saying is that it is only after you cannot go any further, at the moment you fail, that you begin to heal and grow again. In other words, only after you push yourself beyond your limits, and fail physically, is it when you become healthier. I say the same is true with becoming wealthier. I have noticed that most people are not successful because they avoid failure at all costs. Just as the investment advisor advised against starting a business because nine out of ten businesses fail, most people look upon failure as bad. Rich dad taught me that failure was essential to learning and success. I personally have learned more *after* I failed than *before* I failed. Although it sometimes hurt, the healing process after the failure is ultimately what gave me more emotional and financial strength.

I have met many people who are *not* successful simply because they have successfully failed to fail. They have failed to go beyond their own perceived reality on what they think is possible. When they fail to do that, they also fail to find out what is possible in their life. As I said, I think it was my rich dad's ability to continually change and expand his reality that ultimately made him wealthy. Bill Phillips is saying the same thing about becoming healthy. You do not become healthier by staying within your reality of how strong you are. If you want to become healthier and wealthier, you need to go beyond your reality. You need to live your life in the realm of new possibilities. The good news is that if you do consistently go beyond your limits, you gain the best leverage of all. You gain the leverage of becoming healthier, wealthier, staying younger longer, maybe even becoming better-looking . . . and to me, that is leverage worth living for.

If you are willing to expand your reality, you may want to begin by reading books or listening to audiotapes about people who have already achieved what you want to achieve. My poor dad encouraged me to read books on great leaders such as Presidents Lincoln and Kennedy, Gandhi, the Reverend Martin Luther King, and others. So both dads recommended reading to expand your reality, they just did not recommend the same realities because they came from different realities . . . and I am glad I had exposure to both realities.

If you truly want to retire young and retire rich, the place to start is with your own realities.

Chapter 6

What Do You Think Is Risky?

Having two strong men as father figures gave me the opportunity to be aware of different realities. Although at times confusing or even contradictory, having to listen to two different realities was beneficial to me in the long term. I realized that both men thought they were right and occasionally thought the other was wrong.

My real dad was moving rapidly up the ladder in state government. He quickly rose from schoolteacher to the superintendent of education for the state of Hawaii. Noticing his rapid rise, people began to whisper that my dad would someday run for political office.

At the same time my dad was climbing the ladder of government, rich dad had been working hard lifting himself out of poverty on his way to becoming very wealthy. By the time his son and I were in high school, he was rich and getting richer. The plan he had been working for over twenty years was working. Suddenly people began to take notice of him and his activities. He was no longer this obscure figure that no one knew about. People now began to wonder who this person was suddenly buying trophy properties in Hawaii. Rich dad was a man who started with nothing, had a long-term plan, worked his plan, and was now coming on the radar screen of the rich and powerful of Hawaii.

In his forties, rich dad made his move from the small town where we lived and made a play for several large blocks of land on Waikiki Beach. The newspapers were filled with articles about this new player in the resort market. It was not long before he controlled a block of land on the beach at Waikiki as well as other beachfront properties on the outer islands. Rich dad was no longer a poor boy from a little town on a remote island. Rich dad had made his move into the heart of the action and people noticed.

While my two dads were making their big career moves, I was in college at the military academy in New York. Mike, now the son of a rich man, lived in a penthouse apartment right on Waikiki Beach while he attended the University of Hawaii and was being groomed to run his father's growing empire. It sounded impressive that he lived in a penthouse apartment, but in reality, Mike was running the hotel the penthouse was in while attending school.

While at home for Christmas break, Mike and I were in rich dad's office discussing what we had learned at school and the new people we had met. Having met young men from all over the country, I made this comment to Mike and rich dad: "I have noticed how differently people think about money. I have met kids from very wealthy families and kids from very poor families. Even though most of the kids at school are academically bright, the poor and middle class do seem to think differently from the kids that come from rich families."

Rich dad's response to my last statement was swift. "They don't think differently," he said. "They think exactly the *opposite.*" Sitting at his desk, he grasped his yellow legal tablet and wrote down the following comparison:

Opposite Thinking

The Middle Class	*The Rich*
Job security	Build a business
A big house	Apartment houses
Save money	Invest money
The rich are greedy	The rich are generous

After he had finished writing, rich dad looked back up at me and said, "Your reality is defined by what you think is *smart* and what you think is *risky.*"

Looking at his diagram I asked, "You mean the middle class thinks job security is smart and building a business is risky?" I knew this reality well because it was the reality of my poor dad.

"That is correct," said rich dad. "And what else about job security?"

I thought for a while and drew a blank. "I don't know what you're looking for," I replied. "It is true that my dad and many people think that having a safe secure job is smart. What am I missing?"

"You're missing my reality," said rich dad. "I said to you that the middle class and poor don't just think differently. I said they think exactly the opposite. So what is my opposite reality?"

Suddenly more of rich dad's reality crept into my reality. "You mean to say that you think building a business is smart and job security is risky. Is that what you mean by opposite?" I asked.

Rich dad nodded his head.

"You mean you don't think building a business is risky?" I asked.

Rich dad shook his head and said, "No. Learning to build a business is like learning anything else. I think clinging to job security all your life is a lot riskier than taking the risk to learn to build a business. One risk is short-term and one risk lasts a lifetime."

This was the late 1960s. We did not yet know of the word *downsizing*. All most of us knew at that time was that you went to school, got a job, worked all your life, and when you retired, the company and the government took care of your retirement. All we were taught at home and in school was to "Get a good education so you can become a good employee." It was implied but not stated that going to school to become more *employable* was the *smart* thing to do. Today most of us know that job security is a thing of the past, but back then, no one questioned the idea of seeking job security as being the smart thing to do.

I looked at rich dad's comparison of the rich are greedy vs. the rich are generous and I knew at that moment what my reality was. In my family, the rich were considered coldhearted greedy people who were only interested in money and did not care about poor people.

Pointing at his list rich dad said, "Do you understand the difference in thinking?"

"The thinking is opposite," I said softly. "It is beyond just different. That is why it is often so hard for people to become rich. Becoming rich requires more than just thinking differently."

Rich dad nodded and let that idea settle in. "If you want to become rich, you may need to learn to think exactly opposite of the way you think now."

"Just the way you think?" I asked. "Doesn't it require *doing* things differently also?"

"Not really," said rich dad. "If you work for job security, you will work hard for most of your life. If you work to build a business, you may work harder at the start but you will work less and less in the end and you'll probably make ten to 100 to 1,000 times more money. So which one is smarter?"

"And what about investing?" I asked. "My mom and dad have always said that investing is risky and they think that saving money is smart. Don't you *do* things differently when you invest?"

Rich dad grinned and chuckled with that comment. "Saving money and investing money require exactly the same activities," said rich dad. "You will do the same things . . . even though your thinking is exactly the opposite."

"The same?" I asked. "But isn't one riskier?"

"No," said rich dad as he again chuckled. "Let me give you a very important lesson in life." I was now older and he could add more detail to his earlier lessons to Mike and me. "But before I give you the lesson, may I ask you a question?"

"Sure, ask all you want."

"What do your parents do to save money?" he asked.

"They try to do a lot of things," I replied after thinking about his question for a while.

"Well name one," said rich dad. "Name one thing they do that they spend a lot of time doing."

"Well, every Wednesday when the supermarkets advertise their weekly food specials, my mom and dad will go through the paper and plan the weekly food budget. They look for sales and clip coupons on food items," I said. "That is one activity they spend a lot of time on. In fact, our diet at home is based upon what is on sale at the supermarket."

"Then what do they do?" asked rich dad.

"Then they drive around town to the different supermarkets and buy the items they found advertised on sale," I replied. "They say they save a lot of money shopping for food on sale."

"I don't doubt they do," said rich dad. "And do they shop for clothes on sale?"

I nodded. "Yes, and they do the same thing when they are in the market for a car, new or used. They spend a lot of time shopping to save money."

"So they think that *saving* is smart?" asked rich dad.

"Definitely," I replied. "In fact, when they find something on sale, they buy a lot of it and put it in their large freezer. Just the other day they found a sale on pork butt and so they bought enough pork butt to last six months. They were thrilled to find such a savings."

Rich dad burst out laughing. "Pork butt?" he said, chuckling out loud. "How many pounds of pork butt did they buy?"

"I don't know, but they bought a lot. Our freezer is full again. But it wasn't just pork butt they bought, they also bought hamburger from another store that was on sale and put that in the freezer also."

"You mean they have a freezer just for such extra-special sales?" asked rich dad, still chuckling.

"Yes," I replied. "They work hard at *saving* every penny possible. They spend a lot of time clipping coupons and shopping at sales. Is something wrong with that?"

"No," said rich dad. "There is nothing wrong with that. It's just a different reality."

"Don't you do the same thing?" I asked.

Rich dad chuckled and said, "I've been waiting for you to ask. Now I can teach you one of the most important lessons you will ever learn."

"The lesson that you don't do the same things my parents do?" I asked again, waiting for an answer to my previous question.

"No," said rich dad. "The lesson that I do exactly the same things your parents do. In fact you have seen me do it."

"What?" I said. "You shop sales to fill your freezer? I don't believe I've ever seen you do that."

"No you haven't," said rich dad. "But you have seen me shop for investments that are on sale to fill my portfolio."

With that statement I sat quietly for a while. "You shop to fill your *portfolio* and my parents shop to fill their *freezer?* You mean to say that you *do the same activities* but you shop for different things to fill different things?"

Rich dad nodded. He wanted his lesson to sink into my twenty-year-old head.

"You do the same thing but my parents get poorer and you get richer. Is that the lesson?" I asked.

Rich dad nodded his head and said, "It is part of the lesson."

"What is the other part of the lesson?" I asked.

"Think," said rich dad. "What have we been talking about?"

I thought for a moment and finally the second half of the lesson came to me. "Oh," I said. "You and my parents do the same things but your realities are different."

"You're getting it," said rich dad. "What about smart and risky?"

"Oh," I said out loud. "They think that saving money is smart and that investing is risky."

"A little more," said rich dad.

"Because they think investing is risky, they work hard saving money . . . but in reality they are *doing* the same things you are. If they changed their reality on investing and did the same things they do trying to save money on pork butt, they would be getting richer and richer. You do the same things they do but you shop for businesses, investment real estate, stocks, bonds, and other business opportunities. You shop for your portfolio and they shop for their freezer."

"So they *do* the same things but from a different reality," said rich dad. "It is their reality that causes them to be poor or middle-class . . . *not* their activities."

"It's their mental reality that makes them poor," I said softly. "It is what we think is *smart* and what we think is *risky* that determine our socioeconomic standings in life." I was using a new word I had learned from my college economics class.

Rich dad continued, saying, "We do the same things but we operate from a different mind-set. I operate from a rich person's mind-set and your parents operate from a middle-class mind-set."

"That is why you have always said, 'What you think is real is your reality,'" I added softly.

Rich dad nodded and continued, saying, "And because they think investing is risky, they find examples of people who have lost money or nearly lost their money. Their reality blinds them to other realities. They see what they think is real, even though it is not completely real."

"So a person who thinks job security is smart will find examples of why job security is smart and find examples of why building a business is risky. A person will seek verification of the reality they want to believe in," Mike added.

"That is correct," said rich dad. "Is this making sense? Have you got the lesson?"

I nodded, yet I was still letting the lesson settle in. Pointing to the line on the yellow tablet that read, "a big house" and "apartment houses," I said, "So my mom and dad are always shopping for a bigger dream house and you are always shopping for bigger apartment houses. You are both doing the same thing but you are getting richer while my mom and dad only get larger mortgage payments. That is another example of the power of mind-set and reality, isn't it?"

"It is," said rich dad. "And why are your parents always shopping for a bigger house?"

"Because my dad's pay keeps going up so his taxes keep going up. His accountant tells him to buy a bigger house because he gets a bigger tax write-off for larger mortgage payments," I replied.

"And he thinks that is *smart* . . . doesn't he?" asked rich dad. "He thinks it's smart because he believes his house is an asset and he gets a great tax break from the government."

I nodded and added, "And they think that buying apartment houses is *risky*."

"We both get the same tax breaks except that my tax breaks make me richer and your mom and dad's tax breaks make them struggle more and work harder. I have tax breaks for *good debt,* which is debt that makes me richer, and your mom and dad acquire tax breaks for *bad debt*. Now do you understand how *smart* and *risky* determine a person's reality?" asked rich dad.

Both Mike and I nodded. "I understand it better now," said Mike.

"But what about the last line?" I asked pointing to "the rich are greedy" and "the rich are generous."

"First of all, you do not have to be rich or poor to be greedy or generous. The world is filled with poor people who are greedy just as there are poor people who are generous, and vice versa," said rich dad. "And as I have always said to you, there are many ways to become rich. You can increase your wealth by being cheap, but the problem is you are still cheap at the end of the day. You can become rich by marrying someone for money, which is a very popular sport, but we also know what that makes you. You can become rich by being a crook, but why risk going to jail when it is so much easier to get rich out of jail. And you can get rich by being lucky but the problem is you have to count on luck rather than your intelligence when you want to become richer."

I had heard this many times before. At this time I really wanted further clarification on how to become rich by being generous so I pressed by asking, "So what about the differences between 'the rich are greedy' and 'the rich are generous'?"

"Do you remember me telling you boys about doing more and more with less and less?" rich dad asked in response to my question.

We both nodded to his question.

"Well, doing *more and more with less and less* is one form of being generous. In fact, the easiest way to become rich is by being generous," said rich dad.

"You mean to become rich by serving more people," said Mike.

"That is correct," rich dad said. "Anytime I want to earn more money, all I have to do is ask myself how I can serve more people."

Mike then turned to me and said, "My dad has never said this in front of you, but I think you are ready to hear his next lesson. We are old enough to understand a little better."

"Understand what?" I asked.

"Should I tell him?" asked Mike.

"You've already started, so you may as well finish what you started."

Mike turned to me and began to speak quietly. "Your dad has always told you that the rich are greedy. Isn't that true?"

I nodded, saying, "In so many words."

"The reason he says that is because he thinks the rich should pay people more and more the longer they work at a job. He calls it seniority or tenure. Is that correct?"

I nodded.

"But can you understand that, for the most part, the person is often only doing the same amount of work or doing the same job?" asked Mike softly.

"I understand that," I replied. "But my dad does not see it that way. He truly believes in pay raises based on loyalty and longevity."

"So your dad thinks the rich are greedy because they will not pay for loyalty and longevity. Isn't that true?"

"He does," I replied.

"Can you see how wanting more money for doing the same amount of work can be greedy?" asked Mike. "Or wanting to be paid overtime or wanting to be paid extra if the job the person does is outside the job description?"

"But that is how people in my dad's world earn their money," I said. "It is their reality."

"That is the word," said rich dad. "The word is *reality*. We come from different realities. In my world, to ask for more money to do the same job is greedy. In my world, if I want more money, I first need to do more and more for less and less money, for more and more people, then I become rich."

"That is why dad had us read the biography of Henry Ford," said Mike. "Henry Ford became one of the richest men in the world because he provided automobiles for more and more people for less and less cost. Henry Ford from my dad's point of view was a very generous man. Yet many other people think he was greedy because from their reality, he exploited the workers. The conflict comes because of a different reality."

"I understand," I said. "As I have grown up, I have noticed the differences between people who are willing to do more and more for less and less money and the people who want to do less and less for more and more money. In my dad's world, it is the university professors who get paid the most and teach the least. They call it 'tenure' and that is the model of reality my dad subscribes to."

"And they are entitled to think that is *smart* thinking," said rich dad. "But that is not the way I think."

"That is why your dad has a bigger house than my dad," said Mike. "My dad has spent years buying and building apartment houses so he could serve more families with more and more affordable housing. The more apartments he builds, the more the price of rent goes down. If not for people like my dad, many lower income families would be paying more and more rent because there would be so few apartments available. More apartments means lower rents. It is the basic economic principle of supply and demand. Your dad worked hard to buy bigger and bigger houses for himself and his family. He provides houses for no one else, and yet he continues to think that the rich are greedy. It is your dad's reality but it is not my dad's reality."

I sat there silently grateful that Mike and his dad had been as gentle as possible with me on this subject. They were doing their best to point out the differences in the words *greedy* and *generous* to me. At the age of twenty, I was beginning to make a shift in my reality. I knew that I could choose the reality I wanted and the reality I was choosing was the reality of my rich dad. And that reality was that many of the rich were generous. I knew that from here on in, if I wanted to become richer, I first needed to find out how to be more generous. I knew that I could choose to try and become richer by asking for more money for doing less work, but I also knew that I could become richer by doing more for more people. I had that choice of reality. As rich dad said, "The thinking is not different. It is opposite thinking." At the age of twenty I was starting to think in an opposite direction from my own family's thinking. In order for me to retire young and retire rich, all I needed to do was find out how to be more and more generous, not more and more greedy. I began to see that my own family's way of thinking was the greedy way of thinking.

In book number two, *Rich Dad's CASHFLOW Quadrant*, I wrote about the different people found in the different quadrants, illustrated below:

The different quadrants represent different realities. For a person to change quadrants or to be in two or more quadrants requires a change in reality. For example, the E quadrant, which stands for *employee,* is the quadrant that sees the world from the job security reality.

The S quadrant, which stands for *small business* or the *self-employed*, is the quadrant that sees the world from personal independence, the do-it-on-your-own or rugged-individual mentality. Even in this comparison, the comparison between the S quadrant, and the B quadrant, the business quadrant, you find the power of leverage coming into play. One of the main differences between a small businessperson and a big businessperson comes down to how many more people that business owner serves. A big business owner will do his or her best to build a system to serve as many people as possible. A small business owner often depends upon his or her personal touch to serve as many people as possible. The problem with the S quadrant is that the small business owner often runs out of time and is not able to serve as many people as the big business owner. So one of the differences between a small business owner and a big business owner is an S business owner serves people personally and a B business owner uses a system to serve as many people as possible.

The I quadrant, which stands for *investor,* is the playground of the rich. Investors make money with money. They do not have to work because their money is working for them.

A suggestion: You may want to take a quick quiz. The quiz goes like this:

In *your* family, what was their reality on the following subjects?

		Smart		Risky
1. Job security		_____		_____
2. Building a business		_____		_____
3. A big house		_____		_____
4. Apartment houses		_____		_____
5. Saving money		_____		_____
6. Investing money		_____		_____
7. The rich are	greedy	_____	generous	_____

Now you may want to take the same quiz based upon your reality. I ask that you take your family's position first because that reality can be a very strong emotional reality. After comparing your reality with your family's reality, you may understand some of the differences in reality between different members of the same family.

In order to retire young and retire rich, I had to reject some of my own family's reality before I could adopt and find my own realities. For Kim and me to retire young and retire rich, we had to find ways to serve more and more people, rather than be paid more and serve fewer.

Chapter 7

How to Work Less and Earn More

"If you want to get rich," said rich dad, "don't ask for a raise. Instead of asking for a raise, begin to ask how you can serve more people. In fact, if you are serious about becoming rich, you don't really want a raise. If you get a raise you are working for the *wrong* kind of money."

In an earlier chapter, I shared how I retired early by increasing my debt rather than trying to get out of debt, which is what most people try to do. The logic behind that thinking is that there is *good debt* and *bad debt* and most people are loaded down with bad debt. The same is true with income. Most people are *not* aware that there is *good income* and *bad income* . . . and most people do not become rich because they work hard for bad income . . . and when you ask for a raise, you ask for an increase in bad income. If you want to retire young and retire rich, you need to work hard for the right kind of income.

In earlier books I discussed the three different types of income, which are:

1. *Earned income:* Earned income is you working for money. It is the income that comes in the form of a paycheck. It is also the type of income you ask for more of when you ask for a raise, bonus, overtime, commissions, and tips.

2. *Portfolio income*: Portfolio income is generally income from paper assets such as stocks, bonds, and mutual funds. A vast majority of all retirement accounts are counting on portfolio income in the future.

3. *Passive income*: Passive income is generally income from real estate. It can also be royalty income from patents or for use of your intellectual property such as songs, books, or other objects of intellectual value.

Why Rich Dad Did Not Like Earned *Income*

In rich dad's mind, the worst kind of income to work hard for was *earned income.* To him, it was the worst income for four main reasons:

1. It is the highest taxed income and it is the income with the fewest *controls* over how much you pay in taxes and when you pay your taxes.
2. You personally have to work for it and it takes up your valuable time.
3. There is very little leverage in earned income. The primary way most people increase their earned income is by working harder.
4. There is often no residual value for your work. In other words, you work, get paid, and then have to work again to be paid again. Again, to rich dad, there was very little leverage in working for earned income.

Growing up, I always found it interesting that rich dad did not like *earned income*. He often said, "The worst advice you can give your child is to go to school so you can get a high-paying job." The reason he said that was not because he was against school . . . he was against teaching your children to spend their lives working for earned income. Most people I knew dreamed of high-paying jobs with lots of *earned* income. As I said, the difference in realities was more than just different. It was exactly the opposite. Rich dad said, "Teaching people to spend their lives working for earned income is like teaching someone to be a high-paid slave for life."

Why Rich Dad Liked Passive Income

Although he did receive all three types of income, if given the choice among the three, he would take *passive* income all the time. Why? Because it was the income he had to work the least for, it is often the least taxed, and it earned him some of the highest returns consistently over a long period of time. In other words, he worked hard for *passive* income because, in the long run, he worked less and less, served more and more people, and earned more and more the older he got.

In my quest to retire young and retire rich, I had to know which type of money to work hard for. Kim and I were able to retire early because our plan had us working hard for *passive* income and not *earned* income, which is what most people do. Another difference is that we planned on retiring with more *passive* income and not *portfolio* income, which is what most people plan to retire on. While most people *do* retire on portfolio income, it is not always the best income because it is the second highest taxed income of the three incomes . . . and taxes are your largest single lifetime expense. This chapter shall explain why.

My rich dad had all three types of income. The reason he had all three was because each type of income had different advantages and disadvantages. My poor dad worked hard for only one type of income. That difference between the two men made a big difference when measured over their working lifetimes.

My Dads Worked Hard for Different Kinds of Money

My two dads did not work hard for the same kind of money. My poor dad said repeatedly, "Go to school so you can get a high-paying job." My rich dad said, "It is not how much you make that counts but how much money you keep." He went on to say, "Earned income is the income that you work the hardest for and you are allowed to keep the least of."

50 Percent Money

Rich dad often called *earned income*, the income you receive from a paycheck, "50 percent money." The reason he called it 50 percent money was because no matter how much money you earned, the government always took at least 50 percent of it or more in one way or another. If you make $50,000 a year today, then at least $25,000 may go to the government, most of it before you even get your hands on it (through withholding). Even after you receive that remaining $25,000, the taxing continues on. As most people know, you are taxed when you earn, spend, save, invest, and when you die. In fact your taxes at death can be very high if you are not properly prepared for the event. As rich dad often said, "If you do not have a plan for your money after you die, then the government does."

From rich dad's point of view, it was not very smart to work hard and have the government take at least 50 percent of what you worked hard for.

(A few years back, the tax rate was even higher than 50 percent. While the rate has come down over the last few years, many of the tax loopholes have been taken away in order to compensate for the lowering of tax rates. The fact is, when rich dad was in his prime earning years, he often called earned income 80 percent money because that is how much the government took from high-earned-income people.)

My poor dad did not know that there was a difference in the different types of income. And since he did not know there was a difference, he worked very hard for 50 percent money and then bought a bigger house for the tax breaks that he never really got. Rather than finding out more about the different types of income, my dad would go back to school so he could receive a promotion and a pay raise. In other words, he worked hard, studied hard, earned more, and paid more and more in taxes because he worked for 50 percent money.

Rich dad had a difficult time understanding people who spent their lives in search of a higher paying job or a pay raise. He often said, "When you get a raise, so does the government." To him, spending your life working hard for 50 percent money was not the financially intelligent thing to do.

20 Percent Money

Most people today are attempting to retire utilizing what my rich dad called 20 percent money, which is money from *capital gains* or appreciation of stocks and sometimes real estate. The rate used to be a lot higher only a few years ago, which means that working for capital gains is even smarter today. When you hear politicians saying, "My opponent is giving a tax break to the rich," they are often referring to some sort of tax break on investment income.

Many people are financially smarter and not working so hard for *earned* income. Many people are asking for stock options that can be 20 percent money, if the company succeeds. (A certain portion is treated as earned income but the increase in value afterward may be 20 percent money.) A stock option can also be worth nothing if the business does not improve its perceived value to the market. The point is that people are catching on to the tax advantages and the different levels of leverage of the different types of income. The growing gap between the haves and have-nots is because most people are not aware that there are different types of income . . . and they work hard for the wrong kind of income.

0 Percent Money

One of the reasons Kim and I retired early was because we utilized tax-deferred money and many times what my rich dad called 0 percent money. Tax-deferred money is money from capital gains that is not immediately taxed . . . and is deferred for as long as we choose to defer paying those taxes.

For example: We put down $5,000 and purchased a house for $50,000. Two years later we sold it for $100,000. We had a capital gains consequence of $50,000 but we chose not to pay the 20 percent in capital gains, which would have been approximately $10,000. Instead of paying the capital gains tax, as you would if you had made the same amount from a stock or mutual fund, we deferred our gains and rolled $55,000, which was $50,000 in gains plus our original $5,000 down payment, into our next investment. In other words we had a 1,000 percent return in two years and paid no immediate taxes. We legally *deferred* our taxes and used what was technically the government's money as a down payment on a larger apartment house for $330,000. We then used the bank's money and some of the seller's equity to help us finance the remaining $275,000 we did not have. Not only did we use OPM (other people's money), we used government money to help us retire young and retire rich. Between 1988 and 1994, we utilized this investment and tax strategy many times.

In America, one of the advantages of investing in real estate over paper assets is this legal loophole in the tax code. The reason the government allows this loophole is because it wants investors to keep their money invested in real estate to provide a supply of housing for people who choose not to buy or cannot afford their own home. The tax break keeps investors such as Kim and me to provide an abundant supply of rental homes and thus keeps down the cost of housing. These tax incentives also keep the real estate industry vibrant, and help the nation's economy stay strong, since real estate makes up a large sector of the U.S. economy. If the real estate industry hurts, so does the country.

Tax Free Money

There are many ways to earn tax free money. One way is to invest in tax free municipal bonds. An example would be a person who puts $1,000 in a tax-free bond at a 5 percent interest rate. That means that each year this person will receive $50 tax free. While it may not sound exciting, there are many times when such a return is desirable.

Tax Free Money from 0 Percent Money

Another way of deferring taxes is by taking the depreciation from the improvements on your property. For example, let's say I buy a $100,000 rental property. The land is valued at $20,000 and the building is valued at $80,000. The government allows me to depreciate the building and not pay taxes on the amount of that depreciation. Let's say the government allows me to take a twenty-year depreciation schedule on the $80,000 improvement. In many ways, that offsets $4,000 of extra income I do not have to pay taxes on in that year. While $4,000 may not seem like a lot of money, when your portfolio is in the millions of dollars, that amount in just depreciation, when combined with other losses that are *not* really losses, can be significant.

One method the rich use to legally receive tax free money is to simply keep deferring their real estate capital gains and then, at the end of their lives, roll that real estate into something like a charitable remainder trust. The moment they do that, they may *never* have to pay tax on all those capital gains or depreciation they deferred and used for much of their lives. It is due to these legal loopholes that so many rich people donate their mansions or other parts of their estate at the end of their lives. Their families have often become very wealthy through the deferral of the taxes on these assets they donate, and do not need the asset that made them rich anymore. They have made enough money to acquire other assets. Again, it does pay to be generous.

Competent Advice

The best advice at this moment is to seek competent advice. I am not a tax attorney, a tax accountant, or an estate attorney. These are highly specialized and complex areas of law that require the best advice you can find, especially if you are rich or plan on becoming rich. As rich dad often said, "The most *expensive* advice you can receive is *free* advice. It is advice from your friends and relatives who are not rich and have no plans on becoming rich."

Bad Advice

Not only can you receive bad advice from friends and family, you can also receive bad advice from so-called professional financial advisors.

Many people are advised that their home is their best tax deduction. In my opinion that advice falls under the category of bad advice. In America, for every dollar you pay in interest, the government allows you approximately a 30 percent tax deduction. That means, if you give the government a dollar it will allow you to save 30 cents. If that makes sense to you, send me a dollar and I will send you back 50 cents. Another minor point most advisors do not tell you is that after you exceed approximately $125,000 in earned income, you begin to lose that interest tax deduction on your house. That is another reason not to work hard for earned income and buy a big house for its tax advantages.

The Best Loophole of All

In the previous chapter, I wrote about the differences between what some people thought was smart and other people thought was risky. In my first example, I stated that my poor dad thought that job security was smart and that building a business was risky. My rich dad saw it exactly the opposite. Rich dad said, "If you work for job security, you will earn less and less the more and more you work. To me, that is too high a price to pay for a little bit of security."

Today, as it was when I was a kid, the best way to earn more and work less is via owning your own business. It continues to be the best loophole in the world. One reason to start your own business is:

A difference in when you pay your taxes.

Employee	*Business owner*
Earns	Earns
Taxed	Spends
Spends what is left	Pays taxes on what is left

An employee today pays for many of life's finer things with after-tax dollars. For example, most employees have to pay for their car with *after-tax* dollars. A business owner is allowed to pay for his or her car with *before-tax* dollars if it is used for business and meets certain requirements. When you are working for 50 percent money, your car can be far more expensive than your boss's car, even though your car costs less. Even such things as football tickets, trips, or dinners, day care for your kids, and other benefits can often be purchased with before-tax dollars. A business owner can pay for those things with *before-tax* dollars while an employee pays for them with *after-tax* dollars. (They must qualify as legitimate business expenses and may be subject to limitations.) So not only are most people working for 50 percent money in America, most people are paying more for the good things of life with the money that has been reduced by about half. When I studied this difference with rich dad, I quickly realized that the price of job security was very expensive.

A Word of Warning

A word of caution and warning: This book is not a legal textbook. This book is only written to make you aware of some of the differences in income. I caution you because it is legal to reduce taxes as long as you use these tax strategies in *the pursuit of making more money*. If you utilize these same strategies *only to minimize taxes,* then you are technically breaking the law. This is a very important point and is why I recommend you seek the best tax advice possible. I have met too many people who do things only for the purpose of saving on taxes and they have been severely punished by the government. Again, the best professional assistance in this area of law is often priceless.

If you would like more information on taxes, corporations, and other legal tax minimization strategies, you may want to go to richdad.com and look at our $10 library of audiotapes and the Rich Dad's Advisors™ series of books. The audiotapes are information-only interviews with some of my advisors on technical subjects, while the books have been written by our advisors about their individual specialties. Please remember that these are educational products only. I always recommend you first consult professional advisors before taking any kind of financial actions.

Very Few Tax Breaks

When you study and understand the CASHFLOW Quadrant you soon begin to realize that the tax laws are the worst for the employee. In fact it is the *lower* paid employees who pay the *highest percentage in taxes*—so much for the government working to protect the working class. Even the S quadrant has more loopholes than the E quadrant.

The best quadrant is the B quadrant simply because the B quadrant allows you to take advantage of the different tax laws in the different quadrants. For example, as a B quadrant person, I can utilize the tax advantages of the E quadrant, the S quadrant, and the I quadrant. It is not necessarily so for people who are only E or S quadrant people. In other words, if you are an employee or a self-employed professional such as a lawyer or doctor in America, you are not allowed to utilize the same loopholes the B quadrant person enjoys. Yet the B quadrant person can utilize the laws of the E, S, and I quadrants when convenient. Again, competent financial and tax advice and planning are important if you want to use these laws to your advantage.

What Kind of Money Are You Working Hard For?

The question is: What kind of money are you working hard for? If you are working for 50 percent money, you will have to work harder than the person working for less expensive money, and the most expensive money is found in the E quadrant. If you ask any CPA, he or she will tell you that there is very little they can do for you in the E quadrant. The government has locked up most of the loopholes for this quadrant.

For people in the E quadrant, the employee quadrant, your best tax advantage is your 401(k). I have one. Regardless if you are planning on becoming secure, comfortable, or rich, everyone should maximize the advantages of their 401(k). It is for many people in the E quadrant the only true loophole available to them.

The Problem with a 401(k)

Although I recommend that everyone have and maximize contributions to a 401(k), if they qualify for one, there is one major flaw I see in it. The flaw is that although you save your money in it and it hopefully grows free of the 20 percent capital gains tax when you withdraw it at retirement time, you are taxed at the 50 percent tax rate of earned income. Even though you believe you are investing in *portfolio* or 20 percent money, when you cash in, you are still taxed at *earned* income rates. In other words, even though you invest in tax-deferred 20 percent money, you are taxed at 50 percent money rates when you need the money. That means you work all your life for 50 percent money, and when you retire you are still taxed at the 50 percent rate. (Of course, if your employer matches your contributions to the 401(k), it makes sense to maximize your contributions.)

The second problem with a 401(k) is that it only works for people who are planning on being poor. If your income remains high after you retire, you continue to pay higher taxes on your retirement money because your income went up, not down.

When I discuss the three different levels of financial plans, one to be safe and secure, one to be comfortable, and one to be rich, remember that there are different investment vehicles for each type of plan. 401(k) plans and savings are integral parts of my plans to be safe and secure and comfortable. They are not part of my plan to be rich.

The Problem with Social Security

The problem with Social Security is that it only works for people who want to be poor. If after you retire and you find that Social Security is not enough for you to live on, and you go to work for earned income, the government will begin reducing your Social Security payments. In other words, the only way to receive a full payment is to choose to be poor, in most cases.

The Problem with Savings

For people who believe in keeping all of their money in the bank, thinking that saving is smart, their money is working for 50 percent money. I too have money in the bank, but I do not think that saving is as smart as many people do. I have money in savings as part of my financial plan to be safe and secure, not as part of my plan to be rich. This is true even though I do not think it is smart to have my money working for 50 percent money as well as losing ground to inflation.

The Worst Reality

In the following chapters, you will learn why the advice "Go to school, get a job, work hard, save money, put money in your 401(k)" could be the worst advice from a tax point of view. At each step of the way, the advice recommends working hard for 50 percent money. My poor dad was poor because this was his advice to himself and to his kids. It was his only reality when it came to money.

How You Can Earn More Tax-Advantaged Income

If you want to retire young and retire rich you will need to follow my rich dad's advice. And his advice began with the idea of minding your own business.

By simply starting a small home-based business, buying a franchise, or joining a network marketing company, you are moving into more tax-advantaged income. If you can reduce the cost of some of your expenses, just by utilizing tax-advantaged dollars, you are getting ahead financially. But always remember that *your intent must be to make more money* and *not just avoid paying taxes.* One is looked upon as tax planning and the other as tax evasion.

If you are interested in finding out how to work for more tax-advantaged dollars, you may want to check our Web site for other products we have to assist people who want more education; for example, we have two products created by my personal tax accountant, Diane Kennedy, CPA. The products are:

1. *Your First Step to Financial Freedom:* a four-audiocassette program and workbook.
2. *The Loopholes of the Rich:* a book in the Rich Dad's Advisors series published by Warner Books with more in-depth explanation of how owning a business can assist you in gaining more tax-advantaged dollars.

Always remember that as good as these products are, they are not a substitute for finding your own professional advisors. Tax strategy is not a do-it-yourself activity for those people serious about becoming rich and staying rich. These two products may be a great assistance in helping you find competent advisors by knowing who and what to look for as well as allow you to ask more intelligent questions.

Working for Free

In *Rich Dad Poor Dad* I told a story of my rich dad taking my 10 cents per hour away and asking me to work for free. Many people think it is an interesting story but working for free is *not* a part of their reality. I would like to leave you with this thought: If you want to work for tax-deferred or tax free money, it *does mean working for free* in most instances.

Money that comes from compensated labor is the highest taxed of all incomes. That is why I often cringe when I meet bright young people in school who are excited about soon getting a high-paying job. A young person with that mind-set or that reality is a person who winds up working harder and harder for 50 percent money. One day they wake up at age 40 with their high-paying job and begin to wonder why some of their friends have passed them by financially. The reason hardworking employees get passed financially later in life is because they worked hard for earned income. They worked hard for pay raises and bonuses.

Even though my poor dad started out earning more earned income than my rich dad, my rich dad eventually passed and surpassed my poor dad's earning potential. My rich dad said, "You will invest time regardless if you work for earned, portfolio, and passive income. The trouble with working for earned income is that you have to keep working hard for it. Eventually a person working for portfolio and passive income will pass the earning potential of earned income because you can work less, earn more, and pay less and less in taxes when you work for portfolio and passive income."

The reason for this is explained in this table:

Earned Income:	50 percent money
Portfolio Income:	20 percent money
Passive Income:	0 percent money

My poor dad was passed by my rich dad simply because earned income is often income from labor and the other two incomes are income from assets. As time went on, my rich dad slowly but surely kept increasing the number and size of the assets he had working for him. My poor dad only knew how to personally work harder and harder for more and more 50 percent money.

People in the E quadrant have the least control over their taxes and pay the most in taxes, even after they retire. If your income today comes from the E quadrant you may want to consider doing something to earn income from other quadrants. The S quadrant has a few more advantages over the E quadrant, the main one being the ability to deduct some expenses from your gross income, prior to being taxed. The problem with both the E and the S quadrants is that the leverage factor of personal labor is minimal and the taxes are higher. The quadrants with the most control over taxes, the highest leverage potential for labor-free income, and the most legal tax advantages are the B and I quadrants.

If you are serious about retiring young and retiring rich, you may want to consider working for free. The moment you ask yourself the question, "How can I become rich by working for free?" you begin to push your mind into another reality. If nothing comes to your mind on how you can get rich by working for free, keep pushing your reality or begin investing some time and education into studying the lives of people who became rich in the B and the I quadrants.

My rich dad said, "It is hard to become rich working for money. If you want to become really rich, learn how to build, buy, or create assets." He also said, "Working hard for *pay raises* is very risky." It is risky because people often get deeper into the rat race of life working for pay raises and secondly because other people get ahead financially faster than you.

Many of the very rich became rich in their spare time. So, if you have a job because you have financial responsibilities, keep your job but make better use of your spare time. When your friends go to play golf or go fishing or watch sports on TV, you can be starting your part-time business. Hewlett-Packard was started in a garage, as was Ford Motor Company. Keep in mind that today you can go from poor to rich faster than ever before. Michael Dell went from college kid to billionaire in three years. While his classmates were doing their homework or drinking beer in town, he was building a billion-dollar business in his dormitory room. Most of his classmates, now in their thirties, are working hard for 50 percent money. Many are now going back to school in hopes of getting a promotion and a raise, and are still drinking beer and watching sports on TV. Financially they may have a big house, an SUV, kids in private school, and are hoping their 401(k) will have enough money in it when they retire. Some are silently wondering how Michael Dell, a college dropout, got so lucky. His luck began with a difference in reality, a willingness to study, but *not* study for grades, and a willingness to work for free.

The reason Kim and I retired early was because we worked hard to build businesses and buy real estate. That plan allowed us to work less and less and earn more and more. We did not work for money. We worked hard to build, buy, or create assets, as my rich dad had advised. We were not interested in high-paying jobs or pay raises. We were not interested in working at a job without much leverage and working for money that had its leverage reduced by 50 percent. To us that was not smart and, in the long run, it was much more risky. In later chapters, I will go into how you can work to acquire more assets with less risk and higher financial yields. Yet I warn you that you may need to study and work for free in order to learn how to acquire such assets. I warn you now because *studying* and *working for free* are things that very few people do . . . and that is why there are so very few people who retire young and retire rich.

> I am not against paying taxes. Tax is an expense of living in a civilized society. Without taxes, we would not have police, firemen, teachers, sanitation workers, courts, roads, traffic lights, and of course politicians. The point of this chapter is to learn the legal and intelligent control over how much you pay in taxes and when you pay them.

A suggestion: List how much you earn a month in the following types of income currently:

1. Earned Income $ ____
2. Passive Income $ ____
3. Portfolio income $ ____

If you want to retire, you will need passive and portfolio income, in most cases. The sooner you learn to acquire *passive* and *portfolio* income, the sooner you are on your way to retiring young and retiring rich. Not only will you be able to retire earlier; you may also feel more financially secure. You may also feel smarter, since you will be earning 20 percent or even tax-deferred income, rather than 50 percent income, which is the type of income most people are working so hard for.

The final sections of this book will go into ways to acquire more portfolio and passive income with greater safety and higher returns. But again, it may require more study and working for free before you receive those types of income. It often takes dedicated study and working for free to go into another reality. If you should decide to embark upon this journey to acquire the better-leveraged incomes, always remember the Wright brothers. They are prime examples of people who studied because they wanted to learn and not for grades; they worked hard for free without guarantees, took risks intelligently, and pushed themselves and the world into another reality.

Chapter 8

The Fastest Way to Get Rich Quick: A Summary of Mental Leverage

Soon after *Rich Kid Smart Kid* was published, the fourth book in the Rich Dad series, a review of the book appeared in a prominent newspaper. Almost all of the media reporting on the Rich Dad series has been extremely favorable. They have been more than fair, as well as objective, in their reviews of my books. This particular newspaper article on *Rich Kid Smart Kid* did not start out the same way. This journalist began the review with an attack on my inability to write. He more or less said that I needed to go back to school and take writing lessons. The irony is I openly disclose in the book that I failed high school English twice because of my inability to write. Being labeled stupid and a failure at the age of fifteen because I was a poor writer was a very painful event in my life.

Since then I never have claimed to be a writer. Writing could be my weakest skill and the reason I had such a tough time in school. The fourth book in the Rich Dad series is about how I overcame my inability to read and write and still graduate from college. *Rich Kid Smart Kid* is about finding and developing your child's unique genius, even though it may not be in reading and writing, as well as the need to develop their financial survival skills. So the journalist's critique was not on content but on my writing skills, the same problem I had all through school.

The journalist ended the review by throwing out one comment he thought was favorable and would make the article balanced and objective. He wrote, "This book will help your child be more employable." Now, I found the criticism of my writing skills justified. But to put in his article that my book's only socially redeeming factor was that it made your child more *employable* was so far off the mark that I became offended. I doubted if the reporter had even read the book. *Rich Kid Smart Kid* is *not* about making your child more employable. It is about making your child more *unemployable.* If you want to retire young and retire rich, you need to think about how to become *less* employable, not *more* employable. Again the difference is found in mental realities.

How to Become Unemployable

In summary of the importance of mental leverage, I restate that your *reality* is simply what you think is *real.* Or as commonly stated, your perception *is* your reality. When asked, "Is it hard to change one's reality?" I reply with, "It depends." For me, it was a personal struggle to shed my poor dad's reality of what he thought was the smart thing to do and adopt my rich dad's ideas on what he thought was smart. In many ways, changing one's reality from a middle-class or poor reality to a rich reality may be like learning to eat with your left hand after you have spent years eating with your right. While it is not hard to do, and anyone can do it if they persevere, it may not be the easiest thing to do either.

The fastest way to become rich is to be able to change your realities faster. That may be easier said than done for most people, because I have observed that most would rather remain within the comfort of their realities . . . even if it is a reality of financial struggle and constriction. Rich dad said, "Most people would rather live within their means than expand their means." He believed most people would rather be comfortable working hard all their lives rather than be uncomfortable for a few years, working hard at changing their realities, and taking the rest of their lives off. Using the metaphor of switching from right hand to left hand, most people would rather be poor eating with their right hand than become rich by learning to eat with their left hand. In many ways, that is what a change in mental reality requires.

Content Versus Context

Fast Company is a great magazine, and I recommend that everyone subscribe to it. In a recent article entitled "Learning 101," we read:

> "*Learning* is the single most important tool for people, teams, and companies that want to get fast and stay fast in the new economy."

Further on, the article quotes Estee Solomon Gray, who is the Strategic E-Learning Advisor for InterWise, Inc. She says:

> "So where in the old economy, *content* was king, in the new economy, *context* is king."

In other words, learning to shift from right-hand to left-hand dominance is more important than what kind of fork is being used.

The current school system still struggles with giving kids better *content* rather than looking at how the Information Age has changed the *context* of the world we now live in. Just as the book reviewer described earlier felt the only socially redeemable point of my book was to make your child more employable, most schoolteachers are trying to create course content that will hopefully make your child more employable. That is why the school system continues to focus on *content* rather than *context.*

The context of the world has changed. When my mom and dad were growing up in the Great Depression, the context was that jobs were scarce and job security was king. That is why my mom and dad stressed the importance of good grades and a secure job. In my parents' day, if you found a secure job with a good company, and you were loyal and hardworking, you were set for life. The company was responsible for your financial security after you retired. Today, after the downsizing of the early 1990s, most people realize that the *context* or the rules of employment have been changed forever.

Content, Context, and Capacity

Although my rich dad did not use the words *content* and *context* very often, choosing instead to use the word *reality*, he did use the word *capacity* regularly. He would say, "Not only does a poor person have a poor reality, having a poor reality means that person has very little *capacity* to allow money to stay with them."

He meant that when people said such things as, "I'll never be rich," "I can't afford it," or "Investing is risky," it diminished their capacity to be rich. He said, "When a person with a poor or middle-class reality suddenly comes into money, they often do not have the mental and emotional capacity to handle the sudden abundance of money . . . so the money overflows and runs away." Which is why you so often hear people saying, "Money just slips through my fingers." Or "No matter how much I make, I'm short of money at the end of the month." Or "I'll invest when I have some extra money."

Occasionally I will use the example rich dad used to drive his message on context home, to his son and me. Rich dad would take an empty water glass and then pour water from a full and large pitcher into the water glass. It would not be long before the water would be overflowing from the smaller water glass and would continue to overflow as long as he poured. Rich dad would say, "There is plenty of money in the world. If you want to be rich, you need to first expand your reality [context] in order to hold on to your share of that abundance." In seminars, I use this same graphic example to explain the relationship among *content, context,* and *capacity.* I first start pouring water in a one-ounce jigger, then a small water glass, and then a larger water glass. It is a simple demonstration to illustrate the differences in capacity to hold on to money between the poor, middle-class, and rich.

How to Expand Your Capacity

When asked, "How do I begin to expand my reality or context?" I reply with, "By watching your ideas." I also remind people of one of rich dad's favorite sayings, "Money is just an idea." I answer by imparting the same advice my rich dad passed to me. He pointed out statements such as:

1. "I can't afford it."
2. "I can't do that."
3. "That's wrong."
4. "I already know that."
5. "I tried that once and it did not work."
6. "That's impossible. It will never work."

7. "You can't do that."
8. "That's illegal."
9. "That's too hard to do."
10. "I'm right and you're wrong."

Rich dad said, "Cynics and fools are twins on opposite sides of reality and possibility." He went on to say, "Fools will believe any far-fetched scheme and a cynic will criticize anything outside their reality." He finished his explanation by saying, "A cynic's reality does not let anything new in and a fool's reality does not have the ability to keep foolish ideas out. If you want to be abundant and rich, you need to have an open mind, a flexible reality, and the skills to turn new ideas into real and profitable ventures."

Requoting the statement from *Fast Company* magazine:

> "So where in the old economy, *content* was king, in the new economy, *context* is king."

My rich dad would have said it this way: "If you want to get rich quickly, you need to have a mind open to new ideas and have the skills to take on possibilities greater than your current abilities. In order to do that, you must have a reality that can change, expand, and grow quickly. To try and get rich with a poor person's reality or a reality that comes from lack and limitation is a mission impossible."

Why Not Get Rich

Sitting on the mountain in British Columbia in 1985, Kim, my friend Larry, and I decided that we were willing to be very uncomfortable and push ourselves into new realities, in order to retire young and retire rich . . . and believe me, at times it was very uncomfortable. When I am asked how we got rich quickly and retired young, I simply say, "We kept changing our realities." When asked how to change one's reality I simply quote Robert Kennedy's favorite saying:

> "Some men see things as they are and say, 'Why?' I dream things that never were and say, 'Why not?'"

If you want to get rich quicker, it is a matter of going beyond the comfort of your current realities and into the realm of new possibilities for your life. As Robert Kennedy said, "Why not?"

Having a mind that can expand its reality or context quickly is an important form of leverage. In fact, it may be your most important form of leverage, especially in this rapidly changing world. To rich dad, having a mind that could expand its reality quickly was very important. In fact I believe it was his great personal skill and reason for his ever increasing financial success. Now that I am older and hopefully wiser, I more fully appreciate why rich dad forbade his son and me from saying "I can't afford it." In the coming years, your ability to change and expand your reality is your single most important form of leverage. In the coming years, those who can change and expand their context will prosper and move ahead of those who cannot. As the magazine *Fast Company* says, "In the new economy, context is king."

If you want to keep up and retire young and retire rich, you will need to be able to continually change your context quickly . . . because *context* determines *content.* And *context* plus *content* equals *capacity*.

This more or less completes the ideas on the importance of mental leverage. Although this is the end of the mental reality section, much of this book will refer back to this very important concept of the power of one's reality.

The next section of the book is the importance of the leverage of your personal financial plan. The reason having a plan is so important is because most people have dreams but they fail to have a plan. It is important to have a dream of retiring young and retiring rich, but in order for the dream to come true, a person needs to have a plan to bridge the dream into reality.

Your mental leverage will be tested in the next section because we go into dollar amounts that are beyond most people's realities. If the dollar amounts are beyond your reality, or your context, then those dollar amounts will remain only dreams. As stated earlier, it is often difficult for a person who is earning less than $50,000 a year to imagine retiring in a few years with over a million dollars in income. While most people will dream of someday retiring with that much money, less than 1 percent of the U.S. population will. That reality will forever remain a dream for the other 99 percent.

The good news is that if you understand the importance of having the right reality or context, and understand the importance of having a plan, your chances of retiring young and retiring rich are greatly increased.

If you can change your reality and have a strong plan, you may find that making $1 million or more without working can be a lot easier than working all your life for $50,000. All it takes is a flexible reality or context and a plan that is followed. The next section is on creating your plan . . . a highly leveraged plan to retire young and retire rich.

Section II

The Leverage of Your Plan

The following are excerpts from an interview with Robert Reich, Secretary of Labor in the Clinton administration:

> "The widening gap between the rich and the poor is setting us up for serious trouble."
>
> "As Secretary of Labor, my goal was to try and get more jobs and better wages for Americans, and after working hard at that role for a number of years, you can't help but feel jobs and wages are everything. But they're not."
>
> "It's not simply a matter of having a job or even having decent pay anymore."
>
> "In the new economy, with unpredictable earnings . . . two tracks are emerging, the fast track and the slow track and the absence of gradations between."

The question is: Are you and your plan on the fast track or the slow track?

Chapter 9

How Fast Is Your Plan?

"I have the need for speed."

—Tom Cruise in *Top Gun*

The idea of working all your life, saving, and putting money into a retirement account is a very slow plan. It is a good and sensible plan for 90 percent of the people. But it is not a plan for someone who wants to retire young and retire rich. If you want to retire young and retire rich, you need to have a plan that is far faster than the plans of most people.

If you have a chance, rent the movie *Top Gun* and watch the speed at which those young pilots had to fly and make life-and-death decisions. The capacity to handle speed is important to those young pilots because their lives depended upon the *speed* at which they handled *speed.* The same is true in life and business today. The speed at which you can change and expand your context in order to adapt to the changes in the business world today is critical to every one of us who wants to succeed and do well financially. The gap is no longer between the haves and have-nots. Today the gap that is changing the most rapidly is the financial gap between the middle class and the rich. Saying it bluntly, if you have a slow Industrial Age plan, or context, you are being left behind financially . . . not by your peers, but by younger people with faster minds and more accelerated ideas. This accelerating rate of change of contexts is why we have twenty-five-year-olds who are billionaires and we have fifty-year-olds still hoping to find a $50,000 a year job. The sad thing is that many of these same fifty-year-old peers of mine are still advising their kids to follow in their footsteps . . . riding the same slow train their parents rode on.

In book number three, *Rich Dad's Guide to Investing*, I began with the statement that *investing is a plan.* I also said that most people plan on being poor, which is why so many people say as my poor dad did, "When I retire, my income will go down." In other words, they *planned* on working hard all their lives only to become poorer. Rich dad said, "If you want to be rich and retire young, you must have a very fast plan that makes you richer and richer with less and less work."

How Do You Create a Fast Plan?

One of rich dad's basic tenets on money is, "Money is an idea." Adding onto this, rich dad also said, "There are fast ideas and slow ideas just as there are fast trains and slow trains. When it comes to money, most people are on the slow train, looking out the window watching the fast train pass them by. If you want to become rich quickly, your plan must include fast ideas."

If we were to build a house, most people would first hire an architect, and the architect and you work on creating a set of plans. Yet when these same people begin to build their fortune or plan for the future, most people do not know where to begin . . . and they never design a financial plan for their life. There are no blueprints to wealth. When it comes to money, most people follow their parents' financial plan . . . and that plan is often to work hard and save money. Following that plan, millions of people then sit on the train to and from work and watch the limos, corporate jets, and luxury homes from the window of their train.

If you don't plan on spending your life gazing out the window of your train, plane, or car, stuck in rush hour traffic, you may want to begin creating a faster financial plan. The following are some ideas on how to begin to build and develop a faster plan.

1. Choose Your Exit Strategy First

I am often asked, "How do I begin investing?" Or "What should I invest in?" My response to their question is another question, "What is your exit strategy?" And sometimes, my second question is, "How old do you want to be when you exit?"

My rich dad repeatedly said, "A professional investor always has an exit strategy before they invest." Having an exit strategy is an investment fundamental. That is why rich dad also said, "Always start at the *end* before you *begin*." In other words, before you get into investing, you need to first know how, when, where, and with how much you want to exit. For example, if someone came to you and said, "What is the first thing you should do before planning a vacation?" One answer should be, "Well, where do you want to go to?" Or if someone asked you, "What should I study?" the answer would be, "Well what do you want to become after you graduate?" The same is true with investing. Before deciding what you should invest in, you should first know where you want to wind up. That is why rich dad repeatedly said, "Knowing your exit strategy is an important investment fundamental."

Many people invest because they recognize that the company they work for or the government is not going to take care of them after their working days are over. Many people are investing today for their long-term financial security. While it is good that many more people are investing today, I am afraid many investors have not given much thought to their exit strategy before they began investing.

How Much Will You Have When You Stop Working?

A number of years ago, someone gave me the following statistics from the federal government. Although the statistics are a few years old, I do not think the ratios or the dollar amounts have changed much.

Using the benchmark of age sixty-five as when most people plan on retiring, or *exiting,* the question is, how much income do you want when your working days are over? The U.S. Department of Health, Education and Welfare tracked people from age twenty to sixty-five and found:

By age sixty-five, for every 100 people:

36 were dead
54 were living on government or family support
5 were still working because they must
4 were well off
1 was wealthy

These statistics appear to verify my earlier statement that most people seem to have a plan on working hard all their lives and retiring poor. Either they planned on retiring poor or they did not pay attention to their financial plan or their exit strategy.

Looking at these statistics, the question is, when you are age sixty-five, which group do you *want* or *plan* to be in when you exit? My poor dad, although highly educated and hardworking, continually went back to institutions of higher learning for more education, and yet still wound up in the group that was at the bottom of the heap at the end of his life. My rich dad, on the other hand, wound up far, far off the chart in the rich category. Although both men more or less started with nothing, they each had a different plan and exit strategy. One planned on retiring poor and the other planned on retiring rich. Although both men kept working after age sixty-five, the difference was that one had to keep working and the other worked because he enjoyed working.

What Is the Goal of Your Exit Strategy?

After looking at the government statistics, I realized that further distinctions needed to be made in order to obtain a more useful chart to determine one's financial exit strategy. Taking these U.S. government statistics, I added further dollar distinctions to those statistics, based upon year 2000 dollar valuations. Upon retirement at age sixty-five, the income without working falls into these categories:

Poor	$25,000 or less per year
Middle class	$25,000 to $100,000 per year
Affluent	$100,000 to $1 million per year
Rich	$1 million or more per year
Ultra-rich	$1 million or more a *month*

The unfortunate reality is that only one out of 100 Americans will reach the affluent level or higher when they exit the workforce. Chances are that thirty-six out of 100 will be dead, as the U.S. Health and Education statistics state. These thirty-six will exit this earth prior to exiting the workforce. That means that the fifty-nine out of the sixty-four people remaining will exit below the affluent level. Only five go beyond that level. One reason for this is a slow financial plan without a clearly defined exit strategy.

In my investment seminars, I often ask investors, "Which group do you want to be in once your working days are over." In other words, "What is your targeted exit level?" I find it interesting that most people are happy to simply wind up in the middle-class exit category. I then say, "If you are happy there, then keep riding the slow train. The slow train will get you there." I explain further by saying, "The slow train follows the schedule of find a safe job, work hard, live below your means, save money, and invest for the long term."

When I am asked, "Can I get to the *affluent level* on the slow train?" my answer is "Yes . . . you can get there with a safe secure high-paying job . . . but you must begin investing young, live frugally, invest a large portion of your income, hope that the market does not crash, and be willing to retire after age fifty-five." Explaining further I say, "There is a price for using this plan of job security and frugality to reach the affluent level. The price is that it is often difficult to move on to the *rich* and *ultra-rich* level using such a conservative plan." If all you want is to retire at the *middle-class* or *affluent* levels, then you do not need this book. There are many books written for those levels or for people with that context and reality. The middle-class level and affluent level are great levels to exit at. It is the approximately 50 percent of the population that will not reach those levels I feel a deep concern for.

Take the Fast Train

If you are starting life with very little as I did, and want to retire young and retire rich at the *rich* or *ultra-rich* levels, you will most likely need to forsake job security and take the fast train. In order to take the fast train, a person will need an open mind, high-speed ideas, better business and investment education, and a faster plan. In other words, these people will need to operate from a different mental context and content than that of the masses. People who use the job security and long-term investment plan to reach the *affluent* level often arrive without the content, context, and capacity to handle the rigors of the *rich* and *ultra-rich* levels. In other words, they may arrive with money but without the reality required for the rich and ultra-rich levels. As my rich dad said, "There is more to being rich than having a lot of money."

My wife, Kim, and I decided to exit the rat race of life at the *affluent* level. That was our goal. Once we decided on our goal, in 1985, we worked backward and developed our exit strategy, our investment plan, and then and only then did we determine our entry strategy. Once we had our exit strategy we knew what to do and where to begin. For us it was to ride on the fast train to build a business and invest in real estate. It meant giving up a few weekends and watching a little less TV. It meant having friends and relatives asking, "Why don't you get a job?" and "Why do you work so hard?"

The hard work, lack of job security, and following the rigid schedule riding the fast train paid off. We achieved our goal from our investments when she was thirty-seven and I was forty-seven. It took nine years from the time the plan was created until we achieved our goal. We created our plan in 1985 and exited in 1994. In 1985, we chose a plan that would get us to the affluent level quickly as well as give us the required education and experience that qualified us to move on to the rich and ultra-rich levels. The key word here is *qualified*, which will be explained further, in this chapter and in following chapters.

Because our investments brought us more than $100,000 in passive income per year, we were able to move on to the *rich* level simply because we had time, money, and the basic qualifications to move on to the next levels. We went from the *affluent* level to the *rich* level in five years. Next stop is the *ultra-rich* level of residual income. If things go as planned, that should take three years.

In theory, our basic plan through all levels was simple. It was to build businesses and invest in real estate. Today, we continue to build businesses and invest in real estate. While the plan has remained simple, what has increased is our education and experience. It is this education and experience that allows us to increase the speed at which we build businesses and buy real estate. In other words, we made mistakes, corrected, and learned. By making those mistakes and learning, what has changed is the size of our context, our content or knowledge, our capacity to handle larger projects and dollar amounts, and the speed at which we process these larger and more complex facts and figures. Taking the fast train gave us different business and investor qualifications than those reaching the *affluent* level using the slow train.

We started out slowly but we gained education, experience, and friends of the same mind set. As we progressed along our simple plan, our context, content, capacity, and the speed at which we can build a business or acquire income-producing real estate has accelerated. At a time when many of my peers are reaching their peak income-earning years, our income potential appears to be just starting to take off. At a time when many of my peers are happy to be earning $80,000 to $350,000 a year, Kim and my income is boarding the very fast train. The good thing is that we are working less and less, while earning more and more. Things are going according to plan.

When I was in high school, in the 1960s, my poor dad earned far more money than my rich dad. By the time I was in college, my rich dad was earning more than twenty times what my poor dad earned, even though my poor dad was at the height of his income-producing years. By the time both men were in their mid-sixties, my poor dad was barely surviving financially. If not for Social Security and Medicare he would have been living on the streets or moving in with his kids. At the same time, my rich dad's net worth was estimated to be over $150 million and climbing. By the time they were sixty-five years of age, my rich dad was earning more in a year than my poor dad earned in his entire life. Both men's lives had gone according to plan. As former Secretary of Labor Robert Reich said, "Two tracks are emerging, the fast track and the slow track, and the absence of gradations between."

2. CREATE A PLAN THAT WORKS FOR YOU

I estimate that 90 percent of the population follows the same plan. That is why more than 99 percent of the population winds up below the affluent level. There are people who try and reach the affluent or rich level, but they fail to have their plan come true.

I emphasize the importance of creating your own plan because each of us needs to take into account our own strengths and weaknesses, hopes and desires. I knew I had to create my own plan because I was not academically smart like my poor dad. I was smart in other areas, but not in the areas that our educational system recognizes as smart. One of the first steps in creating your plan is to find out what your native genius is and the process via which you learn best.

In my book *Rich Kid Smart Kid*, I write about the seven different geniuses and four different ways of learning. The current system of education recognizes only one genius, the genius of verbal-linguistic, the ability to read and write, and only one way of learning. My poor dad assisted me in finding my genius and my way of learning, even though it was not recognized by the organization he headed, the school department of the government. Today, I earn my money not by what I learned in school, but by what I learned following my own plan.

Even if you are no longer in school, or do not have children, it might be a good exercise for you to find out your own genius and your own personal learning style. If you want to retire young and retire rich, knowing your genius and the unique way you learn is an important part of the plan.

Leaving the Path of Job Security

I clearly remember the day Larry and I left the Xerox Corporation in the late 1970s. That was my last traditional job. Twenty years later, many of my peers at Xerox are now worried about being downsized due to Xerox's technical and financial challenges. The gap in twenty years has widened by more than just money. It is a gap of realities, old and new.

A Change of Context

The previous paragraph was not written to pat myself on the back but to illustrate the change in context in just twenty years. Twenty years ago, the smart thing to do was to find a job and climb the corporate ladder. I remember people not understanding why Larry and I were leaving such a great career opportunity with such a great company. After all, we were both number one in sales for different divisions, the company was still growing, and our future seemed bright. Not only did it not make sense for us to leave during that economic era, the idea of leaving a high-paying job was not the accepted thing to do. The accepted thing to do was to work your way up the corporate ladder, and someday become a manager or even vice president of a region.

When I talk to young people born after 1975, about the same time we were leaving Xerox, many of them do not want to climb the corporate ladder. For many of them, the thing to do is start your own company and take that public through an IPO (initial public offering) and then retire young or start another company and take that public. The change in context in twenty-five years is very big. I have peers who do not even know what an IPO is . . . but their kids do. Their kids talk about becoming an entrepreneur or working with an entrepreneur who will take a company public because they want the fast track to wealth. They want the fast track rather than getting stuck in their parents' rat race . . . a financial rat race that will ultimately lead to the poorhouse for millions and millions of hardworking people of my generation.

How Are You Handling Change?

I have friends who hate changes in fashion, music, and technology. These friends hate rap music, do not have a Web-based business, and are glad that so many dot-coms failed. These are some of the same people who continue to believe in job security, Social Security, and Medicare . . . all Industrial Age ideas or promises.

While there are people who fight change, there are others who run away from change. I have other friends who are actively searching for jobs that cannot be affected or threatened by the World Wide Web. One of them took a job as a teacher, not because he likes teaching kids. He took the job because he wanted a sanctuary from the changes going on in the world. He wanted a job where he could have job security and not be fired. The school system was his shelter from the world of change.

Another friend bought a business that could never be affected by the Internet. She said, "I'm too old to learn how to do business on the Web so I want a business that is Web-proof. I don't have any money for retirement so my plan is to work until I am unable to work anymore."

These examples show realities or contexts that are not changing with the times. These people will most likely fall behind in the ever widening gap between the middle class and the rich. The ship is leaving the dock for the land of greater opportunities, riches, and wealth and many people are choosing to be left behind . . . simply because they are not able to change their mental context. They are stuck in a time that has passed.

How to See the Future

On a flight from London to New York, I sat next to a high-level executive from IBM. After we got to know each other, I asked him, "How do you prepare for the future?" His reply was, "The mistake adults make when looking at the future is that they see the future from their own eyes. That is why so many adults cannot see the changes that are coming. If you want to see how the world will be in ten years, just watch a fifteen-year-old boy or girl. Observe the world from their eyes and you will see the future.

"If you can let go of your vision of the world and actually see the world from a younger person's point of view, you will see a much bigger world, a world filled with tremendous change and an abundance of opportunities yet to come. There are business and investment opportunities coming that will create bigger fortunes than the automobile did for Henry Ford, oil did for John D. Rockefeller, computers did for Bill Gates, and the Internet did for the young founders of Yahoo, AOL, and Netscape."

I then asked, "Will we soon see a high school teenager become a self-made billionaire?"

His reply was, "I'd bet money on it."

If you are not rich today because you missed the last boat leaving the dock, do not worry, another boat to the land of riches and opportunity is getting ready to sail. The question is, will you be on it?

History Repeats Itself

One of my favorite subjects in school was economics and economic history. Economic history is often associated with the leading economist of any given time. Some of these economists are Adam Smith, David Ricardo, Thomas Malthus, and John Maynard Keynes. The stories of their lives and how they saw the world during their periods are very interesting studies in how technology, humans, and economics have evolved.

One period of economic history was named after a group of people called Luddites. Luddites were people who banded together to attack and destroy factories and the machinery in the factory because they were afraid of losing their jobs. Today when someone says a person is a Luddite, it often means a person attacking technological change, or threatened by technological change, or simply hoping the technology will just go away and leave the world alone. While the original Luddites are long gone, modern-day Luddites have replaced them. History does have a way of repeating itself.

Are You Frozen in Time?

Many of us have seen "makeover" programs on TV where the host takes a person who dresses horribly and transforms him or her, from geek to sheik, with a makeover. A team of hairstylists, image consultants, and color specialists swoop in on this person who is a fashion disaster and turn him or her into a fashion miracle. Some of the transformations are truly amazing and some are even life-changing.

A friend of mine is one of the top professional image consultants in the world, which means he gets paid to dress and improve the image of rich people. He is one of the people I pay to dress me. The reason I pay to have someone choose my clothes and cut my hair differently is because I do not want to become frozen in time. Instead I want to be moving with time, being in sync with the changes in context and content, being fashionable with the changes in fashion. The reason I change my image is because it helps me to be in sync with time as compared to being frozen in time, a time that has past.

This professional image consultant, also named Robert, once said to me, "A person often gets frozen in a time when they were most excited about life. It could be that period when they felt the most successful, had the most fun, felt the most alive, the most sexually active, or all of the above. That is why you see men and women of my age who still look like hippies. Many of them felt very alive during the years of protest against the Vietnam War. And on the flip side, that is why you see so many veterans of the same era who still wear their military fatigues. The war was a period when they too felt most alive or that their lives meant something."

When you see people wearing the sweatshirts of their college even though they graduated years ago, it is also a longing for the past through their clothes. Another example of being frozen in time is when people as they grow older begin to act, look, and dress more and more like their parents. The opposite of that is a person who begins to dress in kids' clothes trying to look younger or go back to a time when they were most attractive. Those are cases of being stuck in the past rather than changing with the times. It shows up in the way they dress. It is not really about changing clothes but about being frozen in a context. These people often become more rigid and less flexible the older they get.

Why You Don't Want to Be Stuck in the Past

Now we have all seen people who overdo fashion or people who try to look too trendy or too hip. That is not what I am talking about. One of the reasons I recommend dressing fashionably smart, as my friend Robert would say, is because you want to be in sync with the times. If you are not on the front line of what is happening, then you are in the past.

If you are in the past, then you tend to do or invest in investments that are also in the past. Investments that are of a time that has passed are investments that go down rather than making you rich. One of the reasons people buy investments whose time has passed is because the one doing the investing may also be stuck in the past.

What's Going to Happen

If you want to retire young and retire rich, you need to invest in *what is going to happen,* rather than *what has already happened.* In the world of investing, there is a lot of truth to that old saying "the early bird gets the worm."

Seeing the Future Makes You Rich

Rich dad often said to his son and me, "If you want to be rich, you need to develop your vision. You need to be standing on the edge of time, gazing into the future." Rich dad would tell us stories of how John D. Rockefeller became rich because he saw the growing importance of oil due to the growing demand for automobiles. He also reminded us of how Henry Ford could see the middle class wanting cars of their own, at a time when only the rich had cars. Today in more modern times, Bill Gates became a billionaire because he saw the growth in PCs while IBM's older and wiser men saw the future in mainframes. The older men of IBM did not think like Henry Ford and so they lost the future for IBM and gave it to Microsoft. If I were an investor in IBM, I would have those men of blindness fired and have them pay their wages back. Instead, they received bonuses and the investors lost their future. The young people who brought you Yahoo, Netscape, AOL, and other famous Internet companies became billionaires before they graduated from college because they saw the future.

If you missed the boat heading for the oil fields, the computer age, the Internet age, do not worry, there is another boat sailing. But if you are stuck in the past, your chances of missing the next boat or, worse yet, climbing on the *Titanic* because it is big and safe, are pretty good . . . especially today with the context and content of the world changing so quickly.

In the movie *Top Gun*, there is a classic line that all fighter pilots say, "Take the shot! Take the shot!" If you saw the movie, you may recall that the time available to take the shot at the enemy aircraft is measured in split seconds. If you wait too long, or are unprepared, you will miss the opportunity. The same is true in the world of money. The window of opportunity to take the shot is also narrow. If you are frozen in time, stuck in the past, dressing like your mom or dad, unprepared, lacking the business and investment skills required, you might not even see the opportunity. You will not only miss the window of opportunity, you may take shots at opportunities that are also frozen in time and not going anywhere.

In 1999, a friend came up to me and said, "I took your advice and I invested in a rental property. I bought a $150,000 duplex in a good neighborhood. It's a good start, isn't it?"

I did congratulate the person, for it is just that. It is a good start. The problem is, he is taking a shot at a target whose time has passed. He is late to the party. He did not take the shot when he should have. Yet it is a good start and a good start is often better than not starting at all. It's a good start because even if he loses money, at minimum he will gain priceless knowledge and experience.

Nonetheless he did not take the shot when he should have. I say that because he was with Kim and me when we were taking our shots between 1989 and 1994. Kim and I were buying into a falling market. When we told him he should be buying also, he said, "No, it's too risky. I might lose my job. You know they're downsizing a lot of people. Besides, real estate prices are too low and falling. What if they keep falling? What if we go into a depression?"

The window of opportunity had opened and it had closed. Ten years later, when real estate prices are at their peak, and the stock market is beginning to wobble, my friend realizes that he should begin shooting. He now shoots at targets that are old and going nowhere . . . just like him. He is frozen in time and is now shooting at targets that are frozen in time. At least he is starting to do something but I am afraid he is paying a big price. That price is more than the high price of his overpriced duplex . . . an asset that gives him very little cash flow and will appreciate very slowly in value, if it ever does. At least he finally took his shot, even though it was at a target whose time has passed. I am very proud of him for taking that first step, a step away from his parents' footsteps, the footsteps of the Industrial Age.

Kim and I are still investing in our business and in real estate. The difference is that we are now watching for targets of opportunity that are developing in the future, not in the past. That is why you want to be in sync with the future and preparing to take the shot when the window of opportunity opens, as it did between 1989 and 1993. The windows of opportunity opened in both real estate and stocks between 1989 and 1993. As I write this section of the book, in 2001, the stock market is crashing. The Nasdaq is down by over 50 percent. The stock market only went down 42 percent in 1929. Downsizing is occurring again. My friend is beginning to panic. He realizes that he may have paid too much for his duplex. To me, the windows are preparing to open again.

In my investment seminars, I occasionally have Kim speak of her experience of investing. She often says we began investing in 1989 and stopped buying in 1994. She then adds that between 1985 and 1989, we were *preparing* to invest, according to our plan. During that period we were building our business and studying about investing in real estate. For those of you who remember that era, between 1985 and 1989 was an era of very high real estate prices. Kim and I were preparing to "take our shot" when the window of opportunity opened. When it opened, our friend panicked and we began buying. His plan did not include the preparation for the window of opportunity that had opened. Today, he is late to the party, investing in investments that are too expensive, and worst of all, he is not prepared for what is coming next. He dresses like an old man, although he is younger than me, and invests like an old man.

In American football, the winning quarterback is the person who can throw the football to a place where the receiver isn't. In other words, the quarterback must in his mind see where the receiver will be and throw the ball there, even though the receiver isn't there . . . yet. If the quarterback can do that on a regular basis, he will make the big bucks. A soccer player must also kick the ball to the spot where the opposing goalie isn't. A person who plans on retiring young and retiring rich must also do the same thing. He or she must design their plan to be ready for an opportunity that is not here yet. That is why it is important to be in the present, in sync with the times, and gazing into the future.

A Plan for the Future

If you are sincere about wanting to retire young and retire rich, your plan needs to have a plan for the future, a future that does not yet exist. Just as John D. Rockefeller was prepared for the future of the automobile, and Bill Gates and Michael Dell were ready for the computer age, you too must be prepared for the opportunities of the future. If you are not, you will invest in the investments of the past, and investments of the past often have no future.

How Do You See the Future?

In order to retire young and retire rich, you will probably need to train for the future . . . a future that does not yet exist. As the IBM executive said to me, "The mistake adults make when looking at the future is that they see the future from their own eyes. That is why so many adults cannot see the changes that are coming." Maybe IBM has learned the lessons that young Bill Gates taught them. The lesson of, if you want to see the future, you need to see it through younger eyes. How you respond to changes in fashion, music, and technology reflects how you think and how flexible your mental context is. If you are stuck in the past, or out of sync with the present, you may miss the future entirely.

The other way to see the future is to study the past. In my reality, history does have a tendency to repeat itself, even though it may not repeat itself in exactly the same way. Many adults miss the future, or are run over by the future because their plans for the future have no vision of the past.

In 1998, I was talking to a young reporter in San Francisco who was just out of college. When I told her that mutual funds were risky and that I could see a crash coming, she became very angry. She then began quoting to me words and ideas her stockbroker had said to her. "The fund I am invested in has been the top-rated mutual fund for three years running. It has gone up by an average of 25 percent each year. The stock market is the best investment because even though there are dips in the market, as there were in 1987, the market has gone up consistently for forty years. It is the best place to invest your money." She never aired the interview with me because my views did not fit her view of the future. Today, her sacred funds are down over 50 percent.

While her facts and data are somewhat accurate, the problem is her data does not go far enough back in time. If she knew her history of markets, she would have known that we have a depression every seventy-five years, on average. While this does not mean we will have a depression every seventy-five years, that little bit of ancient history does explain why the market has gone up over the past forty years. The last market crash and depression was in

1929. It took the market approximately twenty-five years to recover to 1929 levels or to year 1955. I was talking to her in 1998, and so her facts were accurate that the market had gone up for forty years. Her view of the future was hindered because her view of the future did not include enough of the past. One of the things my rich dad had me do was read books on economic history. A great book I recommend people read, if they want to understand the future, is the book *The Worldly Philosophers,* by Robert Heilbroner. It is a great book for anyone wanting to see the future by studying the past.

When I teach my investment classes, I have people fill out a financial statement. I then have them look at their past and ask them if what they also see is their future. If they do not like what they see, which is a financial statement filled with bad debt, bad income, bad expenses, bad liabilities, and no future, if that is the picture of the future their financial statement is showing them, I advise them to begin to get unfrozen, get hip, throw out their old clothes, update their wardrobe, change their old friends, and begin to see the future. If you can change your context to be excited about the opportunities in the future, you have a better chance of retiring young and retiring rich.

As simple as some of those changes are, I am always amazed at how hard just cleaning out your closet and updating your clothes is for most people. Many people go out and buy new clothes, but they fail to update them. They just buy new clothes from the old era, the era of their life when life was fun and exciting or an era when they felt most successful. Many people are so afraid of the future, and the possibility that the future could be fun, hip, cool, and exciting, that they would rather stay stuck in the past.

I wrote in the introduction that retiring young and retiring rich was easy. It was not hard to do . . . yet for many people, letting go of their past and stepping bravely into the uncertainty of the future is much harder than becoming rich and retiring young. For millions of people, it is safer and more secure to stay stuck in the context, clothes, and collections of their parents and the past. That is why more than 50 percent of the population will retire at or near the poverty line. They climb on the slow train and ride it to the end of their lives . . . all according to plan.

Chapter 10

The Leverage of Seeing a Rich Future

When I show classes the following numbers for exit strategies, many cannot imagine a financially free future with more than $100,000 or more a year coming in without working.

Poor	$25,000 or less per year
Middle class	$25,000 to $100,000 per year
Affluent	$100,000 to $1 million per year
Rich	$1 million or more per year
Ultra-rich	$1 million or more a month

The reason many people cannot imagine having that much money is because they do not have it in their reality. Many people may dream of such dollar amounts and may say that *someday* they will make that much . . . but in reality, most people are just dreaming. The statistics verify this reality.

Your Future Is Created Today

Many people do not realize their financial goals because they use such words as *someday*, *maybe*, or *in the future*. Rich dad always said, "Your future is created by what you do today, not tomorrow." When you look at the above figures, the question you may want to ask yourself is this: "Is what I am doing today going to get me to the financial goal I want tomorrow?"

The harsh reality is 99 percent of the U.S. population will end up just above the $100,000 mark. Most will follow in their parents' footsteps following their parents' plan. In other words, they did the same thing and wound up on target.

Just after my return from Vietnam, I remember the frustration of earning only $900 as a Marine Corps officer when Mike was earning nearly a million dollars a year from his investments alone. I remember feeling defeated and depressed about the gap between his world and my world, his reality and my reality.

For those of you who read *Rich Dad's Guide to Investing,* you may recall rich dad sitting down with me prior to my leaving the Marine Corps and helping me develop a plan. As the book stated, "Investing is a plan, not a product or procedure."

A Plan Is the Bridge to Your Dreams

Rich dad drew a rough sketch of a large river with me standing on the bank of one side of the river. He said, "A plan is the bridge to your dreams. Your job is to make the plan or bridge real, so that your dreams become real. If all you do is stand on this side of the bank and dream of the other side, your dreams will forever be just dreams. First make your plan real and then your dreams will come true."

Between 1985 and 1994, Kim and I worked on making our plan *real* rather than dreaming of our dreams. What we did is what most combat pilots do. We practiced every day, preparing for the day when our window of opportunity would appear. Once it appeared, we took our shots and then the window closed.

As rich dad said, "Your future is created by what you do *today*, not tomorrow." In other words, what you are doing today is your future. The reason Kim and I did not take jobs, even though we were strapped for cash, was because we had no plans on being employees in the future. Instead we spent our time in seminars learning either how to build a business or invest in real estate. Even though we had no money, each and every day we practiced building better businesses and investing in real estate. We were doing today what we planned on doing in the future. Today, we build businesses and invest in real estate. Tomorrow we will probably be building businesses and investing in real estate. I have no plans on doing what my poor dad did after he retired, which was to look for jobs so he could supplement his Social Security income. He started his life preparing to look for a job and he finished his life looking for a job. By the year 2020, there will be millions of people my age doing the same thing my poor dad did . . . looking for a job to supplement their Social Security income. They will be doing tomorrow the same thing they are doing today.

A Change of Realities

There is another thing my poor dad did almost every day of his life. He always said, "I will invest when I have some money." He also said on a regular basis, "I can't afford it." When pressed to take action, he would say, "Look, I don't have time to do anything about it today, we'll talk about it tomorrow." That was his daily reality and it was his reality at the end of his life. In my opinion, the primary reason he was poor was because he had a poor person's reality, even though he made a lot of money, and he was not willing to change his reality.

As I said, the easiest way to get rich is to constantly change and improve your reality. Yet it is obvious that for many people changing their reality, changing what they do today, is the hardest part of becoming rich. When I go home to Hawaii, I see many of my friends who are doing exactly what their parents did. When my friends ask me what I do, and I tell them I build businesses and invest in real estate, many of them say the same things my parents said, "I can't do that." Or "You know I've been thinking about investing. Maybe someday when I have the money I'll begin to invest." When I tell them about preparing and learning to invest before investing they usually say, "Oh my, do you know how busy I am? I don't have time to learn to invest. The government should have free courses on how to invest. Then maybe I would go take a few classes. Why should I pay to learn to invest? Anyway, investing is too risky. I'd rather keep my money in the bank." My rich dad would say, "Listen to their *words* and you will see their *future.*"

If you want to retire young and retire rich, you may want to begin by listening to *your words* and seeing *your future*. Ask yourself, "If I keep using these words, and thinking these thoughts, at which level will I exit? Will it be poor, middle-class, affluent, rich, or ultra-rich?" If you are truthful and want to change your plans, the first thing to do is change your reality by changing your plans, your words, and your daily actions. Your future is what you do today, regardless of your dreams. As rich dad would say, "It's tough to meet your fairy prince or fairy princess if all you do every day is sit on the couch, watch TV, and eat bonbons."

Start Your Future Today

Why is it that so many people will retire poor and retire old? They cannot stop doing what they are doing . . . even though it has no future. They cannot change their context . . . the context of job security, hard work, and saving money. Many people will grow old, wear clothes from a time that has past, and cling to ideas from their parents and the Industrial Age and then fall out of sync with the present and with the future. It is not a matter of a person's age. It is a matter of a person's context.

So how does a person begin their rich and free future today? Again, the good news is it begins in your mind. It begins with your words, your thoughts, and your actions each and every day. It begins by taking stock of where you spend your time and whom you spend your time with. It begins with knowing that you must make your plan real in order to build a bridge from where you are, over the roaring waters to your dreams. As rich dad said, "Dreamers dream dreams and rich people create plans and build bridges to their dreams." Start your future today by creating a plan to the future. And for many people, one of the first steps on the plan is to *stop doing* today *what you do not want* in your future. If you do not want to work hard all your life for earned income, start asking yourself how you can learn to work for passive and portfolio income. Once you come up with some answers, make those answers a part of your plan. It may mean studying more, reading more books, listening to tapes, attending more seminars, starting a home-based business, and meeting new friends. In other words, do today what you want for your tomorrows.

How Do You See the Future?

I am also often asked, "How do I see the future if I cannot yet see it with my eyes?" Or "How can I see a million dollars a year when I cannot see $50,000 a year today?"

That is an excellent context-expanding question. The answer is found in something my rich dad said to me years ago. He wrote out in big words on his yellow tablet.

SIGHT is what you see with your *eyes.*
VISION is what you see with your *mind*.

When I asked rich dad what improved a person's vision he said, "Words and numbers." He stressed the importance of learning how to read financial statements because you could not see your financial future if you could not read financial statements. In fact, if you cannot read a financial statement, you cannot see your financial past, present, or future. I created the CASHFLOW games to assist people in improving their mind's vision by teaching them the numbers and vocabulary of rich people. One thing that has worked for many people is to get a group of friends together to play CASHFLOW 101 on a regular basis. Once you have CASHFLOW 101 mastered you may want to teach it to others and inspire them to take action, and/or you may want to move on to CASHFLOW 202, the more advanced game. As you play, always remember rich dad's statement, "Your future is today." When people ask me how I became rich so quickly, I say, "I play the game every day." The reality is, the more you play the game, the more you teach the game, and the more you make the game a part of your life, the better your vision of the future will become. As rich dad also said, "If you want healthy teeth in the future, brush your teeth today."

Fast Words for Fast Plans

If you want to create a *fast* plan, you need to learn to use *fast* words. Many people cannot get rich quickly because they use slow words rather than fast words in their plan. If you want to improve your vision of getting rich quicker, you need to use faster words.

If you want to retire young and retire rich, if you want to get rich quickly, you need to use more up-to-date, more hip, faster words of business and investing. Not using faster, more efficient words would be like a professional woodcutter saying, "I don't care if I can chop more wood with a chain saw and make more money. My dad gave me this axe and I plan on using this axe until the day I die." Many people today are going to work and still using their mommy and daddy's axe to make and invest their money.

Are You Swinging Your Daddy's Axe?

After telling the story of chopping wood with an axe rather than using a chain saw, I ask people if they are still swinging their daddy's axe.

After a puzzled moment and some puzzled looks, I am occasionally asked, "Are you asking me if I am still doing things like my parents, when it comes to managing my money?"

My reply is "Yes. That is exactly what I am asking." I continue, saying, "Many people today are not in the same professions as their parents . . . but when it comes to money, investing, and retirement, they do exactly the same things. When it comes to money, many people are still swinging their parents' axe."

If asked to explain further, I say, "Words are tools just as an axe is a tool. When it comes to money, millions of people use word tools that are as slow and antiquated as using an axe to chop wood."

Tools for Your Brain

In one of the classes I taught, a bright young woman asked, "Do you mean to say that when it comes to money, there are fast words and slow words?"

My reply was "Exactly what I mean. If money is an idea, then ideas are made up of words. Most people use slow words, which leads to them having slow ideas, which means they acquire wealth slowly."

"Words are tools?" the young woman said quietly, just loud enough for the people around her to hear.

Nodding, I said, "My rich dad said, 'Words are tools for your brain. The reason so many people struggle financially is because they give their brain old, slow, and obsolete tools to use. If you want to be rich, you first need to update your tools.'"

"Can you give me an example of old and slow words . . . tools?" she asked.

"Sure," I replied. "Most people think it is smart to save money. Saving money is slow. You can become rich saving money, but the price is time . . . your lifetime. So to me *save* is a slow word. My poor dad taught me how to save money. My rich dad did not *save*. Instead he taught me how to *raise capital*."

"But what if someone does not know how to raise capital?" asked another student.

"Then it is best you save money or invest some time, learning how to raise capital. Raising capital is a learned skill."

"But isn't it difficult to ask people for money?" asked a student.

"It was for me at first . . . as learning anything new is. It's just like learning to ride a bike. I was very nervous at the start and made mistakes at the beginning . . . and I still make mistakes today. Yet I learn from those mistakes, so my education and experience make raising capital easier and easier the older I get. There are other people who are getting older and older and are still trying to get ahead by working hard and saving money. That is a very slow plan using old and slow word tools they probably inherited from their parents."

"So while I struggle to save $100 a month, you can raise millions of dollars in the same time," another student chimed in. "That is what you mean by words are tools . . . and that some words are fast and others are slow."

I just nodded and said, "Words are tools for your brain."

Plan to Use Faster Words

If you plan on creating a plan to retire young and retire rich, you may need to update your vocabulary, and if you change your vocabulary, you may speed up your ideas. For example:

Slow Words	*Fast Words*
High-paying job	Cash flow

My poor dad always advised: "Get a high-paying job."

My rich dad always advised: "You want cash flow from assets."

Finding a high-paying job may seem like the fast way to get rich at the start, but in most cases it is the slow way to become rich in the end. Remember my poor dad earned more money than my rich dad at the beginning of their careers, but by the end of their lives, the gap between their incomes was as wide as the Pacific Ocean. In fact, very few people ever become rich via a job . . . even a high-paying one. The following are some of the reasons why cash flow from assets is better than income from a job.

Let's review the three different types of income:

Earned income	50%
Portfolio income	20%
Passive income	0%

Earned income, in most cases, is income that comes from a person's labor or work.

Portfolio income, in most cases, is income from paper assets such as stocks, bonds, and mutual funds.

Passive income, in most cases, is income from real estate.

As always, before making any financial decision, it is very important to have competent professional advice on any matter involving taxes. What may be legal tax planning for one person could be a tax violation for someone else. The point of this section is to know the difference words can make. There is a substantial tax difference between *earned* income and *passive* income. As far as leverage goes, taxes for most people are *reverse* leverage or *negative* leverage. A person who works hard for earned income has to work at least twice as hard as someone who works hard to earn *passive* income. Working for earned income is like taking two steps forward, and then taking one step back.

They Tax You Even After You Stop Working

People who say, "Work hard, save money, and invest in a 401(k)" are working for 50 percent money. Once you retire, and you begin to withdraw money from your 401(k) plan, that money exiting the plan is then taxed at the *earned* income rate, or 50 percent money, as my rich dad would call it. Interest from savings is also taxed at the *earned* income rate.

Many people say, "I must continue to work because my Social Security income from the government does not cover my living expenses." The moment a person begins to work for earned income to supplement their Social Security income, the government not only taxes your earned income, the government often begins to reduce your Social Security payments because you have a job. When my rich dad said, "Most people plan on being poor," he knew what he was talking about. He was aware of the government's laws regarding earned income after retirement. If you aren't poor and you want to earn more money, the government won't help you. Many retired people simply find it better to be poor and not go back to work for tax reasons.

The point is, choosing to use the words *work hard, save money,* and *invest in a 401(k)* is choosing to use very slow words, which causes you to have a very slow financial plan. While choosing to use these words in your financial plan may allow you to reach the affluent level of $100,000 to $1 million a year in retirement income, those same words will in most cases not allow you to go on to the rich and ultra-rich levels of income. As rich dad said, "There is more to being rich than having a lot of money." The rich use a different set of words and those words guide them to different life experiences . . . experiences such as learning how to raise capital rather than save money.

Other words are:

Slow Words	*Fast Words*
Save money	Make money

Rich dad recommended that most people learn how to save money. But he himself did not save money. He said, "Focusing on saving money takes too much of my time and there is not enough leverage in saving money." Rich dad also said, "The money most people save is after-tax money." For a person to save $10, the real dollar amount earned was $20 because it is *earned* income or 50 percent money. On top of that, the interest that you earn on your savings is also subject to higher taxes.

Instead of focusing on *saving money*, rich dad spent his life training himself to *make money.* He said, "If you know how to build businesses and invest money, you can make so much money that your problem will be too much money. When you have too much money, you have *excessive cash* sitting in your bank rather than *savings.*"

In *Rich Dad's Guide to Investing,* I wrote about the two types of money problems. They are not enough money and too much money. Most people only know the first problem, the problem of not having enough money. These people should definitely learn how to save money. My rich dad's financial plan was to have too much money. His problem was that he had too much money sitting in his savings account and he was constantly looking for investments to move his excess money into. His reality or context was that the world had an abundance of money. My poor dad's reality was that money was scarce and that is why he struggled all his life trying to save money.

What is the difference between *working* for money and *making* money?

If you read *Rich Dad Poor Dad*, you may recall the story of me listening to my poor dad (literally) and trying to *make* money. I tried to *make* money by melting down lead toothpaste tubes and then casting quarters, dimes, and nickels in plaster of paris molds. My poor dad had to explain to me the difference between *making money* and *counterfeiting.* My poor dad was not able to tell me how to make money simply because all he knew to do was *work for money.* In the real world of money, many of the rich do become very rich by *making money,* rather than *working for money.* For example, Bill Gates became the richest man in the world not by working for money, but by making money. He became the richest man in the world by building a company and selling shares in his company.

Selling shares in your company is one form of making money. In principle, as long as there is a ready market of buyers and sellers for whatever you may produce, then you are, within this context, *making* money. My books for instance are a form of making money. As long as there is a market for them through booksellers, then my books are *making me* money rather than *me* working for money. If I were a doctor who had to personally work to get paid, then I would be a doctor who worked for money. If I were a doctor who invented a new medicine and sold it in the form of a pill through pharmacies, that pill would be a form of the doctor making money rather than working for money.

In summary, *working* for money in most cases is slow, and finding ways to *make* money can be much faster if you know what you are doing. So if your plan is to *work* for money and then try and *save* money, then you may be swinging your mommy and daddy's very slow and very dull axe.

There are other words that can slow your wealth creation down and there are words that can increase the speed at which you make money.

Slow Words	*Fast Words*
Appreciation	Depreciation

If you do not fully understand the terms *appreciation* and *depreciation* do not worry. It took me a while to fully understand them. If you really want to understand them better, you may want to ask an accountant or a professional real estate investor to explain the concepts to you. A brief example of how each of these terms applies to your financial plan follows.

The other day, a television program ran a story about high school kids learning how to invest in the stock market. One of the students being interviewed said, "I made a lot of money because I bought shares of XYZ company and the price of those shares went up." In other words, he was playing the market in the hopes of capital gains or *appreciation* in the value of the shares that he picked. When most people say "Our home is a good investment" they say that because they expect their house to *appreciate* in value.

I hear friends say to me statements such as, "I bought a lot in this new golf course community. It's a good investment and I expect the lot will double in value in five years." To them such returns are a good investment . . . and hopefully they will realize a doubling of their money in five years.

Rich dad taught his son and me to use different words. When it came to buying any investment, he always said, "Your profit is made when you buy, not when you sell." In other words, he never expected his investment to appreciate in value. If it did, to him, appreciation was a bonus. Rich dad invested for immediate returns on his investment, or cash flow. He also invested for a thing he called "phantom cash flow" aka *depreciation.* An example of depreciation of a building was given in an earlier chapter. He loved immediate *cash flow* and *depreciation* because he did not have to wait for his investment to *appreciate* in order for him to make money. He would say, "Waiting for a stock or piece of real estate to appreciate in value was too slow and too risky."

The point is this, if you are waiting to make money sometime in the future, your plan is a slow plan because you are using slow words, which lead to slow ideas. Repeating my rich dad: "Your profit is made when you buy, not when you sell." I meet so many people who buy a piece of real estate, lose money on it each month, and say to me, "I'll make my money back when the value of property goes up and I sell it."

In Australia, many people buy property, lose money on it every month, and think it is a good investment because the government gives them a tax break for losing money. In my opinion, that is a loser's way of thinking. I often ask them, "Why not buy a property that makes you money every month *and* get a tax break every month." The response I often get back is, "No, my accountant told me to look for a property that costs me money every month and gives me a tax break." Talk about choosing to board the slow risky train rather than the fast more profitable train.

Slow Words	*Fast Words*
Avoid risk	Gain control

My poor dad said, "That's too risky." Or "Play it safe." Or "Why take the risk?" The more he believed in those ideas, the more he lost control over his financial life. By being an employee playing it safe, he lost control over his taxes. By saying that investing was risky and he was not interested in money, he lost more and more control over his financial education. In the end, he paid more and more in taxes, even though retired, and invested only in safe investments that went nowhere or lost money.

I have a distant relative who spent twenty-five years in the military, retired as an officer, and today sits in front of the TV set watching the financial television shows, watching the value of his stock sink lower and lower. He gets more and more depressed simply because he has no control over the value of his portfolio. One day, he saw the president of one of the companies he owns a substantial number of shares in flying in their new private jet, announcing that his staff were all getting million-dollar bonuses. While he joined the chorus of irate shareholders, there was very little that he could do.

In *Rich Dad's Guide to Investing,* I wrote about rich dad's ten investor controls. These controls are vital to anyone who wants to have some degree of control over their life and their future. At present, my concern is that 90 percent of the population of the United States and many other Western countries have very little control over their financial future. That percentage is even worse in developing nations.

Rich dad told me to have a plan on learning how to have more and more control over my financial future. He said, "In order to be a player on the fast track you will need to have a plan on how to gain more and more control. On the fast track, it is control more than money that counts." If you would like to know more about these ten controls you may want to read or reread *Rich Dad's Guide to Investing.*

A final word on risk vs. control: Rich dad said, "The more a person seeks *security,* the more that person gives up *control* over their life." Today I see two worlds evolving. One is the world I call the Responsible Society. It is the group that believes in being responsible for their lives and the ultimate outcome of their lives. There is another world that I call the Victim Society, which is the group that believes that someone else, a company, or the government is responsible for their lives. In any group, family, or company, there are usually both types of societies. Both see the world from their own context or reality and both think they are right. I have found that one of the dividing factors between both societies is their core view on the ideas of risk vs. control. Victims tend to want to give *control* over their lives to someone else in order to avoid taking *risks.* Then they get angry when they feel someone abuses the control they granted the abuser in the first place. In other words, victims are often victims of themselves.

In the coming years, there will be many financial victims. People who gave control over to financial professionals and bought their advice hook, line, and sinker. Many of the future victims will have believed the mantra of "Invest for the long term, diversify, go long and hold, the market has gone up over the last forty years, and play it safe." These victims bought these words of advice simply because they wanted to believe the words. If they failed to choose their advisors wisely, they may become financial victims.

Slow Words	*Fast Words*
Mutual funds	Regulation D, Rule 506

Today, millions and millions of people are betting their financial future and their financial security on stocks and mutual funds. Even I own mutual funds in my retirement plan. Yet, I do not plan on getting rich quickly with those mutual funds nor am I counting on these funds taking care of me once my working days are over. Personally, I do not have much faith in the stock market. I also find that mutual funds are too slow and require me to use my own money. As I said earlier in this book, I would rather use borrowed money to get rich rather than use my own money . . . and banks will not let me borrow money to buy mutual funds.

The other reason I say that mutual funds are slow is because the big profits or appreciation in any paper asset is made at the formation of the company, prior to the company going public. When rich investors begin investing in the share of a company, they are often investing according to the terms and conditions spelled out by the SEC's (Securities and Exchange Commission) Regulation D, Rule 506, and other such regulations. In other words, the rich invest in shares of a company when the company is still a *private* company. The public invests in shares of a company after it becomes a *public* company. The differences can be enormous. For example, if you had invested $25,000 in Intel *prior* to it going public, that $25,000 might be worth more than $40 million today depending upon the ups and downs of the stock market.

The point is, the rich have already made their money *prior* to the public being even aware that the company exists. That means the rich often invest with much lower risk and with the potential of much higher returns. By the time a mutual fund buys shares of the company, the profits have already been made. Then the general public buys the mutual fund that has purchased the shares of the public company, the same company that the rich invested in while it was still private. In other words, instead of investing in a mutual fund or public stock, the rich have invested via a private placement memorandum, also known as a 506 reg d. The difference in the potential speed of getting rich between mutual funds and IPO, or 506 reg d's is astounding. As rich dad said, "Investing in mutual funds is investing at the end of the food chain."

This does not mean mutual funds are not good investments. For most people, mutual funds are great investments. They are better investments if you know what you are doing, know what the risks are, and know the big picture of the whole game of investing in stocks and mutual funds . . . public and private.

I can hear some of you saying, "IPOs were good in the heyday of a bull stock market . . . but not in a down or bear market." There is some truth to that statement, yet regardless of the market, the rich are always offered private investments that are not offered to the general public. That is why knowing the words, vocabulary, and the jargon of the investments of the rich improves your chances of becoming richer quicker.

In the near future, the rich will get richer because they will be involved in pre-IPO offerings. They will not be investing in technology, or computers, or dot-coms. Instead they will be investing in hot new biotech companies, genetic engineering companies, and new companies with the words *system* or *network* after their names. They will be investing in the hot companies of the future, companies that we have not heard of yet. They will invest in companies and real estate projects that the average person will hear about only after the profits have been made. They will be investing in private placement memorandums, or limited partnerships, and other such investment vehicles, rather than mutual funds.

Slow Words	*Fast Words*
Pay retail	Buy wholesale

Most of us are aware enough to know that there is always a wholesale price as well as a retail price. The same is true in investing. The rich get richer because they pay the wholesale price rather than the retail price.

When you look at the board game CASHFLOW, you will see the Rat Race and the Fast Track. The Rat Race is where investors pay retail and the Fast Track is where investors pay wholesale. The rich get richer because they are known as *friends and family* of people who have access to investments that are priced at the wholesale level.

Slow Words	*Fast Words*
Buy shares	Sell shares

Bill Gates did not become the richest man in the world by buying shares of Microsoft. He became the richest man in the world because he is what is known as a "selling shareholder." As explained in the discussion of paying retail or buying wholesale, the rich become rich because they are often selling shareholders of a stock. To become a selling shareholder, you often need to be the *founder* or a *friend* or *family* member of the founder.

Slow Words	*Fast Words*
Go to school	Go to seminars

My poor dad went back to school often. That is why he attended the University of Chicago, Northwestern, and Stanford University, all excellent, prestigious schools. My real dad would come back excited, enthusiastic, and expecting a promotion because he had invested his time going back to school.

My rich dad went to seminars. He said, "You go to school if you want to be a better employee or better professional person such as a doctor, lawyer, or accountant. If you don't care about degrees, promotions, or job security, then you go to seminars. Seminars are for people who want better financial results than a job promotion or increased job security."

I teach seminars rather than teach inside a school. Schools attract a different type of student as compared to seminars. For example, my wife, Kim, and I have an agreement that we go to at least two seminars a year together. We go together because we find that seminars, even bad ones, make our marriage, friendship, and business partnership stronger. Information or education has the power to bind people closer together by the common experience as well as drive a wedge between them, if they do not learn together.

Over the years we have attended many investment seminars, seminars on marketing, sales, systems development, handling employees, and of course investing. We are preparing to attend a seminar on how to borrow money from the government to invest in low-income housing. The seminar costs only $85, put on by the government, and we expect to make millions from what we learn. That is what I mean by people attending seminars for *results* rather than *promotions.*

I meet authors who did well in school as writers but their books do not sell as many as mine do. When I suggest to them that they attend direct marketing courses, or sales training courses, or copy writing classes, many get very indignant. As I said in *Rich Dad Poor Dad*, I am a best-*selling* author not a best-*writing* author.

The other day, I met a friend who sent his daughter to a relatively good state school. He was rather proud of the fact that he paid $85,000 over four years for her education. She has just found a job for $55,000 a year and he is thrilled.

He then asked me how much my seminars cost and I told him about $5,000 for three days. He gasped at the price and said, "I can't afford that. That is too expensive for such a short amount of time." When he asked what I taught in three days, I replied, "On day one we cover how to build a business like Bill Gates did and take it public via an IPO. We also cover on day one how to become a member of the friends and family level of the IPO, just in case you do not want to be like a Bill Gates and you only want to buy stocks at the *wholesale* level." I then said, "On days two and three we cover how to find real estate investments, how to quickly analyze them, and how to finance them. In other words, we teach you to think, negotiate, and analyze deals similar to how people like Donald Trump think and invest in real estate. On the other day we teach people how to use options trading the way hedge fund managers such as George Soros trade, which is not the same way mutual fund managers trade. On top of that we cover how to use corporations to pay less in taxes and protect your assets. You will meet inside investors from the fast track who will tell you how to find the best leveraged investments in the world. And most importantly, you will meet people just like you who think just like you. In other words, you will probably make new friends who are moving at the same speed you are."

All he could say was, "That is too much money for three days."

As I said, there are slow words and fast words. For me, I would rather spend $5,000 and three days to learn how to make millions and possibly billions rather than spend four years and $85,000 to learn how to work for $55,000 or a little more a year for the rest of my life. On top of that, that $55,000 is earned income.

There is one more source of fast, low-cost, high-impact education I use on a regular basis. In 1974, when I left the Marine Corps and knew I was not going to stay in the E quadrant like my poor dad, I began subscribing to audiocassettes from the Nightingale-Conant Company. It has an audio library of some of the great business, motivation, and leadership masters in the world. I still remember buying *Lead the Field* by Earl Nightingale and listening to that tape program over and over as I drove around my sales territory, planning my escape from the E quadrant and the corporate world. In fact I still listen to that cassette program about once a year while at the gym or in my car.

When people ask me "How do I find a mentor?" I often say, "Ask Nightingale-Conant for a catalogue and begin listening to some of the greatest mentors of all time." As rich dad often said, "The truly rich get rich at home and in their spare time." He also said, "It is not your boss's job to make you rich. That is your job."

Some of the great masters in the Nightingale-Conant library are Sir John Templeton, founder of the Templeton Fund, Brian Tracy, Zig Ziglar, Dennis Waitely, Og Mandino, Seth Godin, Harvey Mckay, and others. I have learned more, made more money, found new inspiration to carry on, came up with new ideas, or discovered new ways of doing things just while driving my car, working out in the gym, or going for a walk. The collection of masters at Nightingale-Conant is priceless, yet for less than a hundred dollars you can spend as much personal time as you want with some of the great teachers and masters of the world. All you have to do is hit the rewind button and they will repeat exactly what you want to hear. I never received a college degree from these tapes but I did find financial freedom and, most importantly, the confidence to be true to who I am.

Why Some People Only Seek Content

One of the big differences between those who go to school and those who attend seminars is again the difference between *context* and *content.* I have noticed that when a person who attends schools asks a person who attends seminars, "What did you get from the seminar?" the person who attended the seminar is often not able to explain what he or she got. The reason is, many seminars are more context-expanding than content-increasing. A person who has just had his or her context expanded often cannot say specifically what he or she got. A person who is school-oriented, a person who would rather remain an employee, often cannot understand such vagueness. A person who wants their context to remain the same, and only seeks to have his or her content increased, will not understand a person who is happy to have their reality expanded and is still waiting for the new content to appear. People wanting only content often become very upset if they have their context messed with. That is why they seek content versus an expansion of context. The good news is that both can get ahead, regardless of what they seek. Yet the person getting ahead the fastest is the person who seeks to have both his or her context expanded and content increased.

Is it Time to Get out of the Rat Race?

The other day, a person said to me, "I played your CASHFLOW game once. Now what do I do?"

I replied with, "You played CASHFLOW 101 once? Only once?"

"Only once," he replied.

"How long did you play the game?" I asked.

"About three hours," he replied.

"Did you get out of the rat race?" I asked.

"No, I never did. But I got the lesson."

"What was the lesson you got?" I asked.

"I got bored. I learned that being in the rat race is boring and tiring. I learned that I hate games so I am asking you to tell me what to do next. I don't want to play games. I want to get rich. So tell me what to do next."

I took out the game board pictured below and pointed to the circle labeled the rat race.

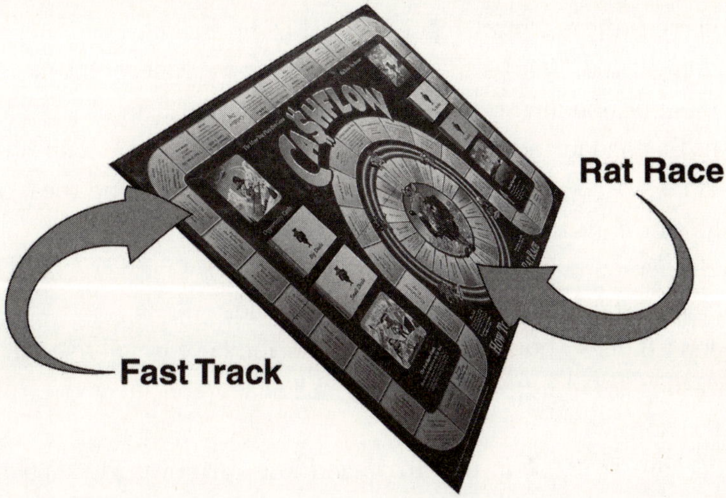

Slowly and deliberately I began to say, still pointing to the rat race circle, "So to you, this game is only a silly game?"

Nodding, he smiled and said, "Yup. And I don't want to play games. I want to get rich in real life."

"And you don't think this game is real life?" I asked.

"Nope," he said with a slight smirk. "That game does not apply to me."

"That's interesting," I said, still pointing to the rat race. "To me this game is real life. Let me ask you this. Which track are you on? The *rat race* or the *fast track*?"

The young man gave me a blank look in return and said nothing.

Continuing, I said, "To me this game is real life. And in real life, each and every one of us is on one track or the other." I happened to have the article from Robert Reich, the former Secretary of Labor, quoted at the start of this section. Taking out the article, I read a quotation from Robert Reich:

> "It's not simply a matter of having a job or even having decent pay anymore.
>
> "In the new economy, with unpredictable earnings . . . two tracks are emerging, the fast track and the slow track and the absence of gradations between."

"You mean the *fast track* really does exist?" he asked.

Nodding, I said, "It does and so does the *rat race*. Ninety-nine percent of the U.S. population invests from the *rat race.* And those in the rat race are falling further and further behind. As Robert Reich says, there is an 'absence of gradations between.' Which means you are either on one track or the other. So which track are you investing from?"

"Well I have a high-paying job and I make a lot of money. Doesn't that mean I'm investing from the *fast track?*" he asked.

"I don't think so but I don't really know. You have to tell me. What are you investing in?" I asked. "Are you a millionaire and do you earn over $200,000 annually?"

"I do have $350,000 in my 401(k) and I do earn over $120,000 a year. Doesn't that mean I qualify for the *fast track*?" he asked.

"I don't think so," I replied. "At least according to SEC regulations, you don't qualify to be on the fast track."

"I don't understand," he said. "Would you tell me what I am missing?"

Taking a deep breath, I was relieved to finally have him open his *context* or his mind to new *content* or information. I have always found it difficult to teach something to someone who thinks they know all the answers. We all know that it is difficult to put more water into a glass that is already full of water; it is also difficult to teach something new to someone whose mind is closed or already filled with other content.

Beginning slowly, I said, "I designed this game with two tracks because to me, this game is the real game of life. In real life each of us is on one track or the other. As Robert Reich says, there is an 'absence of gradations.'"

"You mean we are either in the *rat race* or we are on the *fast track*," he said, now with a little more interest.

"Yes," I said. "And the lesson from the game is how you and I can get out of the rat race. The purpose of the game is to open your mind to the possibility of you becoming rich and financially free . . . free from the rat race most of us know . . . free from the drudgery of spending your life working for money and living below your means. The more you play the game and the more you teach the game to others, the more your mind becomes open to that possibility . . . and the more real financial freedom becomes in your mind and in your content and context. If your mind is *not* open, the chances are you will be one of the ninety-nine out of 100 people who spends his or her life in the rat race."

"Even if I make a lot of money?" he asked.

"Great question," I said loudly. "Best question you could have asked. The answer is money alone will not get you out of the rat race and money alone will not allow you on to the fast track. That is why my rich dad always said, 'Money does not make you rich.'"

"Why?" he asked with a puzzled look. "Doesn't it just take a lot of money to get onto the fast track?"

"Another great question . . . and the answer is no," I said. I was now relieved that his mind was opening to new ideas rather than pretending to know all the answers. "It takes more than money to get out of the rat race and it takes more than money to invest on the fast track."

"I don't understand," he said. "What does it take if it takes more than money? I can understand why it takes more than money to get out of the rat race. But I do not understand why it takes more than money to invest on the fast track."

I collected my thoughts before answering his question. "Do you remember the advertisements in publications such as *The Wall Street Journal* and financial publications that have a picture of a well-dressed affluent-looking man holding up a sign on a street corner saying, 'I have money to invest.'"

"Yeah, I did see those ads. I did not really understand them," he replied softly and a little puzzled.

"Ads such as those were plentiful between 1995 and 1999. The message was that there were many individuals who had made a lot of money in the stock market or from their jobs and they were now looking for investments of the rich, investments found on the fast track. The problem was that even though they had money, they still were not allowed into the better investments on the fast track. Granted there are many flimsy and sometimes crooked deals on the fast track that would have allowed him in, but the best deals are closed to most people . . . even though they have money."

"Even though they have money?" he asked. "Why? I don't understand."

"Because money does not count on the fast track," I said. "In real-life investing, money only counts to those people stuck in the rat race."

"Money does not count?" he said. "Why doesn't money count?"

"Because everyone on the fast track already *has* plenty of money. That is why money no longer counts. In order to get into the better investments on the fast track, what counts is *what* you know or *who* you know."

"You mean it's what you bring to the table that counts . . . not the money," he said quietly.

"You hit it right on the head," I said, smiling. "Things aren't different between the rich and the poor and the middle class. Things are opposite. One side thinks money is important and then once you become rich, you find out money is no longer important."

I spent the next few minutes showing him the different levels of exit strategies. I explained to him that many people are able to achieve the affluent level, which is $100,000 to $1 million of income. Yet if they achieved that level of income by working hard, saving money, and being frugal, they may not be allowed to invest in the investments that the rich and ultra-rich invest in. Many are not allowed to invest simply because they have money but they lack the education and experience required for the investments on the fast track. They have money but they do not bring anything else to the table.

"So that is why there were those ads with affluent people holding up signs that read, 'I have money to invest,'" said the young man whose mind was now gaining some new context. "They had money but no one wanted their money because they were not prepared for the fast track."

"That's correct," I said. "And that is why my rich dad said, 'There is more to being rich than having a lot of money.'"

"So what should I do?" asked the young man.

"Well, the first thing I would do is go back and play CASHFLOW 101 at least a dozen more times. Play until you can get out of the rat race in under an hour, regardless of your profession, your salary, high or low, and what market conditions or setbacks you encounter in the game. Then take a look at the words on the fast track and look up some of the definitions of the words. After learning those definitions begin to seek investors who do invest in *fast track* investments. Spend time with them. Listen to their words and begin to understand what is important to them . . . other than money. The more you can understand their words the more you will be able to communicate with them and begin to see their world . . . the world of the *fast track.*"

"Is that what you did?" he asked.

"No, that is what I *do*. That is what I do every single day of my life. As I said, this game is real life. You are either in the *rat race* or you are on the *fast track.*"

"So how did you get out of the rat race?" he asked. "I know that you started with nothing."

"I had a plan. I had a plan on how to get out of the rat race. The big difference was that my plan was a rich plan from the start. It was a plan that would allow me to gain a lot of money, but more importantly to gain the words, education, and experience required for the fast track. So invest some time by first choosing your exit strategy, and then begin to create and design your own plan . . . a plan that will include the education, experience, and the vocabulary required for the fast track."

The young man nodded. His mind was now open. "So many people retire but they remain in the rat race?"

"Most do," I replied quietly. "Their lives went according to plan. They got on the slow train and stayed on the slow train all their lives. I did not want to get on the slow train, so I searched for a better plan . . . a plan that would work for me. I hope you find a better plan."

The young man nodded his head and said quietly, "I will."

Summary of Leveraging Your Plan

In my opinion, the reason so many people work hard all their lives and still wind up poor or stuck in the rat race of life is because they lived their lives according to a slow plan. An important step if you want to retire young and retire rich is to sit quietly and ask yourself, "What and whose plan am I following?" Other questions you may ask yourself are:

1. What is the exit strategy for my life?
2. How fast are my words and my ideas?
3. What track am I on today and what track do I want to be on in the future?
4. What kind of income am I working for today and is it the kind of income I want for my tomorrows?
5. What is the long-term price of security?

Chapter 11

The Leverage of Integrity

From 1985 to 1989, Kim and I did not have any *passive* or *portfolio* income. We were working diligently at building a business so that we could have more leveraged earned income. All the extra money we earned went back into building the business. We knew what kind of income we wanted, we knew the definition of the incomes we wanted, we knew that we had to convert earned income to passive and portfolio income, but we did not have anything to show when it came to those two incomes. As the years crept on, I could hear my rich dad saying, "The moment you make passive income and portfolio income a part of your life, your life will change. Those words will become flesh."

Both my dads were sticklers for knowing the definitions of words. The difference was, they did not focus on the same words. One dad had me look up words for school and the other dad had me look up words that pertained to money, business, and investing. There was many a night I sat up with my dictionary, looking up the different meanings to different words for both dads.

I meet many people who call themselves investors. When I ask them how much passive or portfolio income they have, many admit they don't have much, if any . . . yet they claim to be investors. Both my dads said, "You're only as good as your word. People who do not keep their word are not much good." One of the reasons so few people retire young and retire rich is they are not true to their word. They use words that to them are not real.

More than Just Definitions

For those of you who have read *Rich Dad Poor Dad,* you will recall the different definitions both dads had for the words *asset* and *liability*. My poor dad assumed he knew the definitions of both words, so he never bothered to look them up. It would not have done much good, even if my poor dad had looked them up, simply because the definitions found in most academic dictionaries fail to clearly explain the differences.

I hated looking up the definitions of words, yet I continue to look up words I do not really understand. Why do I look them up? I look them up because, in my opinion, words are the most powerful tools available to human beings. As rich dad said, "Words are tools for the brain. Words allow the brain to see what the eyes cannot see." He also said, "A person who uses poor words has poor ideas, and hence a poor life." Take a moment to think about the profound difference just knowing the difference between *earned, portfolio,* and *passive* income has made on my life and many other lives. They are relatively simple words, but just knowing the difference can make a big difference in your life.

If you want to change your financial future, one of the most important and inexpensive steps you can take is to know the definitions of the words you use seriously. On television, several large investment brokerage houses have celebrities spouting off words such as *P/E ratio, dividend reinvestment plan, market capitalization* . . . and other investment hip or hype type jargon. These investment houses want you to think that knowing such definitions is important to becoming a better investor, and they are. Yet there are far more basic and more important definitions that one needs to know if you truly plan on retiring rich and retiring young. Some of the more basic, fundamental, and important words to understand are your personal *current ratio, quick ratio, liquidity ratio, debt to earnings ratio,* as well as the difference between *assets* and *liabilities,* and the difference between *earned, portfolio,* and *passive income.*

Harnessing the Power of Words

Why are the later words more important? The answer is, because the words *P/E ratio, dividend reinvestment plan,* and *market capitalization* really have no relationship to you . . . especially when you are just starting out in business or investing. Much more fundamental to you and your life are basic ratios such as *debt to equity* or *liquidity ratios*. Why? Because these ratios are useful to you personally, you can use these definitions in real life. If you understand how those ratios apply to you personally, and if you apply those words to your personal life, then the words become a part of your life . . . the words become flesh . . . and when that happens you harness the power of the words.

P/E ratios apply generally to publicly traded companies, such as IBM and Microsoft. A P/E ratio does not apply to you unless you personally were up for sale and I do believe slavery has been abolished for a while now. For those who may not know what a P/E ratio is, P/E ratio quickly evaluates how expensive or inexpensive a stock is. It is similar to a shopper asking what the price per pound of pork butt is. There is a difference between pork butt selling for $2.99 a pound and pork butt selling for $1.19 a pound . . . and any wise shopper would know that just because pork butt is cheap does not necessarily mean it's a good deal. The same is true for a high or low P/E ratio.

A P/E ratio simply measures the relative price of a stock as compared to its earnings. For example, if the stock paid a $2 per share dividend and the stock cost $20 per share, the stock's P/E ratio would be 10 . . . which would mean it would take you ten years to get your $20 back if all things remained the same. Just because a stock has a high or low P/E ratio does not mean it is a good buy or a bad buy, just as price per pound does not tell you if the pork butt is a good or bad buy. There are other factors you would want to check out before simply buying cheap pork butt.

During the dot-com mania, many stocks had high Ps and no Es . . . which made investing in a dot-com ridiculous, if all you went on was price-earnings ratios. When the market crashed, there were a lot of people wishing they had bought some cheap pork butt and put it in their freezer, instead of buying stocks with high Ps and no Es. Today even frozen pork butt is more valuable than the shares of some of the dot-com stocks. The real butts were the people who believed you could invest in the promise of the future without any reality in today. Many young dot-com promoters had the right context but they failed to have the right content . . . the content called business and investment education and experience.

There are more important, basic, and fundamental ratios to understand . . . and if you understand them and use them, your chances of becoming richer and financially successful improve. A more useful ratio is your debt to equity ratio. Why is it more important? Because each and every one of us can use this ratio . . . and we should use this ratio each and every month. For example, if you have long- and short-term debt of, let's say, $100,000 and you have $20,000 in equity, then your debt to equity ratio would look like this:

$$\frac{\$100{,}000}{\$20{,}000}$$

So in this case, your debt to equity ratio would be a 5. The question is, what does this mean? Well in reality it means very little, yet if next month your ratio is 10, that might tell you that you could be mismanaging your life. A debt to equity ratio of 10 could mean that either your debt has gone up to $200,000 or your equity has dropped to $10,000. In either case, those numbers have more meaning because they are real numbers that relate to your life. As rich dad said, "Mind your own business." And knowing these simple ratios are excellent tools for teaching yourself how to mind as well as manage your own business . . . the business of your life.

Ratios to Apply to Your Life

Just as P/E ratios tend to reflect the confidence the investing company has for the management of a public company, you as a manager of your own life need to have ratios that apply to your life. The following are some ratios you may want to keep track of, if you want to be a better manager of your own financial life.

One of the ratios rich dad had me watch and monitor was what he called the wealth ratio. His wealth ratio was:

$$\frac{\text{Passive Income + Portfolio Income}}{\text{Total Expenses}}$$

The goal of calculating your wealth ratio was to have your passive and portfolio income equal or exceed your total expenses. This would mean you could quit your job (earned income source) and still maintain your lifestyle. Once your passive and portfolio income exceed your expenses, the ratio would be 1 or higher and you would be out of the rat race. This is the goal of playing CASHFLOW 101, my patented board game that teaches you how to create passive and portfolio income.

An example would be:

$$\frac{\$600 \text{ passive} + \$200 \text{ portfolio}}{\$4{,}000} = 0.2$$

If rich dad had seen this ratio, 0.2, or passive and portfolio income which equal 20 percent of expenses, he would have had a strong talking to me about working harder to increase my passive or portfolio income. As rich dad said, "The moment you make passive income and portfolio income a part of your life, your life will change. Those words will become flesh." To him, the more I really knew what passive and portfolio income was, my life would change because my reality of life would change.

Rich dad thought the wealth ratio was a very important ratio to know intimately because it was a great indicator on how well you were managing the business of your life. He said, "Most people retire poor simply because they never know what it feels like to have passive or portfolio income actually in their lives. They may know the definition, but they do not have the integrity to make the words a real part of their life."

For five years, Kim and I knew what the definitions of the words were, we knew we wanted it in our lives . . . but for five years we did not have the two types of income in our lives. Suddenly after the 1987 stock market crash and the seven-year recession that followed, we knew that the window of opportunity had arrived. It was our time to make the words real. It was time to have a wealth ratio that was more than zero. We bought our first property in 1989 and, by 1994, we had a little over $10,000 in passive income a month and our total expenses were less than $3,000 a month. That gave us a wealth ratio of 3.3. Today our wealth ratio is over 12, even though our expenses have gone up significantly. That is the power of making the words a part of your life.

If you are serious about retiring young and retiring rich, you may want to make rich dad's wealth ratio a part of your life. I think you will find it will have more meaning to you than the P/E ratio of IBM or Microsoft. If you will look at that ratio on a monthly basis, I think you will find your life changing much faster when compared to someone who is working for a pay raise. Rich dad's wealth ratio greatly affected what I thought was important for my life.

When I look back upon my life, it was these simple lessons from my rich dad that made me the most money over my lifetime. Today, my personal debt to equity ratio is around 0.7, which means I sleep well at night, even though I have a lot of debt. I am by no means debt free and never plan to be debt free. The point is, these simple lessons from rich dad had a far more powerful impact on my life than all the years I spent studying calculus, spherical trigonometry, and chemistry. The reason rich dad's simple lessons had a profound impact was because his lessons are relevant to my life for as long as I live. I have never used calculus, spherical trigonometry, or a P/E ratio to motivate me to make an investment decision. I don't use them because they are not useful and have very little relevance to my personal financial success.

Add Power to Your Life

There are two points I want to make from this section on words, action, and integrity. One point is that a few simple definitions and simple numbers can add a lot of power to a person's life. Just as any good shopper would want to know the price per pound of pork butt, each of us should be aware of our debt to equity ratios, our personal wealth ratio, and other simple mathematical indicators, which I will not go into here.

The second point is that there is more to success than simply knowing the definitions of words and throwing around jargon in the attempt to sound intelligent. Too many people today use words they really don't understand. Many financial services salespeople use financial words that they don't really understand, words such as "P/E ratios," in an attempt to sound more intelligent than their clients. The main point is, if you want to retire young and retire rich, it is important for you to constantly improve your financial vocabulary. But to fully improve your vocabulary, it is also important to know *more* than just the definition of the word. In my opinion, it is important to make that word a part of your life and your reality. For example, when I say the word *passive income* . . . I say it with passion because it is an important part of my life. *Passive income* means as much to me as *pay raise* means to many employees. The reason I am not passionate about a *pay raise* is because a pay raise for me would be income without much of a future.

I have spent years learning how to convert earned income into passive income. The more time I spend actually converting earned income to passive income, the more real-life experience I gain. The problem I have with many financial services salespeople, such as stockbrokers, real estate brokers, and financial planners, is that while they are selling investment products to you, products that hopefully will someday give you passive or portfolio income, they themselves are only working for *earned* income. To me, that is being somewhat out of integrity.

How Long Is Your Financial Advisor's Nose?

Rich dad loved fairy tales. One of his favorite fairy tales was the story of Pinocchio . . . the wooden puppet that wanted to become a real boy. In the story, Pinocchio lied and the more he lied, the longer his wooden nose grew. It was only after he found his heart and began to tell the truth did he turn into a real flesh-and-blood boy. When rich dad would tell his son and me that fairy tale, he would say, "That is another example of the words becoming flesh . . . or wood."

When I think of the millions of people who are betting their financial future and their financial security on a stock market I cringe. Millions of people are worried about their financial future as the number of layoffs increase and the market continues to fluctuate. In the copy of a newspaper I just read, there are stories of how retirees have lost most of their retirement savings to investment advisors and insurance salespeople they trusted. The newspaper article said the advisors and insurance agents began selling these retirees these bogus investments, not sanctioned by their brokerage houses or insurance companies, simply because the companies they worked for cut back on the commissions (earned income) they paid their agents . . . so the agents found new, bogus products to sell, to people who trusted them . . . people who were hoping for some passive and portfolio income in their old age.

In the coming decades, there will be millions of people who will be in financial trouble in their old age simply because they listened to so-called professional people with long wooden noses. People made of wood, who will continue to say, "The stock market always goes up, mutual funds pay an average of 12 percent per year, invest for the long term, diversify, and dollar-cost-average your losses."

The Power of Integrity

While both dads did *not* stress the importance of the *same* words, they both stressed the importance of the word *integrity.* Both dads agreed that one of the definitions of integrity was the correlation between a person's *words* and a person's *actions.* Both dads said, "Listen to what a person *says* but, more importantly, watch what a person *does.*" In other words, if a person says, "I will be there to pick you up at 7:00 A.M.," and the person picks you up at 7:00 A.M., then he or she is 100 percent in integrity at that moment. Their words and actions are whole. If a person says, "I'll pick you up at 7:00 A.M.," and that person never shows up, never calls, never apologizes, then at that moment, that person has 0 percent integrity. Their actions and their words do not match. Their words and their actions are not whole.

My real dad pointed out to me that one of the dictionary's definitions of the word *integrity* was the word *whole* or *complete.* He constantly said, "You are only as good as your word." He constantly reminded his children about the importance of keeping one's word. He would say, "Ultimately, we are our words. Ultimately, all we have is our word. If your words are no good, then so are you." That is why he also said, "Never make promises you don't plan to keep."

The other day in Dallas, two young people asked me if they could attend my investment seminar. They asked for free tickets because they had no money. Since they were very convincing, Kim and I agreed to leave two free tickets at the gate. They never showed up and I realized why they might have had problems with money, even though they had great jobs.

A Plan with Integrity

One of the more simple, yet powerful parts of my plan to have a life of great wealth was to make sure I had the integrity to be true to my words and respect the power of words by matching my word to my actions. Over the years, rich dad made sure I kept my word on my small agreements. He said, "If you will keep your *small* agreements you will keep your *big* agreements. A person who cannot keep his or her small agreements can never have their bigger dreams come true." I bring this idea in now because there are many people who have big plans but their big plans never come true. The reason is, too many people have big plans but fail to keep their small agreements. As rich dad said, "People who do not keep their small agreements are people who cannot be trusted. If you cannot be trusted with small agreements, people will not help you make your big dreams come true. If you cannot keep your word, then people fail to trust you and have little confidence in you and your words."

I have watched the wisdom of both dads' advice on the power of words unfold. I have seen so many people show their core behavior when the pressure is on. I have one friend that will not keep his time appointments with me and then he wonders why I don't want to do business with him. He also breaks his agreements with other people such as his partners, employees, and bankers, and often legally cheats them. Although he is successful, he must always look for new people to do business with. Instead of building upon his relationships, he destroys them and has to start again with completely new people. He has no problem finding new people but his wooden nose keeps getting longer and it's getting harder to hide.

Another ex-friend of mine is a person who lies under pressure. Instead of telling the truth, she lies and thinks she can get away with it. When cornered or confronted, she says, "It's not my fault. I couldn't help it. Besides, I did not lie. You did not hear what I said." As my rich dad said, "People who do not keep their small agreements are people who cannot be trusted. If you cannot be trusted with small agreements, people will not help you make your big dreams come true."

So I pass on the words of wisdom from both my dads and those words are, "Be sure your words and your actions are one." In mentioning the fast words and slow words, I assure you that part of my plan was to fully understand each of those words mentally, emotionally, and physically. Rich dad insisted that I make plans to know the meaning of new words mentally, emotionally, and physically. For example, he said, "Your life will change forever once you learn to buy stocks at *wholesale* versus paying *retail*. When you know how rich you can become buying wholesale, you will never want to pay retail again." He also said, "Your life will change forever once you know the difference between *saving* money and *making* money." And "Your life will change forever once you know why it is better to have *depreciation* rather than hope and pray for *appreciation.*" He said, "If you will dedicate your life to making words real and a part of your life, your life will be far different than someone who only knows the words by their mental definition."

A significant part of my plan was to make sure the new and faster words I learned or became aware of became an active part of my life. From my rich dad's point of view, I would be out of integrity if I simply threw those financial words around only to sound intelligent, only to impress other people, and did not actually use them in my life.

So the lesson I pass on to you from my rich dad and my poor dad is that when creating your plan, make it a part of your plan to fully use and understand the power of the new faster words you want in your life. Don't just know the definition or, even worse, not know the definition and sling the words around as jargon, hoping to impress the uninformed. Make the words a part of your flesh and you will harness the power of the word.

Rich dad often said, "There are preachers and there are teachers. Preachers are people who tell you what to do but *they do not do* what they *tell you to do.* Teachers are people who tell people about what they are doing or what they have already done." Rich dad also said, "In the world of money, business, and investing, we have far too many preachers."

In Summary

If you want to retire young and retire rich, take the time to constantly upgrade your financial vocabulary and have the integrity to walk the talk rather than just talk. Always remember that words are tools for the brain and that there are fast words and slow words to wealth.

The Most Destructive of All Words

Rich dad often said, "The most life-destroying word of all is the word *tomorrow*." He said, "The poor, the unsuccessful, the unhappy, the unhealthy are the ones who use the word *tomorrow* the most. These people will often say, 'I'll start investing tomorrow.' Or 'I'll start my diet and exercise tomorrow.' Or 'I'll start reading tomorrow.' And so on." Rich dad said the word *tomorrow* is the word that destroys more lives than any other single word. He said, "The problem with the word *tomorrow* is that I have never seen a *tomorrow.* Tomorrows do not exist. Tomorrows only exist in the minds of dreamers and losers. People who put off till tomorrow find that the sins and bad habits of their past eventually catch up with them." He finished his comment on tomorrow by saying, "I have never seen a tomorrow. All I have are todays. *Today* is the word for winners and *tomorrow* is the word for losers."

In the coming chapters and lessons, you will learn how to do simple things today . . . simple things that can greatly improve your tomorrows.

Chapter 12

The Leverage of Fairy Tales

From Ugly Duckling to a Swan

Rich dad loved the story of the Tortoise and the Hare. He once said to me, "I am successful because I have always been a tortoise. I did not come from a rich family. I was not smart in school. I did not finish school. I am not particularly talented. Yet, I am far richer than most people simply because I did not stop. I never stopped learning or expanding my reality on what was possible for my life."

Rich dad loved fairy tales and biblical stories. At the beginning of this book, I shared with you the story of David and Goliath. Rich dad loved the story that a little guy could beat a giant by using the leverage of a slingshot. Rich dad loved fairy tales, yet he was not a great reader . . . but he absorbed the lessons from those fairy tales, and those lessons guided his life . . . a life where he started with nothing and ultimately became a financial powerhouse.

There were many times, when Kim and I were broke and living on very little, I would find a place to sit quietly and again hear rich dad telling me the story of the tortoise and the hare. I remember him saying, "Many times in life, you will meet people who are smarter, faster, richer, more powerful, and more gifted than you. Just because they have a head start on you does not mean you cannot win the race. If you will keep the faith in yourself, do the things that most people do not want to do, and keep making progress on a daily basis, the race of life will be yours."

Another fairy tale that rich dad loved was the story of the Three Little Pigs. He would often intertwine the story of the tortoise and the hare with the story of the three little pigs. When I was around twelve years old, rich dad said, "Poor people build financial houses made of straw. The middle class build financial houses made of sticks. And rich people build houses of brick." He would then add, "To be a successful tortoise, it's okay to be slow but be sure you are slowly building a house of bricks."

In 1968, while at home for Christmas leave from the academy I attended in New York, rich dad and his son invited me to their new home, which was the penthouse of his new hotel. "Remember me telling you those stories?" he said, as we gazed from his balcony over the white sand beach and crystal blue ocean. "The stories of the Tortoise and the Hare and the Three Little Pigs?"

"I do," I said, still amazed at the beauty of their new home, high on top of their new hotel. "I remember them well."

"Well here is the house of bricks," he said with a grin.

That day in 1968, rich dad did not have to say much more than that. He had told and retold the fairy tales so often I knew that the fairy tale had become real. He was the tortoise who took the longer, slower, less secure road, but now he was on top and climbing higher. He was forty-nine years old, and he had passed many rabbits along the way.

I also knew that my real dad had built a house of sticks, an expensive house of sticks in a very affluent neighborhood of Honolulu. My poor dad had just been promoted to the head of the school systems for the state of Hawaii. He too had reached the top of his ladder. He too had become visible to the public, as had rich dad. The difference was that one controlled his future and the other did not. One lived in a house made of sticks and the other a skyscraper made of bricks. In three years, my dad would lose his safe, secure job and all he would have was his house of sticks.

The Value of Being an Ugly Duckling

In 1968, while standing on the balcony of his penthouse, rich dad reminded me of another fairy tale. It was a fairy tale that I did not realize had meant so much to him because he never recounted it to his son and me when we were kids. "Do you know the story of the Ugly Duckling?" he asked.

I nodded my head as I leaned over the balcony.

"Well, most of my life, I saw myself as the Ugly Duckling."

"You're kidding, aren't you? How could you see yourself as an ugly duckling?" I found it hard to believe because rich dad was a very handsome man.

"When I dropped out of school at the age of thirteen, I saw the world as an outsider . . . someone who did not fit, someone who had been left behind. While working in my parents' store, high school boys who were on the football team would come in and push me around or damage the store. Many a day, these older athletic bullies would come in and knock cans off the shelves or throw oranges out on the road and dare me to do something about it."

"Did you ever fight back?" I asked.

"Twice I fought back, but I got pretty badly beaten," said rich dad. "But I'm not just telling you this story to tell you of athletic bullies. In this world there are other kinds of bullies."

Wondering where rich dad was going with this, I just looked down from the balcony and listened as he continued.

"I've also known people who were intellectual or academic bullies. They would come in the store and talk down to me because they were better educated. It seemed that just because they thought they were smarter than other people, they could look down upon those of us who did not go to school."

"I have a school filled with those guys," I added. "It seems that just because they think they are smarter than you or had better grades, it gives them permission to sneer when they talk to you, or snub you altogether."

Rich dad nodded. Continuing, he said, "While working in the store, I also met the social bullies. They looked down their noses because they were from rich families, or they were pretty, sexy, handsome, popular . . . and in the in crowd. There were many times when these kids would laugh or smirk at me as I waited on them. I remember asking one of the girls in the in crowd for a date, and her friends laughed at me for even asking. I still remember one of the girls saying, 'Don't you know that rich girls do not go out with poor boys?' That really hurt."

"That still goes on," I said. "I met a girl who said she would not go out with me because I didn't attend an Ivy League school."

"Well, at least you are in college," said rich dad. "When the kids my age went off to college, I felt alone, left behind, and unwanted. And that is why, for all these years, I have seen myself as the ugly duckling."

Rich dad had never shared this part of his life with me before. I was now twenty-one years old, and I realized that his son and I had the advantages he did not have. I knew that at times his life was physically hard but I had no idea how mentally and emotionally tough it had been for him.

Standing on the balcony of his prestigious hotel, I began to realize that he was not telling me the story of being an ugly duckling for me to feel sorry for him. He was smiling and too happy to be doing that. So I asked him, "You used the story of the ugly duckling to keep you going. Didn't you? You did not use that fairy tale to feel sorry for yourself, did you?"

"No," he agreed. "I used the story of the ugly duckling, the story of the three pigs, the story of David and Goliath, the story of the tortoise and the hare to keep me going. Instead of letting those few kids who were athletic, social, or intellectual bullies get me down I used their snobbish actions to inspire me to do better. Today, I have a house of bricks and we are in the penthouse of that house of bricks. If not for those fairy tales or biblical stories, I would not be here today. I am no longer the ugly duckling. By taking my time to build a house of bricks, using as much leverage as David did, and taking my time as the tortoise did, I stand here on top of the streets I grew up on."

"You became the swan?" I said with a smile.

"Well, I wouldn't go that far," rich dad chuckled. "The point is that we can all grow, evolve, and make dramatic changes in our lives, if we want to. The other point is that fairy tales can come true. Ugly ducks can become beautiful swans and slow tortoises can win the race."

Ugly Ducklings into Rich Swans

In my investment seminars, I often put up the following exit strategies:

Poor	$25,000 or less per year
Middle class	$25,000 to $100,000 per year
Affluent	$100,000 to $1 Million per year
Rich	$1 Million or more per year
Ultra-rich	$1 Million or more a month

I ask the class to not be Pinocchio and instead tell the truth of what is real for them, if they continue to do the same things they are doing. I ask them,

"If you keep doing what you are doing today, which financial level will you exit at, at age sixty-five?" I also remind them that less than one out of 100 exit at or above the affluent level.

Many admit that they would be happy just to exit at the middle-class level. Their primary concern is that they do not exit at the poor level. Yet there are a few who ask the question I am looking for, which is, "What do I have to do to go beyond the affluent level?" The moment someone asks that question, they have the possibility of evolving from an ugly duckling and emerging as a financial swan.

At this stage of the investment course, I may retell the fairy tales or biblical stories rich dad told me. I ask them, "Can you embrace the lessons from these stories and embody them in your life? Can you see the lessons from these stories as real and possible for you? Can you imagine going from a financially poor duck and emerging as a rich and powerful swan?" Some can and others just stare blankly, wondering why I am talking about fairy tales in an investment class.

Then I say, "For me to move from a middle-class mind-set and go on to the affluent mind-set was a change as large as changing from an ugly duckling into a swan."

From Slow Plan to Fast Plan

In one of my classes, a young woman asked, "What is the first step?"

Before replying, I draw on my flip chart the following picture.

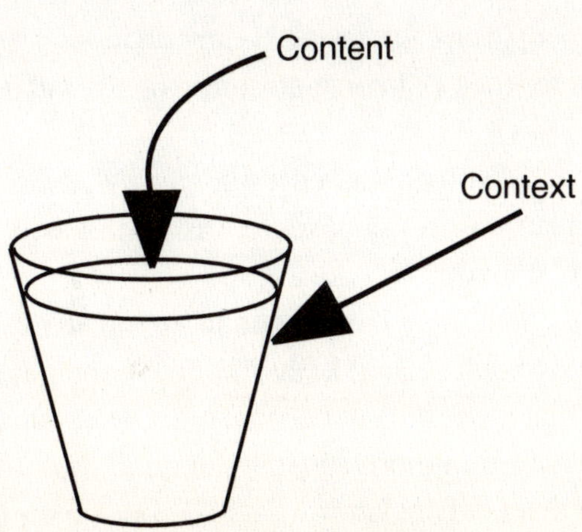

I then say, "In 1989, two years after the market crashed and a recession had set in, Kim and I were working our plan. It was a slow plan. Kim and I had agreed that we would buy two pieces of real estate a year for ten years. As the market crashed, we found more and more deals as more and more people panicked. In less than a year, we had purchased five small rental properties, each with a positive cash flow. I estimate that we had looked at over 600 properties just to find those five small houses that made investment sense. But now the market was getting worse and more and more deals were appearing. The problem was, we were out of money."

"So you had opportunities but you were out of money?" the young woman asked.

Pointing to the glass on the flip chart, I said, "I realized that we were at the limits of our context . . . our reality."

"So it was time to change your reality?" asked another student.

Nodding, I said, "Yes. It was time to change or miss a window of opportunity."

The class was quiet and listening intently. Knowing that I had their attention, I asked, "How many of you have seen an opportunity but were unable to take advantage of it?"

Most of the class raised their hands.

"When that happens," I said, "it means that you are at the boundaries of your *context*, what you think is possible for yourself, and your *content*, which is the accumulated knowledge via which you handle problems and challenges."

"Then what happens?" asked a student. "What should we do?"

"Most people give up, saying, 'I can't do it,' or 'I can't afford it.' Many will ask friends for their opinion, and some friends will tell them to play it safe, don't take risks."

"So what did you do?" asked a student. "What did you do when you realized your plan was too slow, there was a window of opportunity, and you were out of money?"

"Well, the first thing I did was admit to myself that I was being a tortoise who wanted to quit . . . and it was not time to quit, it was time to push on. I also knew that it was time to become more of a swan than a duckling. Keeping the lessons from those fairy tales in mind, I continued instead of giving up. I knew that I did not know what to do but I knew I had to do something.

Days of not knowing what to do turned into weeks. One day after Kim and I had just come back from a trip, I was putting our suitcases down when the phone rang. The phone call was from my favorite real estate broker, who said in an excited voice, 'I just found the deal of the day. If you are interested in it, I'll give you a half-hour head start before I tell another one of my clients.'"

"What kind of deal was it?" asked a student.

"He told me it was a twelve-unit apartment house that was in a great area and it was only $335,000, $35,000 down, and the seller was anxious to sell. The broker then faxed me the sales data on the property with a rough pro forma on income and expenses."

"Did you buy it?" asked the student.

"No," I said. "I told the broker to give me half an hour and I would drive out immediately to look at it. When I got there I realized why it was such a great deal so I dashed to a pay phone and told the broker I would take it."

"Even though you did not have the money?" asked another student.

"We had nothing," I said. "We had just purchased the last of our five units and we were really strapped for cash because we were investing in real estate as well as reinvesting in our business. Even though we had no money, I offered the sellers what they were asking for, which was $35,000 down and they would carry the $300,000 at 8 percent interest for five years. It was such a great deal that I could not pass it up."

"Why was it such a great deal?" asked another student.

"There were many reasons. One was because the owners lived on the property and they had never raised the rents. The tenants were their friends and they did not have the heart to ask them for more money, so the rents were at least 25 percent below market. Another reason was the couple was too old to manage the property and they just wanted to move out. Not being sophisticated investors, they did not appreciate the value of their property. They were also afraid that the value of their property would fall in value with the recession so they were very anxious to sell. Another reason it was a good investment was because there was also a new computer chip factory being built just a mile from the property and more than a thousand new employees were going to be moving into the area, which again meant higher rents. But it was the fact that I did not have to go to a bank to borrow the money that really made the deal a good one. So I called my broker and I told him that I would give them their full price and terms. My only problem was now to find the $35,000 in thirty days, which was when the couple wanted to move out."

"So for thirty days you kept asking yourself, 'How can I afford it?'" asked a student.

"Well for two nights, Kim and I tossed, turned, sweated, and worried," I said. "We were not asking how we could afford it. We kept asking ourselves why we were so crazy. I kept asking myself, 'Why am I doing this? We're doing fine. Our investments are working. Why do I have to push the boundaries of my comfort zone?' I kept thinking about the $35,000. I realized that $35,000 was more than many people earned pretax in a year and now I had to come up with $35,000 cash in a month. I wanted to quit. My self-confidence was challenged, I felt inadequate, stupid, and foolish. After four nights, I finally calmed down, and then I began to ask, 'How could we afford it?'"

"So how did you afford it?" asked a student. "Or did you afford it?"

"Finally, after sweating, praying, and doing our best not to quit, we took the paperwork to our bank and presented our story to the bank manager. After he turned us down, I asked him why he turned us down, and what I could have done better. After he told me, I went to the next bank, with the first banker's improvements, and was again turned down. After being turned down, again we asked the banker why. By the fifth bank, I had learned a tremendous amount about what information banks wanted, why they wanted it, and how they wanted it presented to them. Even though our presentation was much better, we were still turned down by the fifth bank. Almost ready to quit, Kim and I went to the sixth bank. This time, we were much better prepared. We also knew why the investment was a good investment. In trying to convince the five bankers, we had convinced ourselves even more of this investment's soundness. This time our presentation was clearer and much more professional. We spoke the words bankers wanted to hear. Our numbers were clear and we included our track record with our five other properties. We could now explain in banker's words and numbers why it was a great investment. The sixth banker said yes. He had the $35,000 check for us in two days and with three days to spare we went to the escrow office and bought the twelve-unit apartment house."

"What happened after that?" asked a student.

"The real estate market continued to slide and we kept buying," I replied. "Even though we still had very little money, we kept buying. By 1994, the market turned up and we were financially free for the rest of our lives. That twelve-unit apartment building sold for over $500,000 in 1994 and had put over $1,100 a month in our pocket during that period. The $165,000 in capital gains were rolled tax-deferred into a thirty-unit apartment house, which is one of the apartment houses we still have today. That thirty-unit apartment house began putting a little bit more than $5,000 a month in our pocket. With the other properties and investments we had, we were earning over $10,000 a month in passive income, which put us at the *affluent* level, and we retired. We had about $10,000 in passive income and about $3,000 in monthly expenses. We were financially free."

"So it was not luck," said a student. "It was your plan that got accelerated."

"We were prepared for the window of opportunity and we took it," I said. "Soon after 1994, the prices of real estate skyrocketed and it became a little harder to find such bargains and willing sellers."

"So you made quite a bit of money without any of your own money?" asked a student.

"Yes, on that deal, but I *do not* recommend you doing what we did. Investing in real estate without any money down can be very risky, if you do not know what you are investing in, and if you do not have the cash reserves if things do not go the way you expect them to. I have met many people who bought a property with nothing down, only to find out that the expenses of the property were far greater than the actual income they received. I have had friends who have gone bankrupt because they purchased property or businesses that were too highly leveraged. That is why I do not openly endorse buying no-money-down real estate. I recommend having some experience buying, selling, and especially managing real estate before going after highly leveraged deals. We had looked at hundreds of other properties before buying this particular twelve-unit property and we also had the cash flow from our business to support any unexpected losses from the investment. The trouble with no-money-down real estate deals is that there is often too much leverage and that type of highly leveraged investment can easily eat you alive if anything should go wrong. So I repeat myself: I do not recommend anyone do what we did. I tell you this story for one reason."

"And that reason is?" asked another student.

Going to the flip chart, I then added to the drawing I had up there previously.

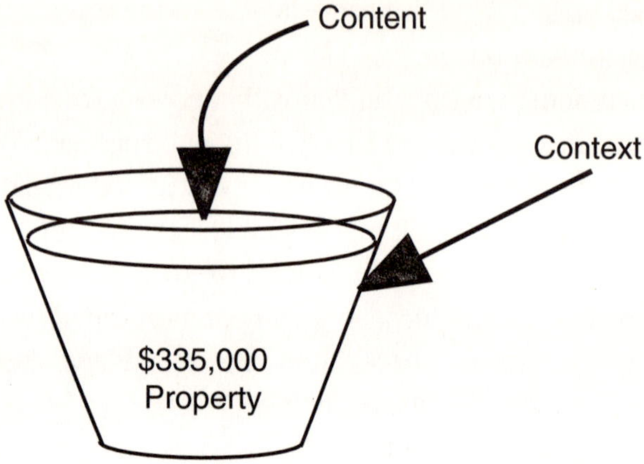

"The reason I tell you this story is to explain to you the importance of being willing to expand your context as well as add to your context."

"So today, affording a $335,000 property is easy for you because you increased your reality and your education. Is that what you are saying?" asked a student.

"Very easy," I replied. "Looking back upon it now, it seems silly to have let a $35,000 down payment seem like a lot of money, and a twelve-unit apartment house as a big deal. But back then it was a lot of money, and it was a very big deal. The important thing for Kim and me was the willingness to go beyond our context and our content."

"So most people do not push beyond their comfort levels," said another student. "Most people find it easier to play it safe and say, 'I can't afford it.'"

"That has been my experience," I said. "I believe that one of the main reasons why less than 1 percent of the population goes beyond the affluent level is simply because most people find it very uncomfortable going beyond their personal reality, their context, and their content. Most people try and solve their financial problems with what they know, rather than expand what they know so they can solve a bigger problem. Rather than taking on bigger financial challenges, most people wrestle all their lives with financial problems they feel comfortable with. They remain poor but pretty swans rather than risk becoming an ugly duckling again."

"Have you become an ugly duckling again?" asked a student a little cynically.

"Sure," I said. "After the $335,000 apartment house, we found it easy to invest up to the $2.5 million level. From 1994 to 2001, we did well in that range up to $2.5 million and our passive income increased to about $16,000 a month without much effort. We were definitely at the affluent level and it was time to move on to be rich. For those of you who know our past, you may recall that *Rich Dad Poor Dad* was in rough draft, written between 1995 and 1996, I designed and created the board game CASHFLOW in 1996, and I got back into the world of business. Simultaneously in 1996, I knew it was time for me to learn how to take a company public, through the IPO process, which is when I met Peter, as described in book number three, *Rich Dad's Guide to Investing*. Also in 1996, Kim and I met Sharon Lechter, and *Rich Dad Poor Dad* was published. Sharon, Kim, and I founded CASHFLOW® Technologies, Inc. in the fall of 1997. We were entering a new world with a new context, content, and friends. Our real estate investing context remained at $2.5 million in investments."

"So you moved to expand your context in other areas but did not expand your real estate reality. Is that what you are saying?" asked a student.

"That is exactly what I am saying," I said. "With Sharon as a co-author and partner in the business, our little company grew far beyond our wildest dreams. Without Sharon, we would not be as successful as we are today. After working for five years with Peter, we have four to six companies going public through the IPO process in the next few years. Both in business and in the IPO process, our reality on what is possible has expanded considerably. Our context as to business and the IPO process has taken quantum leaps."

"But your reality in real estate remained the same," said a student. "It has remained the same since the $335,000, twelve-unit apartment house. It has remained stuck between $335,000 and $2.5 million. That is your lesson, isn't it?"

"Exactly," I said. "Just because a person improves in one financial arena does not mean they expand in all arenas. That is why in 2001, Kim and I decided it was time to get back to real estate and push the walls of our context again."

Getting Rich Gets Easier

Years ago, rich dad said to me, "One of the reasons the rich get richer is because once you've found the formula to getting rich, it gets easier to get rich.

If you never find the formula, getting rich always seems hard and staying poor seems natural."

The reason I have spent so much time on this subject of reality, context, and content is because it was rich dad's formula. It was his basic formula to never say, "I can't afford it" or "I can't do it," and choose instead to expand his reality. As you already know, rich dad used fairy tales and biblical stories as his life-guiding lessons to keep him going through times of doubt and fear. But it was his lesson on acceleration of wealth that was most interesting to me. He would say, "Once you know that the formula to getting rich is to continually expand your reality, which increases your leverage, then getting rich becomes easier and easier. For people who become stuck in one reality, thinking their reality is the only reality, the speed at which they can become rich goes down."

In other words, rich dad taught me that once you become rich, getting rich gets easier and becomes faster. If you never become rich, life becomes harder and slower. Knowing this, I knew it was time for Kim and me to expand our reality on real estate again. We had invested over five years expanding our reality on business and the IPO process and we had become rich much quicker and faster than ever before. I knew that at the next level getting richer would become easier and faster. I knew because I saw it happen to my rich dad.

After $5 Million It Gets Very Easy

Late in the year 2000, the stock market was crashing, our business was expanding rapidly, our books and games were selling worldwide, the companies we were bringing public were taking shape nicely and were soon to be profitable. Kim said to me, "I want to get back into real estate. We need to invest in more stable assets if we want to maintain our wealth." With that, we went back out into the market and ran into our old reality, our old context and content. It felt like we were back at trying to find $35,000 for a $335,000 apartment house. Even though we could easily write a check for three $335,000 apartment houses, paying cash without needing a loan, we were having trouble again. Things were not coming our way. At that point, I knew it was time to expand our reality one more time.

Up to then, Kim and I were looking for projects that ran around $4 million. We felt comfortable with that number since we knew we had over $1 million for the down payment, if we needed it. We thought we knew a lot, but we could not find a property or the financing that made sense or that worked according to our new plan. It was then I called an old friend named Bill, who does hundreds of millions of dollars in real estate. After finally tracking him down, I asked him what was wrong with our approach. Bill's reply was, "Four million dollars is a tough market. Banks don't like investments that big and projects of that size are not exciting enough for sophisticated private investors. But after $5 million, it gets easy again."

The moment he said that, I knew I was at the boundary of my reality, my context. Four million dollars was easy and comfortable but $5 million was now just outside my comfort zone. My mind began to scream, saying, "If I can't get a bank interested in a $4 million project, how will I get them interested in a $5 million real estate investment?" I could hear my reality speaking loudly to me. I could also hear rich dad telling me to remember the fairy tales and to also remember that getting rich gets easier the richer you get, if you just follow the formula. I knew it was time to follow the formula and push beyond my reality.

It Got Very Easy

At the start of this book, I wrote about how easy it was to retire early by borrowing money from the banks. Once Kim and I were willing to push beyond our reality, our comfort zone, we found out that it is just as easy to borrow money from the government.

I have written about the tax laws being in favor of those who are in the B and I quadrants and against those in the E and S quadrants. I also wrote that most of the people who complain about taxes are the E and S quadrant people. The reason is, on the B and I side, the government wants to be your partner, simply because it is the B and I side that creates jobs and provides housing. I had always known this, because my rich dad had told me, but I had no idea how much the government helps those that help the government, until I began looking into real estate investments over $5 million . . . until I was willing to expand my context.

Our search was on. We were now looking for larger projects that were far beyond our comfort zone. At our first meeting in 2001 with a real estate sales person who specializes in low-income government-sponsored housing, Kim and I showed the salesperson our existing real estate portfolio. In our portfolio we had millions of dollars in real estate, mainly in unit sizes of thirty to fifty apartments.

"You know how to manage multifamily apartment houses," said the real estate agent, a young woman in her late thirties. "That's good."

"Why is that good?" asked Kim.

"Because one of the requirements of the government is that anyone it lends money to must have a successful track record at managing multifamily apartment houses. You've been doing that for over ten years and have run them profitably. Many people want these government loans but only very few people qualify for them," said the agent. "As you know, most people who do own a few investment properties want to manage their own real estate, collect their rents, and do their own repairs. That is why they never learn how to manage larger properties as you do."

Kim and I nodded. We knew there was much more to real estate than simply collecting rent and fixing a few toilets. We had learned a lot in the last ten years. But now it was time for us to move on. If we were to move on, we had to meet new people, learn a new vocabulary, and be willing to play a much bigger game. Listening to these two new people in our lives, I realized that over the past ten years we had become hares and swans in the real estate market up to $4 million. We were the proverbial big fish in a small pond. It was now time to move on and again become uncomfortable, become slow tortoises and ugly little ducklings in a much bigger game.

Sitting next to the agent was an investment banker who specialized in tax-exempt, rated and nonrated government housing bonds. When I asked him what kind of financing programs the government had, he replied, "If you and your project qualify, the government will offer you 95 percent to 110 percent financing."

"You mean they will lend us all of the money to buy our next investment? The government will give us the money to buy our asset?"

"Even more if you qualify," he said. "The government will even lend you the money to fix up or rehabilitate the project if you qualify."

"You mean if the project costs $10 million they will lend us all of the $10 million or more? And if it takes $3 million to fix the place up, they will also lend us that money? They will lend us all the money for our property?"

The investment banker nodded. "They would prefer to lend you $20 million or more, but $10 million would be a good place for you to start. Once you do a $10 million project, a $20 million or even a $50 million project would not be out of line . . . if you have a proven track record."

I could hear rich dad saying that things got easier and easier. But I could not believe it could become this easy. Still in a little disbelief I asked, "At what kind of terms?"

"I might be able to secure interest rates between 5 percent to 7 percent, fixed for forty years, and nonrecourse."

"Nonrecourse?" I gasped. "You mean the government won't come after everything I own personally if the project goes bad and I can't pay the money back? My banker hates nonrecourse loans. Every time I borrow money from him, he makes sure everything I own is also on the line."

"That's correct," said the investment banker. "But you realize that there are many terms and conditions that apply here that do not apply to conventional bank financing."

"I realize that," I said. "But I had no idea how good the government could be."

"Occasionally, there are even better programs in these tax-exempt government bond issues. There are occasionally *forgivable loans,* where the government simply forgets you borrowed money from them if you do certain things well. It is very similar to a *grant.*"

"Why does the government do this?" I asked.

"Because one of the great problems facing this country is low-income affordable housing. The government is afraid that without people like you, millions and millions of people will go homeless and be forced to live in substandard, crime-ridden slums. The government is going after slumlords and is taking some of them to jail. These slumlords prey on the poor and the government wants to put a stop to them. At the same time, the government is willing to offer billions of dollars to individuals like you who have proven themselves to be responsible managers of large multifamily projects."

"They are willing to give me the money to become even richer."

"That is correct," said the investment banker as the real estate broker smiled on. "It's more than just money. It's big money. If you do well over the next few years, I can help you borrow billions of dollars, if you want to get that big and that rich. Last year, one of our divisions had to return over a billion dollars because they could not find anyone who qualified for it."

It was Kim who said, "The best thing about getting rich this way is that we do a lot of good for a lot of people. It excites me to think about turning a slum into safe housing for people with families."

"That is exactly what the government wants you to do. It is from our slums where most of our problems come from. It is from our slums where crime breeds and grows. If you can change slums into safe housing, you will have more and more money available to you. As much as you want."

"So we become rich by becoming partners with the government?"

"As rich as you want to be," smiled the investment banker. "All you have to do is do what you have been doing for the past ten years, which is own and manage multifamily apartment houses. All you have to do is capitalize on your ten years of experience. And we would love to help you get even richer. Do you know how hard it is to find people with your years of experience? Just let us know when you're ready. She'll help you find your property and I'll find you all the money you want."

The meeting was soon over. Kim and I thanked them and headed for our car. Once in the car, we sat quietly in almost stunned disbelief. It took a number of miles before we said anything. Finally Kim said, "Do you remember the twelve-unit apartment house we bought ten years ago?"

"I was just thinking about it," I replied.

"What would have happened if we had chosen to say, 'I can't afford it'?" she said. "What would our lives be like if we had let $35,000 stop us?"

I thought for a moment and said, "I think we would still be saying the same thing today. If $35,000 had stopped us back then, it would probably be stopping us today." As we drove out of the parking lot, I could hear rich dad saying, "Your future is determined by what you do today, not tomorrow." Turning to Kim I said, "If we had said 'I can't afford it' ten years ago, we would probably be saying 'I can't afford it' today."

We drove home in silence, feeling excited and blessed. As the car drove up to our home, I could hear rich dad telling me that once you became rich, getting rich became easier and easier. I could hear him saying to me that the reason many people never went past the middle-class level of life was because they did not believe in fairy tales. Since they did not believe in fairy tales, they failed to learn the lessons from the stories. As I got out of the car, I silently thanked my rich dad and could hear him saying to me, "Always remember that fairy tales do come true . . . in one way or another."

Chapter 13

The Leverage of Generosity

Who Is Really Greedy?

The other night, one of the more famous weekend news commentators said in a heated tone, "I did not go into business because I am not a greedy person."

For much of my childhood I heard comments like that one. Many of the people who visited my parents' home were people who either worked for the university, the educational system, the labor union, the Peace Corps, or for the government. Although not stated as blatantly as the TV commentator, it was often said or implied that people in business were in business simply because they were greedy.

My rich dad had a different point of view. He often said, "All of us are greedy to some extent. It's only natural to desire basic survival, a better life, and enough life support to live well once we stop working. But just because someone is in business or is rich does not necessarily mean they are any greedier than anyone else. In fact, it could be just the opposite." He then said, "The reason most people are not rich is simply because they are not generous enough."

In the previous chapter, when Kim and I decided to increase our real estate holdings, the floodgate of money from the government also opened up.

In our desire to become richer, one of the first steps was to find ways of being more generous . . . in this case to provide better housing for more people at a better price.

When you look at history, the richest people have been very generous in one way or another. As mentioned earlier, Henry Ford became a billionaire by providing affordable cars for the masses, at a time when cars were only for the rich. In fact, many of the car companies that only built cars for the rich are no longer in business today. The car companies for the rich went out of business, while the Ford Motor Company grew into a worldwide industrial power, fulfilling Henry Ford's mission. So if you want to retire young and retire rich, it's okay to be greedy, just as long as you constantly work to find ways to give more to more and more people. If you will do that, you will find your own path to great wealth.

Ratios of the Rich

Rich dad liked ratios because, as he said, "You can tell a lot just by a little comparison." To rich dad, ratios were simply comparisons, just as a P/E ratio is simply a comparison. When it came to money, rich dad said, "One of the main reasons the poor and middle class struggle is because their ratios have no leverage." He would use the ratio 1:1 to illustrate the leverage ratio of a poor or middle-class person.

One day, while I was still in college, rich dad showed me his ratios. On a paper he wrote:

Businesses	1:5
Workers	1:300
Real estate	1:450
Dollars	1:6 million
Shares	1:2 million

In other words, his business ratio meant he owned interests in five businesses. He had over 300 workers working for him. In real estate, he had over 450 tenants, and that did not include his industrial real estate, stores, or restaurants. As the years went on, the numbers on the right side of the ratio continually increased, which is why he got richer and richer, while working less and less.

My poor dad's ratio started out at 1:1 and ended with 1:1 . . . which is why he got poorer and poorer. As you can tell by the leverage ratio, my poor dad believed in a day's pay for a day's work. There were times my poor dad worked at two different jobs. Even though he worked at two jobs his ratio remained at 1:1 according to my rich dad's definition. Rich dad said, "If most people have two jobs, they are just working more hours at the same ratio."

Between 1985 and 1990, the ratios for Kim and me looked like this:

Businesses	1:1
Real estate	1:0
Dollars	1:not much

We had one business we were building, we owned a home but we did not count it as an asset, since it took money from us every month, and we had almost nothing in savings. Stocks or other paper assets were inconsequential, since they cost us money and never put any money in our pockets.

By 1995, our leverage ratios looked like this:

Businesses	1:0
Real estate	1:70
Dollars	1:300,000

By this date, we had sold our business, bought more income-producing real estate, and put some money in the bank. The important thing was that the real estate provided us enough money to live at the affluent level and never work again.

By 2000 our leverage ratios looked like this:

Businesses	1:7
Real estate	1:70
Dollars	1:millions
Shares	1:1.5 million

While the ratios paint an interesting picture of financial progress, the real gains are in the business arena, the arena where the true dollar valuations, or cash flows, are not reflected in the ratios. I do not present these numbers to impress, for they are not that impressive, nor do I present them to brag. In fact, I hesitate to show these numbers because they are personal and I would rather not show them. I show them simply to illustrate our path and our plan. I also present them to let people know it is possible to start with very little and yet build a financial house of bricks, as in the story of the Three Little Pigs.

Even though the numbers are not big, when compared to the world of the ultra-rich, our plan is to continue the acceleration of wealth for a few more years. If things go according to plan, we should move into the world of the ultra-rich in a few years.

You may notice from the numbers that our plan over the past few years was to move into building businesses rather than acquiring real estate. For the next five to ten years, our plan is to continue to build more businesses, but focus more on acquiring larger pieces of real estate, with the help of government funding.

The point I would like to impress upon you now is the idea of the continual expansion of context, or reality, and the constant search for faster and better content, or education. If you want to follow a similar path to wealth, I cannot stress enough the importance of having an open mind, going beyond personal doubts, limitations, and complacency, being willing to learn, and taking action. I have met many people who want to grow financially at this rate, or faster, but many are not willing to expand their context or increase their content. So these are the people who struggle at one thing or go from project to project, hoping it is the project that will make them rich. I contend that if a person has an ever-increasing context and content, the person will become richer and richer, regardless of what the project is. It is not the product or new idea that will make you rich. It is your context and content that makes you rich. As I have said in other books, Ray Kroc became a billionaire selling billions of average hamburgers and Starbucks became a world-famous brand selling cups of coffee.

Rich dad often said, "If you do not change your context or your content, your ratios will remain the same." I have a friend who always has the next new idea to make millions of dollars. The other day, he called me and asked me to invest in his latest scheme. He had a great idea for a line of clothing that the store he works part-time for does not sell. He said, "Every day people come in to this store looking for this brand of clothing. My boss does not want to carry it. Why don't you give me some money and I'll open a shop right across from this one. We'll split the profits 50-50."

When I asked this friend if he would attend classes on cash flow management, retail management, sales, marketing, and hiring and firing people, he declined. His response was, "Why do I need to do that? I've worked in this store for years. I don't need to learn anything more to run a store." After I turned him down, he called again with another project and again I turned him down.

I turned him down simply because I doubt if he is willing to change his context and content. He just wants to make money . . . and given his age, if he were good with money, he would already be rich. So he continues to think that it is the next hot idea, or business opportunity, that will make him rich, rather than his limited context and content that holds him back. Even if he did open that store, and his new products were successful, I suspect that his ratio would continue to be 1:1. In other words, he would probably have to be in the store all day and all night with very little chance of expansion, given his existing context and content.

Why It's Hard to Get Rich

It's hard or nearly impossible to get rich with a context and content that limits you to a 1:1 leverage ratio. It's hard to get rich because there is no leverage. When you look at the CASHFLOW Quadrant shown below:

you may begin to understand why it is harder for the left side of the quadrant, the E and S side, to get rich because of the leverage ratios. For the most part, the E and S side is all 1:1 ratio, with few exceptions. For example, most employees can only work for one company at a time. While they may hold a second job, that still falls in the 1:1 ratio. The same is true for many small business owners or self-employed people. That friend of mine who wanted to open a clothing store would most likely have been chained to one store. I sincerely doubt if he could handle more than one store. A dentist can only drill in one mouth at one time and a lawyer or accountant only has so many billable hours in a day.

When talking to my tax advisor, Diane Kennedy, she said, "A vast majority of high-income professional people from the S quadrant get stuck at an income cap of $100,000 to $150,000." Diane goes further, saying, "The ones that make more do so because they are highly specialized and charge a lot more per hour or by the project. This group caps out at around $500,000 per year. Very few make much more than that." Again the problem is the 1:1 leverage ratio.

In the previous chapter on fairy tales, one of the fairy tales mentioned was the story of the Tortoise and the Hare. One of the ways the hares or rabbits of life get off to a fast start is because they have some special gift, intelligence, or talent. They may be great scholars, fast learners, or great athletes, or artists such as movie stars. Many do well early in life. Yet for a tortoise like me, I knew that the way I would win my own race was to win the race using the ratios of leverage. It was the same plan my rich dad used. Maybe if I was really smart, and was a rocket scientist, maybe I could have been successful in the more traditional world of business and climbed the corporate ladder. But early in life when I began having trouble in school, I knew that I had to find my own way of winning my race. Today my income is greater than many of my peers who got the high-paying jobs early in life. My income is higher because I used the *leverage of assets* rather than the *leverage of my labor.*

For those of you who want to retire young and retire rich, one of the decisions that you may need to make is to find out which race you have the best chance of winning. For example, if you are like baseball star Alex Rodriguez, who was paid $252 million for a ten-year contract, plus commercial endorsements, then obviously the E quadrant is the best for you. Even though Rodriguez's ratio is 1:1 for ten years, it is a pretty good ratio when the dollar signs are added in. If you can be a movie star like Julia Roberts, who makes $20 million a movie, then that is obviously the best path for you. Secretary of the Treasury under George W. Bush, Paul O'Neill, received over $100 million in shares and stock options as an employee of Alcoa. Even though he was in a work situation with a 1:1 ratio, his compensation was very leveraged. If you think that your chances for success are best on the path to the top of the corporate ladder of a major corporation, then that is the best path for you, even if it is a 1:1 ratio. The reason Kim and I followed the same path rich dad used was simply because we felt we had the best chance for financial success on his path. It was a path that required us to acquire assets. It was a path that required us to work at constantly increasing our leverage ratios.

A Good Path for Turtles

There is another reason why I personally chose rich dad's path. The reason is found in the diagram of the CASHFLOW Quadrant below:

(Limited) (Infinite)

Years ago rich dad pointed to the left side of the quadrant and said, "The earnings potential on the E and S side is *limited*. The earnings potential on the right side is *infinite.*"

Rich dad explained further, saying, "The trouble with selling your labor for money is that there is only so much you can do. If you learn to acquire or build assets to generate money, you can slowly but surely increase your income. In fact, the right side of the quadrant is a great side for turtles, turtles who slowly but surely acquire more and more assets."

Rich dad also said, "The trouble with selling your labor is that your labor has no long-term residual value. If you buy a rental property and you profitably rent it out, the labor you used to acquire that rental property can be rewarded over and over again, for years. In other words, you can be paid for years for something that may have taken less than a week of work to do." An example is, in 1991, Kim and I bought a property in a resort area for $50,000 cash. It was a great deal, since it originally sold for $134,000. We bought it out of foreclosure from a bank. Since 1991, we have been paid over $1,000 a month net income or over $12,000 a year for years. The total time it took to buy and put the property in a rental pool was less than eight hours of work. We have thought of selling the property and taking the appreciation, but that would be too much trouble at this time.

The trouble with working at a job for money is that you have to start over selling your labor each and every morning. In most cases, your labor has no long-term residual value, if you are working for money. On top of that, if you are working for money, then your earning potential is limited. If you work slowly acquiring assets your income potential is infinite and that income can be passed on for generations to come. Your job or profession is not something you can pass on in your will to your children.

Life Gets Easier

Rich dad pointed out that working for money by selling your labor often means that life gets harder simply because you have to work harder to make more money. He said, "If your leverage ratio for life remains at 1:1, then your life will get harder. If you work for an ever increasing leverage ratio, then life gets easier and you make more and more money."

A Quantum Leap in Wealth

Most of us have heard of the term a *quantum leap.* Others may use the term *exponential,* meaning beyond a linear increase in something. In other words, 1+1 does not equal 2. In a quantum leap of wealth or an exponential increase of money, 1+1 can equal 5, 6, 7, or more. In other words, if you work diligently and build a strong house of bricks, I have found that there are often sudden quantum leaps of wealth, quantum leaps that people who follow a 1:1 do not seem to have.

For example, from 1985 to 1990, life for Kim and me was pretty much a life of financial struggle. Suddenly, between 1990 and 1994, Kim and I had a sudden and exponential burst in wealth and financial success. From 1994 to 1998, life again was pretty stable. We worked diligently building assets, more specifically businesses. We did not buy much in the way of real estate, since the price of property had gotten too high and finding a great deal took too much time. Then suddenly in 1999, not only did my books and games begin to take off, many of our other businesses and investments began to catch fire.

It seemed like a sudden surge of good fortune, new friends, and new opportunities, yet in reality, it was the years of working without much results and occasional financial setbacks that were the source of the surge in exponential wealth. The reason this happens is because the value of assets often increases exponentially while the value of your labor only increases incrementally. For example, my accountant told me that the value of one of my companies grew to $40 million in the year 2000. That was the price she thought we could sell it for if we wanted to. At the same time one of my attorneys raised his hourly rate by $25 an hour. That is an example of assets increasing *exponentially* and income increasing *incrementally.* That is another example of the earning potential of the left side of the quadrant being limited and the earning potential of the right side being almost infinite.

Another example of a quantum leap occurred in the number of shares of companies we owned. From 1996 to 1998, we worked at acquiring shares of a public company. That company suddenly went broke and we lost everything we had in that company. Our shares became virtually worthless. Yet, due to the experience we gained working on acquiring a major stake in that company, we transferred what we had learned to acquiring shares in better companies, at very low prices. Hence we have gone on to acquire many shares in good start-up companies and those shares have gone on to do very well, even in a down stock market.

At the start of this book I wrote about the journalist who criticized me saying that most new companies fail at the start. Today, even though the risks are still high in starting a business, the experience gained from running those small struggling companies that failed has added to my ability to start companies that are more stable and have a better long-term chance of success. When I look at the success of *Rich Dad Poor Dad* and our company, richdad.com, much of our current success is due largely in part to my failures of the past. Sharon and Kim also had their setbacks, disappointments in business, and yet those setbacks became the lessons learned that contributed to our combined success today. It is what we as a group learned from our individual pasts that gives us what seems to be the sudden and quantum leap of success we enjoy today.

I mention all this as a way of encouraging you to keep going, even though you may encounter some setbacks along your life's path. If you will learn from each setback, rather than blame or make excuses, your wealth of knowledge will increase. If you steadily work to be more and more generous, work to serve more and more people, work to increase your leverage ratios, I am quite certain that you too will experience these sudden bursts, quantum leaps, or exponential jumps in wealth. It seems that even turtles can push along with a sudden gust of tailwind.

The Power of Networks

I came across a law known as Metcalfe's Law that partially explains the quantum leap or exponential burst of wealth. Robert Metcalfe is one of the founders of 3Com, the company that brought you the PalmPilot. His law states that *the economic power of a business is the square of the number in the network.*

The story of the fax machine helps us understand this concept more clearly. In my early days at the Xerox Corporation, we were tasked at selling fax machines. The problem in the early 1970s was that very few people had fax machines and even fewer people knew what they did. Since there were so few fax machines, their economic value was low. Yet as time went on and more and more people used them, there was a sudden burst in their popularity. Today, most of my friends have fax machines in their homes as well as their business.

So Metcalfe's Law is this: If you have only one fax machine, your economic value is one, according to the formula,

1:1 (squared)

The economic value of 1 squared is still 1. But the moment you have two fax machines, the economic value of the network does not go up linearly. It increases quantumly. The moment you have a second fax machine the economic value goes up to 4, not 2:

$1{:}2^2$ = economic value of 4

When there were 10 fax machines in the network the numbers looked like this:

$1{:}10^2$ = economic value of 100

The S Quadrant Suffers

For people who operate as sole proprietors, or other forms of self-employed small business owners, they often do not have the benefit of Metcalfe's Law. One of the reasons a franchise group such as McDonald's is more powerful than a mom-and-pop hamburger stand is again due to Metcalfe's Law.

I have found that people who work hard at being rugged individuals often have to work much harder just to maintain their autonomy. That is why many professionals join associations in order to have more clout in the world.

The E Quadrant Unionizes

For years, people in the E quadrant have known the value of getting organized into a labor union. By joining together, employees in the E quadrant have much more power than trying to negotiate as individuals. Today one of the richest and most powerful labor unions in America is the NEA, the National Education Association. One of the reasons our educational system is slow to change is largely due to the power of the teachers union. They know the power of a network.

The Power of Monopoly

Rich dad often said, "The formula for great wealth is found in the game of Monopoly." Many of us know this formula, the formula of buy four green houses and trade them in for one red hotel. The formula for wealth found in the game of Monopoly also follows Metcalfe's Law. When you look at the comparison of my poor dad's and rich dad's ratio, you may understand why my rich dad's economic power continued to increase and my poor dad's economic power remained the same.

	Poor Dad	*Rich Dad*
Real estate	1:1 never changed	1:450 always increasing

In other words, my poor dad's economic power remained at 1. One squared is still 1. All he had was his house. In this example, my rich dad's economic power was 450^2. He controlled over 450 rental units. His economic power was going up exponentially. When you look at my poor dad's ratio of 1:1, and then factor in the affect that taxes had on his income, earned income at 50 percent, you can actually see why my poor dad's economic power did not increase, although he worked harder and harder. My rich dad's income was going up, his economic power was going up, and he was paying less and less in taxes.

In 1985, Kim and I had a plan to acquire two new rental units a year. We began buying our first property in 1989. Once we had five units, our economic power was 5^2 or 25. Not only did our economic power go up, our confidence had also gone up as our experience went up. When we purchased that twelve-unit apartment house, our leverage ratio was 1:17 and our economic power was $1{:}17^2$ or 289. Others who only had their home, and did not purchase investment property during the downturn, had their real estate ratio remain 1:1 and their economic power remain at 1. For Kim and me our goal for the year 2005 is to have 1,000 or more rental units in our portfolio. The question is, what is the economic power of $1{,}000^2$?

This example explains how a person who operates in the B or I quadrant can soon pass a very smart, talented, or well-educated person in the E or S quadrant, even though the person in the E or S quadrant earns more money. Metcalfe's Law explains why my rich dad was eventually earning more in a year than my poor dad earned all his life. Metcalfe's Law also explains why tortoises can beat hares if they continue to acquire assets rather than work for money as many a rabbit often does.

Network Marketing Business

After understanding Metcalfe's Law, the law of networks, I knew why network marketing organizations offer such a powerful tool to average people like you and me. Applying Metcalfe's Law to a network marketing business, you begin to see the power of this form of business.

For example:

A person from the E or S quadrant decides to join a network marketing organization and learns to move to the B quadrant. They work for a year or two, gaining the required education and mind-set. Let's say for two years, nothing much happens. People come and people go from their business, rather than stick it out. So after a year or two, their leverage ratio or economic power is the same. It is not much different from being in the E or S quadrant:

$$1:1^2$$

Economic power of 1

Suddenly, in the third year, this person's context is expanded and they have new content and all of a sudden they now attract and train three strong candidates who also want to build the business.

Their leverage ratio and economic power looks like this:

1:3

Economic power of 9

In three years that is a quantum leap of power.

After five years this person now has a network of ten and their leverage ratio looks like this:

1:10

Economic power of 100

And now let's say this person decides that ten people are enough and he or she focuses only on the ten people in their business. Soon after just a few years, let's say the ten people in his network also have ten people (1:10:10). That means the original person now has 100 people in his network.

Then with his or her excess cash, this person begins to buy apartment houses. He begins with a 100-unit apartment house:

Business	1:10:10
Real estate	1:100

Within five to ten years, this individual has not only made the shift from the E and S side of the quadrant, he has jumped his economic power in both the B and I quadrant, something that is hard to do in the E and S quadrant. Suddenly, the person who made the shift is far wealthier, making much more money, and has more economic power than the peers he or she left behind in the E or S quadrant.

After fifteen years, the numbers could be staggering.

That is an oversimplified example of why I recommend some of the network marketing companies. As the name says, it is a network . . . which harnesses Metcalfe's Law, which is the law that measures the power of networks.

Today, when I talk to people who are worried about their retirement or their mutual funds in their retirement account, I often recommend they add to their portfolio a network marketing business. I say to them, "If you really follow the lessons taught by some of the network marketing businesses, and you build a solid business with solid people in your network, you will find that business to be far more secure than the mutual funds found in your retirement fund. If you truly work hard to make those in your network rich, they in turn will make you rich and very secure. In my mind, a network marketing business is far more secure than the stock market because you are counting on people you have grown to love and trust and all of you are harnessing the power of Metcalfe's Law . . . the law that measures the power of networks."

Networks Harness the Power of Generosity

The rich and powerful understand the power of networks. McDonald's is a network of hamburger stands linked throughout the world. General Motors is a network of car dealerships throughout America. Exxon is an oil company with oil fields, tankers, pipelines, and gas stations linked throughout the world. If the rich and powerful use networks, shouldn't you? Safeway is a chain of food stores that distributes food throughout the country. CBS, NBC, ABC, CNN, PBS, CBN are very powerful communication networks.

Rich dad said, "If you want to be rich, you must build networks and link your network with other networks. The reason it is easy to become rich through networks is because it is easy to be *generous* through networks. On the other side, people who act alone or as individuals limit their chances for economic success." He went on to say, "Networks are people, businesses, or organizations that you are generous with because you support them and they support you. Networks are powerful forms of leverage. If you want to be rich, build a network and network with other networks."

Our business plan for richdad.com is based on networking with, rather than competing against, organizations, especially if they are larger than we are. Today, we network with AOL Time Warner, Time Life, Nightingale-Conant, PBS, publishers in forty different countries, many church organizations, and several network marketing companies. We work together to make each other stronger and more viable, as well as wealthier. There is a give and a take, a sharing of strengths and minimizing of weaknesses that makes us all stronger.

We have found that through being cooperative and focused on making sure the people we do business with do well financially we grow exponentially. I have noticed that individuals or businesses who primarily focus *only* on making themselves rich or taking more than they give do not make good network partners. I have noticed that people who want only to *take* and are only concerned about themselves often have to work harder and earn less in the long run.

I was once on a board of a company where it was obvious that the president did not care about the company. All he cared about was his pay package and his golden parachute. He did not care about the network, in this case a business with hundreds of employees that gave it life. All he cared about was himself. Needless to say, we brought in a new president. The key point to being successful in networking is to be sincerely interested in first making sure the individuals or organizations that you network with are also doing well. You cannot only care about yourself, as too many people and organizations seem to do.

Over the years, Kim, Sharon, and I have met individuals, consultants, or organizations that would only work with us if they were certain that they got paid first. In other words, it was the fee we paid them that seemed to be more important than the service they delivered.

Recently we hired a consulting firm to come in and look at our internal marketing systems. They asked for a sizable fee before they would do any kind of work. We paid them and three months later their report came back. After shifting through the mumbo jumbo of the report, we realized that all the report said was that we should retain their firm and pay them for three more years. There was not one recommendation on how to improve our marketing systems. There was only a proposal for more work. That is an example of a vendor putting the vendor's fees in front of the client's needs. Needless to say, we did not sign the contract.

When I was in high school, rich dad asked me to come and watch him hire a new man to manage one of his industrial parks. At the meeting in his conference room, there were three applicants. After rich dad got through explaining the task, he asked if any of them had any questions. The questions were interesting. They were:

1. "How much time off will I have each day?"
2. "How much sick leave?"
3. "What are the benefits?"
6. "When do I get a raise and promotion?"
7. "How many paid holidays?"

After the meeting, rich dad asked me what I noticed.

I replied, "They were only interested in what was in it for them. Not one asked you how they could help you build your business or what they could do to make the business more profitable."

"That's what I noticed," said rich dad.

"Are you going to hire any one of them?"

"Sure," said rich dad. "I'm looking for an employee, not a partner. I'm looking for someone who wants to make money, not get rich."

"Didn't it sound greedy to you?" I asked. For those of you who have read my other books, you may recall rich dad always had me work for free, rather than for money.

"Yes it does," said rich dad. "But we're all greedy to some extent. The reason they will probably not ever become rich is not because they are greedy; they will probably never become rich because they are not generous enough."

In other words, their leverage ratio will probably always be 1:1. Repeating what rich dad said, "Most people will not ever become rich because all they think about is a day's pay for a day's work. There is not much leverage in a day's pay for a day's work because no matter how hard you work or how much you get paid, the ratio is still 1:1."

One of the reasons rich dad had his son and me learn to work for free was so that we would learn to give and build an asset before we received. Years ago, rich dad drew this diagram to explain his point. Rich dad called this the "Who Gets Paid First and Who Gets Paid the Most" diagram:

5. Business owner
4. Investors
3. Specialists (accountants, employees, consultants)
2. Employees
1. Asset (business or other investment)

Rich dad said, "A business owner must pay the asset first. That means continually reinvesting enough money and resources in order to keep the asset strong and growing. Too many business owners put themselves in front of the asset, the employees, and everyone else. That is why their business fails. The reason the business owner gets paid *last* is because he or she starts a business in order to be paid the *most*. But in order to get paid the most, the business owner must make sure that the rest of the business is paid first. That is why I am training you to not work for money. You are learning to delay gratification and work to build assets that grow in value. I want you to learn to build assets, not work for money."

Too many dot-coms and other start-up companies fail to follow this diagram or the advice of people like my rich dad. I have met so many people who form a business by borrowing money or raising capital from friends, family, and other investors. They immediately rent a big office, buy a fancy car, and pay themselves huge salaries from *investors' capital* rather than from *income* from the business. Because the investors' capital is mismanaged, and there is still no income, they then try to pay the business, their employees, and specialists as little as possible. In such ventures, it is often the investors that get stuck with the bill, as was the case in many dot-com start-ups.

Rich dad said to his son and me, "The people who must get paid *first* ultimately get paid the *least.* The business owner should pay himself last because he is in business to build an asset. If he is in business for the big paycheck, he should not be in business . . . he should be looking for a job. If the business owner has done a good job at paying everyone else to build his asset, the asset should be worth far more than he could ever have paid himself."

Rich dad said, "Most people are not in the world of business to build or acquire assets. Most people are in the world of business as employees or self-employed specialists because they want a paycheck. That is one of the main reasons that less than 5 percent of the U.S. population is rich. Only 5 percent of the population realize the value of assets over money." Rich dad also said, "The business owner or entrepreneur gets the big bucks at the end of the day because he or she must be the most generous at the start of the day. The business owner takes the most risks, and also gets paid last. If they have done a good job, the amount of money can be staggering." That is why I continue to follow rich dad's diagram when starting any business and why I continue to work for free. I work for free because I want the big money at the end of the day.

Too many people in the E or S quadrants are limited as to how many people or organizations they can serve . . . hence their income is limited. A true business owner in the B quadrant who focuses on building a business that continually serves more and more people will become richer and richer. They get the big reward simply because he or she builds a system or asset to serve more people. That is why a business owner can become rich *exponentially* and people who work for wages become rich *incrementally*.

How Fast Can You Get Rich?

The good news is that it has never been easier and less expensive to become rich. All you have to focus on is serving more and more people. In John D. Rockefeller's day, it took him approximately fifteen years to become a billionaire. For him to become a billionaire, he had to acquire many oil wells and create a network of gas stations and gasoline delivery systems. That took a lot of time and a lot of money. Today it would take billions of dollars to build what Rockefeller built.

It took Bill Gates approximately ten years to become a billionaire. He had the foresight to use IBM's network to grow rapidly. It took Michael Dell and Steve Case, founder of AOL, less than five years to become billionaires. One entrepreneur used the growing demand for computers and the other used the explosive power of the World Wide Web to tap into the power of an explosive network. For each new generation of entrepreneur, it took less time and less capital to become billionaires, due to the advent of new networks. You can too.

If you understand the power of networks and the importance of leverage ratios, you too can become exceptionally wealthy in a short period of time and at a fraction of the cost. If you have solid business fundamentals and experience, you can market to the world over the World Wide Web. As the cost of doing business on the Web goes down, the power of the network goes up. One of the reasons Steve Case and AOL (a much younger person and company) could buy Time Warner and CNN (an older company with older directors) was simply because AOL had a bigger network. The bigger the network, the more economic power.

I have often written about people who became very rich in their spare time. Many of today's ultra-rich started their business at home on their kitchen table, just as Hewlett-Packard was started in a garage, Dell Computer was started in a dorm room. So even if you have a low-paying job, you can still become very, very rich if you start a business at home, or in your garage, all in your spare time. Remember, "It is not your boss's job to make you rich. Your boss's job is to pay you for what you do, and it is your job to make yourself rich at home and in your spare time."

It has never been easier to become rich beyond your wildest dreams for less effort and less start-up capital. I know that many of the high-flying dot-coms went broke . . . as many of us thought they would. In my opinion, the dot-coms that went broke may have had the right context, but they did not have the right content. Many dot-coms had the right idea but too many lacked true business experience and business basics. Many were simply trying to get rich on a mania, rather than to truly serve more people.

I recently read that a company paid its president a salary equivalent to over a billion dollars of investors' money and that president ran that company into the ground. Another dot-com company paid their employees a Christmas bonus equivalent to three months' salary in 1999. That same company was out of business and bankrupt before the Christmas of the year 2000. That is definitely a case where the mission of the company was making entrepreneurs and employees rich rather than serving the customer first. It was the investors who paid for the flaw in the company's mission and purpose. They failed to follow rich dad's prior diagram of who gets paid first and who gets paid last. These people, investors included, focused on being greedy rather than on the purpose of a business, which is to be generous.

Today our Web site receives over 50 percent of its business from customers who live in countries outside the United States. We are working on developing our game CASHFLOW to be deliverable over the Web. It is our vision to have CASHFLOW being played by someone in Africa, Asia, Australia, Albania, and America simultaneously. The site will be a community of players who pay a nominal monthly subscription fee to learn as they play, taking distance learning courses designed to teach them to be *rich* rather than teach them to be *workers.* The purpose of the Web site is for the community to help each other retire young and retire rich. All of this work is being done for one purpose and that purpose is to serve as many people as we can. By focusing on being generous, we build an asset that builds a network worldwide.

6.5 Billion Potential Customers

Now if you apply the ratios and potential markets not yet realized by an online game, see if you can estimate the value of this asset that richdad.com is building: Today in the world, there are approximately 6.5 billion people. Of the 6.5 billion, approximately 2 billion are potential customers. CNN, founded by Ted Turner, has an estimated 30 million subscribers worldwide. That 30 million subscriber network made Ted Turner rich enough to donate a billion dollars to the United Nations.

If we at richdad.com attract 1 million customers to join the service and pay this nominal monthly fee, then according to Metcalfe's Law, what would the economic value of richdad.com be? What would it be if it grew to 5 million, 10 million, 30 million? The question really is, what is the worldwide market of people who want to learn to be rich? What will happen when the Internet is able to do simultaneous translations so people from different countries and languages can play against and learn with people from different countries and languages? (Which is our plan for the online game!) What will happen to the investment market when a Web site begins to tout hot investment trends in cities like Phoenix, Tokyo, Seoul, Detroit, Virginia Beach, Singapore, Kuala Lumpur, Hong Kong, Portland, Dubai, Cairo, Sydney, Perth, Shanghai, Johannesburg, Florence, York, Brussels, São Paulo, Mexico City, Hanoi, London, Lima, Toronto, New York, and on and on? How many people would that Web site attract and what would the economic value of this business then be? How much will it cost to build such a worldwide network? Will it cost as much as it cost Rockefeller, Ford, or Ted Turner to build their networks?

Another network that richdad.com is targeting is the educational institutions. By developing course content that could teach young people how to manage their money responsibly, invest, and manage their own portfolios, how many educational networks could we tap into? If we could become part of the curriculum of school networks throughout the world, what would our economic value be?

In the future, when the new technology of bandwidth hits the World Wide Web, what will our economic value be when we become one of the thousands of businesses that have our own private television network over the Web? I know it is still in the future, but as rich dad said, "Your job is to position yourself and be ready when the opportunity presents itself." He also said, "It is okay to be five years early, but not one day late."

I am not stating our business plan to brag or say that it will come true. It is a plan and as we all know, not everything goes according to plan. I realize that we may change it as we go or we could fail . . . but as you know, I have failed before, and if I fail again, our company will correct, learn, and rise again smarter and stronger. The point of sharing our business plan is to illustrate the explosive power of leverage to more and more people today via different networks. Not many of us can afford to build a television network as Ted Turner did. But most of us can afford a used $500 computer and begin to build a worldwide network.

In a few years, those that are prepared and positioned will take advantage of the explosive power that bandwidth will bring. The people who take advantage of the new technology can become far richer than Ted Turner did with television, or Bill Gates did with computer software, or Jeff Bezos did with the Internet.

Years ago, rich dad said to me, "People on the B and I side of the quadrant have access to infinite wealth. People on the E and S side are limited by the limitations of their physical labor. For people on the E and S side to move to the B and I side, the first shift is the shift to generosity . . . the desire first to serve more people, rather than get paid first."

If you look at Sam Walton of Wal-Mart, all he did was build a network of large discount stores, stores that brought great products for lower and lower prices, to millions and millions of people. That is why Sam Walton was worth far more than an attorney who charges $750 per hour. The key is generosity.

A Final Word on Generosity

During the dot-com mania, there was much talk about old-economy businesses and new-economy businesses. Regardless whether the business is old-economy or new, all successful businesses and individuals must follow certain age-old principles and laws.

Generosity falls under the age-old law, the Law of Reciprocity. It is the law that states "Give and you shall receive." It is not a law that states, "Receive . . . and then you give." It is a law that has survived the test of time and it will survive the test of the future. Today, more than ever before, it is very important to want to look after yourself and your loved ones . . . but if you want to be rich, you must first think about serving the needs of as many people as you can . . . first. It's the law.

Rich dad believed in the Law of Reciprocity and in the idea that being generous was the best way to becoming very, very rich. It was his context on life and his actions were in integrity with his context.

Rich dad often gave us examples on how to use the Law of Reciprocity. He constantly reminded us of the need for us to be generous. He would say, "If you want a smile, be the first to give a smile. If you want love, be the first to give love. If you want to be understood, then be the one to be understanding." He also said, "If you want a punch in the mouth, be the first to give someone else a punch in the mouth."

Not only did rich dad believe in being generous by serving more and more people, he also believed in being generous with his money. In that line of thinking, he truly believed in the power of tithing, or the power of giving money. That is why rich dad gave generously to his church, charities, and schools. He gave money because he wanted more money. He would often say, "God does not need to receive, but humans need to give."

He would say, "Many people say they are generous with their time because they do not have money. People who are generous with their time have lots of time because they give their time. They do not have much money because they do not give money. They do not give money because they are tight and stingy with money, always afraid that there is not enough money . . . so their fear becomes reality. If you want more money, give money . . . not time. If you want more time, give time."

If you have a hard time giving money, you may want to start giving a little at a time on a regular basis. Each time you give, you will hear your context, or your reality, speaking loudly to you. At the moment you hear your reality speaking to you, and it's a poor person's reality, you have the opportunity to choose and rechoose your reality. The moment you give if only a dollar away to your church or your favorite charity, your world has changed. The moment you sincerely build a business or invest to increase your service to more people, you have forever increased your chances of becoming extremely wealthy and retiring young and retiring rich.

Our Company Policy

For those of you who have played CASHFLOW, you may have noticed that there are many squares dedicated to charities or other socially responsible events. The game was created that way in keeping with rich dad's lessons.

Also, at holiday time in December, we honor every employee of rich dad.com by tithing or donating a certain amount of money to the church or charity of their choice. We have the employees help us decide where the company's donations will be made. The donation is given by the company but in the employees' honor because we recognize that our company's success is from the efforts of the entire team—therefore the team should help determine where the company's charitable donations are given. It is our way of being in integrity with the lessons and philosophies of rich dad and our products. It is also one of the most joyous things we do in our company. We have found that one of the best leverages of all is the leverage of being generous.

Start by Being Generous to Yourself

Rich dad always said, "Start small and dream big." When it comes to improving your leverage ratios, rich dad's advice holds true today. In book number four, *Rich Kid Smart Kid,* I wrote about the three piggy bank system for kids, a system Kim and I use today. One piggy bank is for savings, one is for investing, and the other for tithing, giving to church and charity. Improving your leverage ratios can begin with something as simple as three piggy banks, putting ten cents, fifty cents, or $1 a day in each bank. At the end of the month your ratios will look like this, if you put $1 a day in each bank:

Savings	1:30
Investing	1:30
Tithing	1:30

This is a great start. In one month your ratios are increasing each and every day. Imagine what might happen in thirty years. The point to remember is that you are really increasing the habit or discipline of paying yourself first or being generous to yourself. Rich dad said, "One of the reasons poor people are poor is because they treat themselves poorly." And by that he did not mean to run out and buy a new dress or new golf clubs. He meant that poor people do not do things that financially enrich themselves. By paying yourself first, you are financially enriching yourself, your soul, and your future.

Section III
The Leverage of Your Actions

"Just do it."

—Nike

"Talk is cheap. Learn to listen with your eyes. Actions do speak louder than words. Watch what a person does more than listen to what they say."

—Rich Dad

Can Everyone Become Rich?

I once asked rich dad if anyone could become rich. His response was, "Yes. What a person must do to become rich is not that hard. In fact, getting rich is easy. The problem is most people would rather do things the hard way. Many will work hard all their lives living below their means; invest in things they do not understand; work hard for the rich rather than work hard to make themselves rich; and do what everyone else is doing rather than do what the rich are doing."

The first two sections of this book have been primarily about the mental and planning process of acquiring great wealth. Both processes are important to retiring young and retiring rich. This next section is what one must and can do in order to retire young and retire rich. Although the mental and planning processes are important, ultimately it is what you do with what you know that counts. As rich dad said, "Talk is cheap."

There are many books written on how to become rich. The problem with many of them is they tell you to do things that are often too hard for most people to do. This section of this book is about the simple things that almost everybody can do. After reading this section, you will know that you have the ability to become very rich . . . if you want to. Or at minimum, you will find one or two things you can do that will make you richer, if you choose to do them. After reading this section, the only question will be: How badly do you want to become rich?

Chapter 14

The Leverage of Habits

Rich dad said, "There are habits that make you rich and habits that make you poor. Most poor people are poor because they have poor habits. If you want to be rich, all you have to do is train yourself to have rich habits."

If you are serious about becoming rich, you must do the following things over and over again, from now until forever, for the rest of your life. Everyone in the Western world can do and can afford what is recommended. The problem is, only a few people will do them, and do them, and do them.

HABIT #1: HIRE A BOOKKEEPER

At the start of this book, I wrote that it is easier to borrow a million dollars than to save a million dollars. There is one catch. Before your banker will lend you the million dollars, your banker will want to know that you are trustworthy with the money. One of the ways the banker will feel comfortable lending you that much money is if you have clean professional financial records, in the form of a financial statement.

Most people cannot qualify for large loans because they have poor records. Many people pay higher than necessary interest rates simply because they have poor financial records. In *Rich Dad Poor Dad*, I wrote about the importance of financial literacy. The basis of financial literacy is a financial statement and it is what your banker will want to see if he or she is to lend you substantial amounts of money.

Even if you do not have a business, your personal life is a business and all real businesses have bookkeepers. That is why I strongly recommend you hire a bookkeeper and keep a bookkeeper for life. By having a bookkeeper keep your income, expenses, assets, and liabilities in line, you begin to keep professional records. I also strongly recommend you sit down with your bookkeeper and go over your numbers each and every month. Repetition is how we learn, and by repeatedly going over your monthly numbers, not only do you establish a good habit, you gain more insights into your spending patterns, you can make corrections earlier, and you ultimately take control over your financial life.

Why not do it yourself? Why hire an outsider? Some of the reasons are:

1. You want to start being a professional B or I quadrant person. All professional B and I quadrant people have professional bookkeepers. So treat your personal financial life as a business now. As described in *Rich Dad Poor Dad,* one of rich dad's six lessons was "mind your own business," and that begins with hiring a professional bookkeeper.

2. You want a disinterested outside third party to look objectively at your money and your spending habits. As you know, money can be an emotional subject, especially if it is yours. By having a person who is not emotionally attached to your finances, he or she can put things in order and speak to you clearly and logically. I remember my mom and dad not discussing money. They argued and cried about money. That is hardly objective money management or discussion.

3. My poor dad did not want to look at his financial situation. He kept our financial troubles a personal secret, a secret from himself, his family, and from anyone else. As kids we knew our family was in financial trouble . . . but we did not discuss it and we kept our financial problems a secret. Psychologists will tell you that *family secrets become toxic,* which means secrets poison the family. I know the emotional pain from our financial struggles did indeed affect all of us, even though we kept it a secret.

4. By hiring an unemotionally attached professional bookkeeper, you can bring your financial challenges out into the open. By being able to discuss your financial statements with your professional bookkeeper, you bring the subject of money and the business of your life out into the open. If it is in the open, and you discuss your finances with a professional, you are more

able to make the changes or tough decisions you need to make . . . before the financial problems become toxic.

5. If you earn less than $50,000, and are in the E quadrant, a professional bookkeeper should not cost more than $100 to $200 a month. I hear people say they would rather spend that money on food or clothing. The problem with that thinking is spending your money on food or clothing will not solve your money problems and will not make you richer. As rich dad always said, "There is good debt and bad debt, good income and bad income, and good expenses and bad expenses." He told me that hiring a bookkeeper and other professional financial advisors was money that went for *good expenses,* simply because these were expenses that made you richer, your life easier, and prepared you for a better future.

If you truly cannot afford a bookkeeper, then find one and trade services. You can clean their house or their yard and in exchange they can do your books. The most important thing is to do it, regardless of the price . . . because the long-term price is too high. As rich dad said, "Your greatest expense in life is the money *you do not* make."

6. Most importantly, hiring a professional bookkeeper reaffirms to yourself that you are taking your personal financial life seriously. It means that at least once a month, you sit down with your bookkeeper, are held accountable, and learn, correct, and redirect the financial future of your life.

In *Rich Kid Smart Kid*, the introduction begins with "Why your banker does not ask you for your report card." What your banker asks for is your financial statement. Rich dad said, "Your financial statement is your report card once you leave school." In school, we received report cards at least once a quarter. Even if you had bad grades, the report card gave you and your parents the opportunity to know what you were good at and weak at . . . and then gave you the opportunity to make corrections. In real life, people without financial statements, or report cards, cannot make corrections if they do not know where they are that month, quarter, or year. Think of your financial statement as your report card and work diligently to have your financial report card be measured in millions or maybe billions of dollars. That is why your bookkeeper is important. Your bookkeeper gives you your report card once a month.

There are three steps to follow:

1. Find and hire a bookkeeper.
2. Have an accurate accounting each month of your financial condition.
3. Review your financial statements each month with your advisor so you can make corrections quickly.

HABIT #2: CREATE A WINNING TEAM

In *Rich Dad's Guide to Investing,* I wrote that the B quadrant and I quadrant were team sports. One of the reasons people from the E and S quadrants occasionally have trouble transitioning is because they are not used to having a team assisting them with their financial plans and financial decisions.

As a child, I noticed that my poor dad shouldered the financial problems by himself. He sat quietly at dinner if he was troubled, argued with my mom if he was frustrated about money, and sat alone late at night, trying to make ends meet. There were many times I came home to find my mom crying because she knew that we were in financial trouble, and she had no one to talk to. When it came to money, my dad was the man of the house and he never discussed his financial challenges with anyone.

My rich dad on the other hand would sit around a table in his restaurant, surrounded by his team, and openly discuss his financial problems. Rich dad said, "Everyone has financial problems. The rich have money problems, the poor, businesses, governments, and churches. What determines if someone is to be rich or poor is simply how well he or she handles those problems. Poor people are poor simply because they handle their money problems poorly." That is why rich dad discussed his money problems openly with his financial team. He said, "No one person can know everything. If you want to win the game of money, you want the best and smartest people on your team." My poor dad lost because he thought that he should know all the answers . . . and he didn't.

After your bookkeeper gives you your monthly financial statements, meet with your team on a monthly basis. You may want a banker, accountant, attorney, stockbroker, real estate broker, insurance broker, and others. Each professional comes to the table with a different set of eyes and different ways of solving your problems. Just because you have many opinions does not mean you have to follow any of them. The most important thing is that you do not keep your money problems a secret, you listen to people smarter than you in different areas of expertise, and ultimately, you make your own decision.

When people ask me how I learned so much about money, investing, and business, I simply reply, "My team teaches me." I have learned more about business and investing outside of school simply because I use my life as my real-life school. I have found that I am more interested in solving my own problems than sitting in school trying to solve fictitious ones.

The following is an example of how I use my team to teach me. The other day, I met with one of my attorneys who tried to explain to me how to use government tax-exempt bonds. His explanations were way over my head and his vocabulary was filled with words I have never used before. Rather than waste his time sitting there pretending I understood, I stopped the meeting and scheduled another. At the next meeting, my accountant and this attorney sat down with Kim and me and the two of them helped explain what he was saying to us, in our language.

I said earlier that words are tools for the brain. Each profession uses different words. For example attorneys use different words than accountants or bookkeepers. By investing the time to fully understand the words, by having the meanings translated for me, I am better able to use the words and make those words a part of my life. In other words, I use the different professionals as translators so I can use their words in my life. The more words I can understand and use, the faster I can make more money and the better my financial future becomes.

That meeting cost me a few hundred dollars in fees, but I know the return will be exponential. It helped me understand how to borrow tens of millions of dollars from the government at very low interest rates. The combined education from my attorney and my accountant on this subject will greatly accelerate my leverage ratios. As I said earlier, you can increase your income incrementally or exponentially. By investing in my vocabulary and understanding, my wealth will increase exponentially.

So start gathering your team. If you cannot afford a high-priced team, you may want to find a retired person who enjoys helping and guiding people. Many times, all you have to do is buy them lunch. You would be surprised how many people simply enjoy being asked to share their life's experience in helping others. All you have to do is be respectful, not argue, and listen intently. Do this once a month, and your future will be enriched forever.

HABIT #3: CONSTANTLY EXPAND YOUR CONTEXT AND YOUR CONTENT

We now live in the Information Age, not in the Industrial Age. In the Information Age, your greatest asset is not your stocks, bonds, mutual funds, businesses, or real estate. Your greatest asset is the information in your head and the age of your information. Too many people are falling behind because the information in their head is ancient history or they cling to answers that were right yesterday, but wrong today. If you want to retire young and retire rich, you will need to keep up with a world of rapidly changing information.

So how do you keep up with the Information Age? The following are some of the things I do to keep learning. I am not telling you to do the exact same thing I do, I simply share with you what I am doing. If it works for you, fine and if not, then find what does work for you.

1. Nightingale-Conant's Audio Library. In 1974, after I decided to follow in my rich dad's path, I knew I needed to find more mentors than just my rich dad. I knew I needed information not found in traditional realms of education. In 1974, I came across audiocassettes packed with priceless information, information that added not only to my information *content*, but also expanded my *context.* These cassettes gave me pertinent and relevant information and also expanded my reality so I could use the information.

Today, more than twenty-five years later, I continue to use Nightingale-Conant's products. Whenever I need timely information I go through their catalogue looking for an audio- or videotape program that will teach me what I want to learn. When I need timeless and priceless information from some of the greatest masters in the world, I look through their catalogue.

Some of the audiotapes you may want to begin with are:

1. *Lead the Field* by Earl Nightingale. This is one of the all-time classics that will forever be relevant. Earl Nightingale is one of the leaders in modern business and motivational education. Age-old wisdom on leadership is what we all need if we want to stay abreast of the Information Age.
2. *Making Money on the Web* by Seth Godin. This tape set is filled with practical, basic, and useful information on how to begin your worldwide business network. Even if you do not plan on doing business on the Web, this tape is filled with commonsense business basics essential for anyone who wants to be rich.

3. *Thinking Big* by Brian Tracy. This tape set is essential for anyone who realizes that they might be thinking too small. One of the reasons people have a context of scarcity or not enough money is simply because they habitually think too small. This tape set will help open your mind to bigger possibilities for your life.

4. *The Art of Exceptional Living* by Jim Rohn. This is a great context-expanding educational tape program. The reason this is a great tape set is because many people think they have to do great things, or overcome huge obstacles, to be great. Jim Rohn points out that there is a difference between doing great things and living an *exceptional* life . . . doing the simple things of life *exceptionally*. As stated in this book, I do not feel I was gifted with any great talent, looks, personality, or brains. After listening to this tape, I stopped focusing on doing great things and focused instead on doing what I did, exceptionally well.

5. *How to Be a No-Limit Person* by Dr. Wayne Dyer. This is a great tape set on how to make each and every day of your life count, on expanding your context or reality to allow in more opportunity, better health, greater happiness, and to face problems with a better attitude.

Whenever I go to the gym or drive in my car, I often have one of the Nightingale-Conant library of great mentors' audiocassettes playing. When I am asked about finding mentors, I emphatically recommend the person get a tape catalogue and seek the mentor you want to learn from.

2. I subscribe to these financial and business newsletters:

a. *Louis Rukeyser's Wall Street* by Louis Rukeyser. I find his information insightful. This newsletter is important for anyone who wants to stay abreast of what is happening on Wall Street.

b. *Strategic Investment* by James Dale Davidson and Lord Rees-Mogg. These two men have a global perspective on the world economy. I find their information insightful, often contrarian, and especially good for the rich investor.

c. *Audio-Tech Business Book Summaries*. This organization publishes on a monthly basis a printed book summary and an audiocassette program on the latest business books. I find it better to read the summary and listen to the tape before deciding if I want to read the book.

We are moving into an era of unprecedented opportunity . . . we are moving into the Age of the Entrepreneur. If all you want is a bigger paycheck, you may miss this era while others become super-rich. If you do not want to miss this era, I suggest you make it a habit of being ahead of the pack and seeing the future the pack cannot see.

HABIT #4: KEEP GROWING UP

The other day, a friend of mine was complaining that he had lost several million dollars in the stock market. He had never invested before 1995, had borrowed money to buy stocks, and now had lost almost everything, including his house, after the market crashed. He kept complaining loudly and I finally had enough. I said, "Grow up. You're a big boy now. What made you think that the stock market would always go up?"

My comment did not stop him. He kept on saying, "Why didn't Alan Greenspan lower interest rates earlier? Why did he have to raise them? It's his fault and my stockbroker's fault that I have lost everything. How will I pay back all that money? Why doesn't the federal government do something about the losses on the stock market?"

As I walked away, I repeated what I said earlier, which is: "Grow up."

Rich dad often said, "People get older, but they do not necessarily grow up. Many people run from mom and dad's shelter to the shelter of a company or the government. Many expect someone else to take care of them, or be responsible for their lack of wisdom and common sense. That is why they seek job security or government sanctuaries. Too many people spend their lives looking for guarantees and spend all their lives avoiding risk, avoiding growing up, and always looking for a surrogate parent to take care of them." I know many people who are not able to survive without Social Security. I know of people who are not yet old enough to collect Social Security, yet they are counting on Social Security and Medicare to be there for them in the future. Those government safety nets were created in the Industrial Age and were created only as safety nets for the very needy. Today, unfortunately, many people, even highly educated and highly paid people, are still counting on the government to take care of them. We are in the Information Age and it is time that we as a culture begin to grow up and mature financially. Leave the government safety nets and social programs for those that really need them.

When I left high school, I thought I was grown-up and knew all the answers. Today, I often say, "I wish I knew back then what I know today." There are many things I did in my past that I am glad I did, but I would not do them today. I believe that growing up is realizing that growing up means doing things differently as we grow older. To continually do the same old thing every day of your life is in many ways arrested mental and emotional development. The world is changing, growing more sophisticated, and so should we.

One of the ways the world is changing is that there is not much job security and financial security anymore. Companies are pushing people out into the cold cruel world and saying to them, "Don't expect us to take care of you once you stop working for us." They are also saying, "You'd better count on the stock market to take care of you once you stop working." Yet in the real cold harsh world, to expect the stock market to always go up is childish fantasy and as silly as expecting the tooth fairy to pay for your dental bill. Growing up means being willing to be more and more responsible for yourself, your actions, your continuing education, and your maturity. If you want to have a rich and secure financial future, it is imperative to know that markets go up and markets go down and no one is there to protect you. The faster we grow up and face that reality, the better we can then face the future with greater maturity. In the Information Age, more of us need to grow up and grow away from old Industrial Age ideas of expecting someone else to be responsible for our job security and financial security.

I am afraid that in less than twenty years it will be obvious that the Industrial Age is dead and gone. We will know this when the government finally admits that it is broke and will not be able to keep many of its financial promises. If in twenty years too many people panic and begin draining their 401(k)s, the stock market will crash, many people will be disappointed, and America may go into a deep recession, possibly a depression. If this happens, millions upon millions of baby boomers and their children will finally have to grow up. Growing up means that you become less and less dependent upon others, and are more and more able to take care of yourself, your needs, and the needs of others. To me, growing up is a lifelong process, a process that many people are avoiding by still seeking job security and financial security provided by someone else . . . someone other than themselves.

Continually growing up is an important habit. If you are to retire young and retire rich, you will need to grow up much faster than most people are willing to.

HABIT #5: BE WILLING TO FAIL MORE

One of the biggest differences between my rich dad and my poor dad was that my poor dad was unwilling to fail. He thought making mistakes was a sign of failure . . . after all he was a teacher. My poor dad also thought that in life there was only one right answer.

My rich dad constantly ventured into areas that he knew nothing about. Rich dad believed in dreaming big, trying new things, and making small mistakes. He said to me at the end of his life, "Your dad spent his life pretending he knew all the right answers and avoiding mistakes. That is why at the end of his life, he began to make big mistakes." Rich dad also said, "One of the great things about being willing to try new things and make mistakes is that making mistakes keeps you humble. People who are humble learn more than people who are arrogant."

Over the years, I watched rich dad go into businesses, ventures, and projects he often knew nothing about. He would sit, listen, and ask questions for hours, days, and months as he gained the knowledge he required. He was always willing to be humble and ask stupid questions. To this he would say, "What is stupid is to pretend you are smart. When you pretend to be smart, you are at the height of stupidity."

Rich dad was also willing to be wrong. If he made a mistake, he was always ready to apologize. He did not try to be right all the time. He would say, "In school there is only one right answer. In real life there is more than one right answer. If someone has a better right answer than you, take it. Then you have two right answers." He would also say, "People who have only one right answer are very often three things. One, they are usually argumentative or defensive. Two, they are often very boring people. And three, they often become obsolete because they fail to notice that their once right answer is now wrong."

So rich dad's advice was, "Live a little. Do something daring and a little risky every day. Even if you do not become rich, this habit will keep your life exciting and keep you younger for years longer."

Unfortunately, my poor dad spent his life doing all the right things. He did the right thing when he went to school. He got a job teaching because in his mind it was the right thing to do. He worked hard and climbed the ladder because it was the right thing to do. He ran against his boss because he was upset with the corruption in government because it was the right thing to do. At the end of his life, he spent twenty years in front of the TV set angry because he did all the right things and no one seemed to care that he had done all the right things. He got very angry when he thought about all of his peers who he thought did the wrong things, but now were rich or in positions of power.

Rich dad said, "Sometimes what is right for you at the beginning of your life is not the right thing for you at the end of your life. Too many people are unsuccessful simply because they are afraid of changing or are unable to change with the times. The reason they are unable to change is because they are afraid of being wrong. Sometimes to be right, we all need to be wrong. If we want to learn to ride a bicycle, we must go through being wrong for a while. Most people are unsuccessful simply because they want to be right but they are unwilling to be wrong. It is their fear of failing that causes them to fail. It is their need to be perfect that causes them to be imperfect. It is their fear of looking bad that causes them to ultimately feel badly about themselves."

For people who are afraid of failing, or are afraid of making mistakes, I created an audiocassette program with Nightingale-Conant entitled *Rich Dad Secrets*. Rich dad's secret was that the world was designed for us not to fail. The world was designed for us to win. The challenge was to be willing to first fail so you could win. The problem this tape set helps overcome is a person's fear of failing. Once you understand *Rich Dad Secrets*, you will be more willing to fail, in order to win. As rich dad often said, "People who avoid failing also avoid success. Failing is an integral part of success."

In summary, what my rich dad did daily was be willing to fail a little each day. My poor dad did his best not to fail at all. The difference in these little habits made a big difference toward the end of their lives.

HABIT #6 LISTEN TO YOURSELF

The last and most important habit for anyone who wants to retire young and retire rich is to listen to yourself. Rich dad often said, "The most powerful force I have is what I say to myself and what I believe." This habit is another way of expressing your reality or your context. What rich dad meant by *your most powerful force* goes back to the biblical concept that your words become flesh. In other words, pay close attention to what you are saying to yourself, because what you are saying to yourself is what you are becoming each and every day.

Rich dad would say, "Losers focus a lot on what they don't want in life, rather than be specific with what they do want. That is what they do differently. It's a habit. The same is true with money."

"So there is a big difference between someone who constantly says, 'I don't want to be poor' and someone who says, 'I want to be rich,'" I replied.

Rich dad nodded and said, "It seems to me that the human mind does not hear *do* or *don't*. It just hears the subject being discussed . . . words such as fat, healthy, poor, and rich. Whatever the subject is, is what you become."

"So when someone says, 'I don't want to lose money' all the mind hears is, 'I want to lose money'?" I asked, seeking further clarity from rich dad's lesson.

"That is how it seems to me," said rich dad.

"So what many people do is talk about what they don't want, or talk about what they can't have," I said.

"That is correct. But I do something more than that. It is one of my habits," said rich dad.

"Something more than just say what you want?" I asked.

Rich dad nodded and gave me one of the most important habits for my life. He said, "We all feel frightened, uncertain, and doubtful at times. That is part of being human. When I feel that way, the first thing I do is check my thoughts. If I feel bad or afraid, I know I am saying or thinking something to cause myself to feel that way."

"Okay," I said. "What is the next step?"

"I change my thoughts or words to words I want," said rich dad. "For example, if I am afraid of losing, I say to myself, 'What am I afraid of, what do I want instead, and what do I need to do to get what I want?' If you notice, they are all questions that first open up my reality to new possibilities and realities."

I nodded and said, "Then what?"

"Then I sit quietly until the feeling of fear leaves and the feeling I want comes into my heart, chest, and stomach area. Once I can feel the feeling I want, and I have the thoughts I want, I then take action. I prepare myself first, I get into the right frame of mind, the emotional feeling I want rather than what I don't want, then I take action."

The summary of this process is:

1. Notice thoughts you don't want . . . change to thoughts about things you want.
2. Notice feelings you don't want . . . change to feelings you want.
3. Take action, and keep going, correcting if necessary, until you get what you want . . . rather than what you don't want.

Putting It into Practice

A few years ago, I was in Las Vegas for the night. I do not gamble much, but with time to burn, I decided to play some blackjack. As soon as I got to the table, I noticed my body begin to tense up with the fear of losing and my mind began saying, "You can only lose $200. Then you have to stop."

Immediately, I changed my thoughts to "I have $200 to play with and when I win $500, I will stop." I had my entry and my exit strategy in place. Then I sat at the table, watching the dealer deal, but I did not put up any money. I could feel the fear of losing deep inside my chest. I focused my attention on changing the losing feeling to the winning feeling. Only when I could feel the confidence of a winner in my chest, heart, and stomach did I begin gambling. Even though I lost the first few hands, all I did was focus on winning thoughts and winning feelings. After an hour, I walked away with my $500.

The other night, I found myself again back in Las Vegas. Again, I went through the process. The trouble was, this time I could not win, no matter how I focused my thoughts and my feelings. Once my $200 was gone, I had to fight my feelings to not put up more money. Walking away from the table was one of the hardest things I had to do. I wanted to chase my money.

As I walked away, I could hear rich dad saying, "Even with the best thoughts and best feelings, sometimes things just do not go your way. A winner knows when to quit and walk away. A winner must know that losing is part of winning. It is only a loser who stays at the wrong table forever, losing everything, hoping to prove that they are not a loser."

Happy Relationships

This process of choosing how you think and feel works in relationships as well. I have noticed that I feel terrible when I think about all the things my wife, Kim, does not do . . . and I feel madly in love with her when I think about all the wonderful things she does do and we do together.

The Righteous Brothers had a hit song entitled "You've Lost That Loving Feeling." When it comes to business and investing, many people have "Lost That Winning Feeling."

Keeping the Faith

During the period from 1985 to 1994, Kim and I focused on what we wanted and we did our best to feel the way we wanted to feel and the way we would feel when our dreams did come true. Even though there were times when things did not go the way we wanted them to go, it was focusing on what we wanted and feeling the way we wanted to feel that got us through the tough times. Choosing how you want to feel and choosing to think what you want to think is a very important habit rich dad taught me. Now if only I could feel and think that way about the cold green salad sitting in front of me.

The point of this habit is that I go through the thought and feeling process especially when I feel afraid or doubtful of myself. To me, doing that is a better habit than allowing your feelings of doubt and uncertainty run your life. While the process does not always assure that I win, it is still a good habit that has allowed me to occasionally win when the odds were stacked against me and I wanted to run. Always remember that all winners lose now and then . . . but that does not mean they have to feel or think like a loser.

As Nike says, "Just do it." In life, it seems that what winners do is focus on what they want and losers seem to focus on what they don't want. That is why it is important to make a habit of listening to yourself on a regular basis. Winners keep those winning feelings and winning thoughts, even though they are not winning. That is a very important habit.

Can You Adopt These Habits?

Before going any further, I want to reemphasize how important I believe these basic habits are. These are easy habits that virtually anyone over the age of eighteen can follow. Yet even though they are easy, I am afraid only a very few will make them habits.

If you can make these simple habits your lifelong habits, the action steps in the following chapters will be easy for you and may make you richer than your wildest dreams. As rich dad said, "The story of the Three Little Pigs is more than a fairy tale. It is a story filled with truths. If you want to build a house of bricks you need good habits . . . for good habits are the bricks of the rich."

Chapter 15

The Leverage of Your Money

Who Works Harder? You or Your Money?

On March 12, 2001, the financial channels were crying the blues about the crash of the stock market. On March 10, 2000, just a year earlier, the NASDAQ was at an all-time high of 5048.62. On this day, March 12, 2001, the NASDAQ was at 1923, a 62 percent fall in approximately a year. Also on this single day, shareholders lost $554 billion on all exchanges. Obviously, many people were very concerned, afraid, or angry.

On one of the channels, a commentator said something I have been concerned about for years. He said, "Many rich investors are only getting richer in this market fall. They get rich because they go in and out of the market. I feel for the working person that has just had their pension plan wiped out. They left their retirement money in the market because they have to."

My wife, Kim, was also watching the program and listening to the commentator. Kim said, "Watching your retirement plan get wiped out must be like watching your house burn and not having a hose to put the fire out."

In *Rich Dad's Guide to Investing,* I wrote that the poor and middle class invest in mutual funds and the rich invest in hedge funds. While many people claim hedge funds are too risky, I tend to disagree. I think mutual funds are far riskier, simply because most mutual funds tend only to do well when the markets go up. At least with some hedge funds, you can make money in an up market as well as a down market. Which one do you think is riskier in the long run? How would you feel if you were getting ready to retire and you just watched your retirement fund get cut in half? At least if you have fire insurance, you can rebuild your house in less than a year if it burns down. For many people, they may not have enough time to rebuild their retirement fund if it is wiped out late in their life.

Is Your Money Just Sitting There Doing Nothing?

One of the reasons people work so hard all their lives is simply because they were taught to work harder than their money. When most people think of investing, many just *park* their money either in a savings account or in their retirement account, as they continue on with their life of hard work. While they work, they hope their money is working too. Then when something like a financial disaster comes along, their parked money gets decimated and most people have no financial disaster insurance.

Rich dad said, "Most people spend their lives building financial houses of straw, houses which are susceptible to wind, rain, fire, and big bad wolves."

That is why rich dad taught his son and me how to keep our money moving. To further illustrate this point, one day on a camping trip, he had Mike and me repeatedly jump through and over the roaring campfire. He said, "If you're moving, even fire will not hurt you. If you're standing still near the fire, even though you're not in the fire, the heat will eventually get to you." That morning, as I watched the stock market sink lower and lower, I could hear rich dad telling his son and me this story. It is the people who are standing still with their money parked that are feeling the heat. If you want to retire young and retire rich, you will need to work harder and faster. Your money will have to do the same thing. To leave your money sitting in one place is like watching a pile of dry autumn leaves, waiting for the spark . . . the spark that will turn the leaves into a bonfire.

How Fast Is Your Money?

One of the reasons Kim and I retired early was because we kept our money moving. Rich dad often referred to this concept as the *velocity of money*. He said, "Your money should be like a good bird dog. It helps you find a bird, catch the bird, and then goes out and gets you another bird. Most people's money acts like the bird that just flies away." If you want to retire young and retire rich, it is very important that your money be like a bird dog, going out every day and bringing home more and more assets.

Today, many financial planners and mutual fund managers say to the average investor, "Just give us your money, and we'll put your money to work for you." Most investors nod and repeat the mantra, "Invest for the long term, buy and hold, and diversify." Their money gets parked and they go back to work. For most investors, these are pretty good ideas, given that most investors have no interest in learning how to put their money to work, since they seem to prefer working harder than their money. The trouble with these plans of average investors is that they are not necessarily productive investment strategies, nor are they necessarily safer.

Kim and I did not keep our money in a retirement account in order to retire young. We knew that we had to keep our money working, working hard to acquire more and more assets. Once our money acquired an asset, that money was soon reemployed to go out and get us another asset. The strategy we used to keep our money moving and acquiring more and more assets is a strategy that almost everyone can use. As promised, this book will list things that almost everyone could do to become rich.

Keep the Money Moving

One of the strategies we used to keep our money moving was to buy a rental property, and within a year or two, borrow out our own down payment and buy another rental property. That was following rich dad's advice of using money like a bird dog. The average person calls this process a *home equity loan*. Some people call it a *bill consolidation loan* to pay off credit card debt. You may notice that Kim and I borrowed money to buy investments and the average person uses debt capital to pay off bad debt. This is an example of the bird flying out the window. While it is still velocity of money, it is velocity of money away from you, rather than acquiring assets for you.

A Simple Example

The following is an example of how we invested and then borrowed money to invest in other assets. In 1990, Kim and I noticed a house for sale in a beautiful neighborhood in Portland, Oregon. The owner was asking $95,000 but the property did not sell. The economy was bad, people were being downsized, and there were many houses on the market. We would have put in an offer earlier, but this house did not fit our investment profile. It was too expensive and too nice a house to be considered a long-term rental property. If this house were in San Francisco, it would have been a $450,000 home. Yet we watched this property because we could see it had a lot of value and potential.

On our way to and from the airport, we would drive by the house to see if it was still for sale. After about six months we finally knocked on the door and found that the owner was very anxious to sell and ready to listen to any offers. He owed $56,000, so I offered $60,000 and we settled on $66,000. I gave him $10,000, and we took over his existing mortgage. A month later, the owner and family had moved out and were on their way to California, happy to have sold their home. They did not make much money and they did not lose much money. The house rented immediately and we wound up making about $75 a month positive cash flow after paying all debt and expenses. About two years later, the market had improved and many people were making us offers to buy it, the best offer being $86,000. Kim and I did not take the offer, although it was tempting. If we had sold we would have realized approximately a 100 percent per annum return on our down payment as illustrated by the following numbers.

$86,000	offer
−66,000	purchase price
20,000	gain

20,000 = approximately 200 percent in 2 years
$10,000 down payment 100 percent per annum cash-on-cash return. (I say approximately because there would be other expenses involved in the transaction and it does not take compounding into account.)

Although the 100 percent return was attractive, we did not sell. The house was in a great neighborhood and we felt the house could eventually reach the $150,000 range in three to five years. Instead of selling this house, we decided to begin buying more, now that the market was turning in sales price and also rental income.

Given the strong market indications, Kim and I applied for a home equity loan. The balance on the mortgage was now less than $55,000 and the appraisal came in at around $95,000. The rent could cover a mortgage of around $70,000, so we refinanced the house and put approximately $15,000 in our pocket. We had gotten our money back and we still had the asset. The dog had gotten the bird and we could now go out and find another bird. On top of that, the dog was now worth $15,000.

Within a few months, after looking at several hundred properties, we found our new target. It was a great house in the same neighborhood. The house did not show well since the owner had let his children live in it rent free for years. The asking price was $98,000 and after several offers and counteroffers, we purchased it for $72,000, put $4,000 into paint and repairs, and put it up for rent.

Late in 1994, we sold both houses for just under $150,000 each and took that money to buy a larger apartment house in Arizona, where the market prices were still depressed.

Besides keeping our money moving, there are a number of points I would like to point out.

1. We did well because the market was down and that gave us time to look for and negotiate sensible investments. If the market were up, we would tend to look harder and be even more cautious.

2. The investments had to make sense *today*, not tomorrow. I say this because too many people have the *buy*, *hold*, and *pray* strategy. Rich dad always said, "Your profit is made when you buy, not when you sell." Every property we bought had to have a positive cash flow on the day we bought it and it had to have a positive cash flow even in a bad economy. If the market had not gone up, Kim and I would still be happy with the investment.

3. As stated earlier in this book, every investor has an exit strategy before they enter the market. Since this was a new type of market, even though it was investing in real estate, it was a different type of real estate investment. This difference required we start over again, doing our research and coming up with different entry and exit strategies.

4. Those two houses would sell for $200,000 to $250,000 today, now that the Portland market has recovered. The reason we sold early was to leave some money on the table for the next buyer, also to take advantage of

a market that was down and about to move up, in this case, Phoenix, and because our investment portfolio had changed. We no longer held single-family homes; we had now graduated to larger and larger apartment houses, again for more leverage.

5. Know the difference between being an *investor* and a *trader*. We were investors when we were willing to buy and hold the properties for their cash flow. We were traders when we knew our entry as well as our exit strategy. In other words, an investor buys to hold and a trader buys to sell. If you want to retire rich, you need to know how they are different and how to be both.

In my opinion, one of the reasons so many people lost money in this latest stock market crash is because they were actually being traders who thought they were investors. Again this further illustrates the importance of knowing the definition of words.

6. Kim and I invest for the long term. But to us investing for the long term does not mean parking your money, leaving it in one big pile, thinking you're diversified when in reality all of your investments are in one vehicle, a vehicle such as mutual funds, and then hoping that the wind does not blow or a fire does not break out. Investing to us means being in the market every day of our lives, gathering more information, gaining more and more real-life experience, and keeping our money moving, over the fire. We do not buy, hold, and pray, which is what *long-term* means to millions of people.

"I Want My Money Back"

Most shoppers know that they can get their money back if they do not like the product they just bought. Most wise retailers offer a money-back guarantee if the customer is not satisfied. The problem with most money-back guarantees is that in order to get your money back, you have to give the product back first. If you are a sophisticated investor, what you want is your money back and you want to keep the asset too. That is the reason I love investing. I get to keep what I purchased and get my money back. That is why rich dad said, "One of the most important things a real investor needs to say is, 'I want my money back. I also want to keep my investment.'"

If you can understand this principle of investing, you will understand what the velocity of money means. It means you want your money back as quickly as possible so it can be reinvested to acquire other assets.

More Than One Way to Speed Up Your Money

This idea of the velocity of your money does not apply only to real estate. The idea of velocity of money is really a principle or mental tool of the rich. Once you understand the principle, you want to be able to apply it in everything you do. Velocity of money is an important aspect of leverage.

Another way of increasing the velocity of money is through knowing the tax laws and using corporate entities. For example, let's say someone owns a business and also owns part of a second business that invests in real estate. The diagram and explanation look like this.

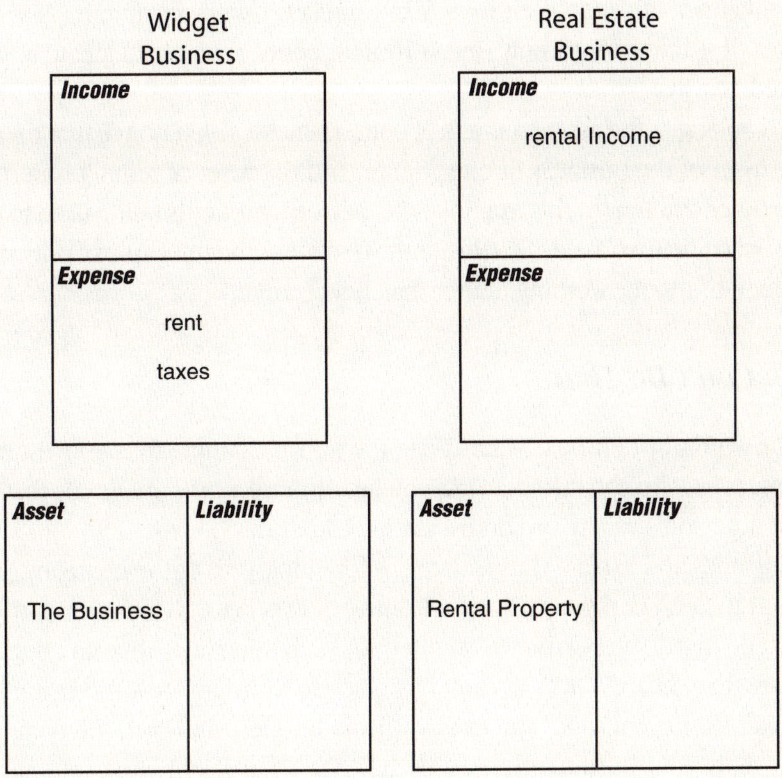

Rental expense from one company flows to the *rental income* of the other company. You may not recognize why this is important. As you may know, a business is taxed after expenses, while the individual is taxed before expenses. So an individual who rents a house pays for that house with after-tax dollars. The business can pay that rent with pretax dollars. The rental income goes to another corporate entity but this income is now classified as *passive* income, rather than *earned* income. (There is an exception where the ownership of the two companies is the same, where the income must be treated as earned income. For example, if you have a business in your home and pay yourself rent, you would have to treat that income as earned income.) Passive income, if managed properly, can flow to the individual or the business paying substantially less in taxes. As always, we recommend competent tax and legal advice before doing anything like this.

A person who manages his or her business and investment portfolio in this manner can keep their money moving faster while paying much less in taxes. If it flowed into only one corporate entity, it would stagnate and be taxed heavily.

Looking at the asset columns of both businesses, you notice that there is the asset of the business in one column and the asset of rental property in the other column. In this example, this person's money is being used to create or acquire two assets tax-efficiently. That is another example of velocity of money, or money working, rather than being parked.

You Can't Do That

Four words I often hear when I use the above example in my investment classes are "You can't do that." As you know, these words are words that define a person's reality or context. In my earlier days, I would go into small companies and explain these strategies for employees of the company.

At the end of my talks, I would almost always hear, "Great ideas but you can't do that." The person would often say such things as, "You can't buy real estate that cheap." Or "You can't buy a house without a new mortgage or a banker's approval." Or "You can't own the business and own the company that rents your business the real estate." Or "That might work in America, but that can't be done in my country."

I no longer do such investment talks to employees or self-employed people. I only do such talks to people who are or want to be business owners or investors. I leave traditional investment advisors to talk to groups of employees or groups of self-employed individuals not because of the individuals involved, but because of the collective consciousness of such groups. As stated earlier, the words "I can't" are often the words that define the quadrant a person comes from.

The example used above is done every day throughout the world. In all of the countries I have done business in, it is common practice to buy a building just by taking over the mortgage. But it is done primarily in larger investments. The idea of a business renting real estate from another business owned by the same person is also done all the time. It is common practice. McDonald's uses that very formula. It sells a franchise business to an individual. The individual then pays McDonald's a franchise fee as well as pays rent to McDonald's for the real estate. From *Rich Dad Poor Dad*, you may recall that Ray Kroc, McDonald's founder, said, "My business is not hamburgers. My business is real estate." Ray Kroc and his team obviously understood the velocity of money and how to use money to acquire more than one asset.

Velocity of Money with Paper Assets

The idea of the velocity of money applies to all assets, including paper assets. When someone looks at a stock's P/E ratio, they are looking at the velocity, in many ways. When someone says the stock's P/E ratio is 20 it means it will take you twenty years to get your money back, based upon today's price and earnings. For example if a stock's price is $20 today and is paying a $1 annual dividend, then it will take you twenty years to get your money back.

The Rule of 72

The Rule of 72 is another measure of money's velocity. This rule measures the interest or annual percentage growth of something. For example, if you receive 10 percent interest on your savings, your money will double in 7.2 years. If your stock is appreciating in value by 5 percent per year, that means it will take 14.4 years to double your money. If it appreciates by 20 percent per year, then it will take 3.6 years to double in value. The Rule of 72 is simply dividing the number 72 by the interest or the percentage of gain in value to give the relative speed your money will double.

During the economic boom of the late 1990s, many financial planners and investment advisors were touting the wisdom of the Rule of 72. A number of years ago, I had this one young investment advisor tell me that his portfolio was doubling in value every five years. I asked him how he knew that since he had only been investing for three years. His reply was, "Because the mutual fund my money is in has *averaged* over 15 percent per annum for the last two years." I thanked him for his enthusiasm in his attempt to sell me more mutual funds but I declined. I wonder what he is saying today? I thought about telling him the story of the bull and the bear. The story of the bull and the bear states that the bull comes up by the stairs but the bear goes down by jumping out the window. In other words, as rich dad would say, "Averages are for average investors."

Playing with House Money

This is one more way an investor can use the velocity of money in their favor and that is by *playing with house money.*

There are two reasons I love small cap stocks. Reason number one is because I am an entrepreneur rather than a corporate person. I like and understand the problems of small start-up companies and can sense if the business has a chance for growth or not. Reason number two is because a small cap stock can double and triple in value much faster than a blue chip stock. Since a small cap stock has a better chance of doubling or tripling faster than many large cap stocks, in the right market conditions it is easier to play with house money. The following is an example of playing with house money.

Let's say you buy 5,000 shares of XYZ company for $5 a share. You now have $25,000 in the market. The market shines on you and, in less than a year, the price of XYZ is now $10 a share. You now have a market valuation of $50,000. A greedy investor, which I have been, will say, "The market will keep going up so I'll hang on." Again, an exit strategy is important before getting into the market.

Instead of hanging on and just parking your money, one way to increase the velocity of your money is to simply sell $25,000 worth of stock. That way, you still have $25,000 worth of stock, although half the shares in this case, and you have your money back. The remaining shares which have the $25,000 valuation at that time is *playing with house money*.

I use this strategy often, but not all the time. There have been times when the price of the stock went from $5 to $8, not reaching the exit price of $10, so I held on. Many times, the stock has not held and dropped below $5, leaving me with all my money either lost or still on the table. I will admit that the times I have used this strategy of selling shares to recoup my initial investment, I have felt much better about my investment, even though I may not have made as much money, due to the fact that I did pull some money from the table.

Bye-Bye Money

My friend Keith Cunningham often recites a short poem that goes:

> Money talks I can't deny.
> I heard it once,
> It said bye-bye.

I have never understood why people cry about losing money in the investment market. They don't cry when they go to the grocery store and spend money they don't get back. They don't cry when they buy a car and lose money when they sell it. So why should investing be any different?

I often hear investors say, "You haven't lost any money as long as you don't sell the stock." When I hear someone saying something like that, it often means they bought high and now the price is low and they are waiting for the stock price to go back up. There is some validity to thinking that way, but only in special-case situations. A thought opposite to that thought is cut your losses early. There are times when I have invested wrongly and the price of my investment drops rather than climbs. If the price of a stock drops more than 10 percent I will more often than not cut my losses and look for something new. There are two reasons I may do this.

Reason #1: If my attention is focused too much on the loss and I feel badly for making a bad decision, I will sell. I just want to cut and move on. As I have said in other books, I know that out of ten investments, the odds are two to three will be bad, two to three will be good, and everything in the middle just lies around like a lazy dog. I will occasionally let the lazy dogs lie as long as they are not losing money. If they become real dogs, I cut and review my mistakes and take the lessons.

Reason #2: I love shopping. So even if I have less money to shop with, I am happier shopping rather than buying, holding, and praying that the investment will go back up someday. As I said, most people don't cry when they sell their formerly new, now used car for a loss. The reason they don't cry is because they're usually shopping for a new car.

How Long Are Blue Chips Blue?

There is another investment strategy I often hear and that is to "Invest for the long term and only buy blue chip stocks." To me, that is an obsolete idea, again because it worked in the Industrial Age but doesn't in the Information Age. The reason that old strategy is not working is because blue chip stocks are not blue chips anymore. For example, if you had invested in Xerox twenty years ago, you would be hurting today, even though it is a blue chip stock. The real question each of us needs to ask is how long will a blue chip stock be blue?

Many of today's Fortune 500 companies may not exist ten years from now, due to technological changes and other innovations. Blue chip companies, which used to last for sixty-five years, are now lasting only ten. These points demonstrate that the old strategy of business is no longer working in today's world.

In this age of faster moving technology, a company may rise and fall in just a few years. This speed of change then requires all of us to be more vigilant and to focus on keeping our money moving, rather than just leaving it parked waiting for the market to rise and rise forever. The buy, hold, and pray strategy is okay for the average investor, but it is not a great strategy for anyone who wants to retire young and retire rich.

Chapter 16

The Leverage of Real Estate

Investing with Your Banker's Money

I had dinner with a friend and her father the other night. He's a retired airline pilot. The stock market had just fallen another 3 percent that day and he was very upset because his retirement account was losing all its gains. When I asked him what he thought of the market he said, "My other daughter called to let me know that I could move in with her if I lost everything."

Cautiously I asked, "Do you mean to say that the only investments you have are in the stock market?"

"Well yes," he said. "What other kinds of investments are there? The stock market is the only place I know of. What else is there to invest in?"

De-Worsify Your Portfolio

The common mantra heard everywhere today is, "Invest for the long term, dollar-cost-average, diversify your portfolio, etc., etc, etc." This is a great mantra for people who do not know much about investing. The word I have always questioned is *diversify*. When I hear someone say they have a diversified portfolio, I often ask them what they mean by that word. More often than not, they will say something like, "I have some growth funds, bond funds, international funds, sector funds, mid cap funds," and so on.

My next question is, "Are they all in mutual funds?" Again, in most cases, the response is, "Yes, most of my investments are diversified in different mutual funds." While their mutual funds may be diversified, the reality is their investment instrument of choice, in this case mutual funds, is not diversified. Even if they say, "I do dabble in stocks, invest in REITS, and I do have some annuities," the hard fact is that most people are only in the paper asset category. Why? . . . because paper assets are easier to get into and manage. As rich dad said, "Paper assets are more sterile. They are neater and cleaner. Most people are not from the B quadrant and will never build a B quadrant business and most people will not invest in real estate because of the acquisition, liquidity, and management challenges."

There are over 11,000 mutual funds to choose from in the United States alone, and that number is growing. There are more mutual funds than there are companies that mutual funds invest in. Why are there so many mutual funds? Because of the same reasons listed above. They are sterile and often sterilized in the name of protecting the public. The problem the public has is figuring out which of the 11,000 funds is best for them. How do you know if the hot fund today will be the hot fund tomorrow? How in the world do you choose the winning fund today for your retirement tomorrow? And if over 80 percent of your investment portfolio is in mutual funds, is that really diversification and is that smart? Personally, I don't think so. Anyone who has 80 percent or more of their portfolio in different funds is not really diversifying, they are really *de-worsifying* their portfolio.

The Tragic Flaw of Mutual Funds

Some of you may be aware of the hidden tax flaw of mutual finds. Unfortunately there are many mutual fund investors not aware of the mutual fund tax flaw, the flaw that passes capital gains tax through to the investor. That means, if there is a profit and a capital gains tax consequence, the fund does not pay that tax, the investor does. This flaw is especially pronounced in a bear market. There are exceptions, however; for instance, gains on mutual funds held in certain retirement funds are deferred.

Let's say the fund has had great success for a number of years. It has bought well and many of the stocks it has picked have greatly increased in value. Suddenly, the market turns down, investors panic, and they begin asking for their money back. The fund must then sell its best stocks quickly in order to give the investors their money. When the fund sells its stock, there are capital gains to pay on that stock. For example, the fund purchased XYZ Corp. ten years ago for $10 a share, and when they sell it, it sells for $50 a share. So the fund manager did well by picking the stock early, but now at time of sale, the investor must pay the capital gains tax on the $40 profit. In times like this, the investor can lose money because the value of the fund may have gone down while, at the same time, the investor must pay capital gains taxes. So an investor in mutual funds can be required to pay capital gains taxes, even though he has lost money rather than made money. Personally, I do not like having to pay taxes when I have in fact lost money. That is like paying income tax on income you did not receive. In early 2001, there are many investors who had the value of their mutual funds cut in half and at the same time they will have to pay capital gains taxes on gains reported to them by their mutual funds. To me, that is a tragic flaw.

Am I saying not to invest in mutual funds? No, I have money in mutual funds. In *Rich Dad's Guide to Investing*, I talked about financial plans to be secure, comfortable, and rich. Mutual funds can play an important role in your financial plans to be secure and comfortable. Find competent financial advisors to assist you in developing the right financial plan for you, but the more you educate yourself about each financial investment available the more financially literate you will become. There are some very good mutual funds that use systemized approaches in selecting the companies to invest in by studying the underlying fundamentals.

The Beauty of Investing in Real Estate

My friend's father, the retired airline pilot who thought the only kind of investment is paper assets, is only now finding out about mutual funds' tragic flaw. As the dinner neared an end, he said, "I've lost much of my savings because the share value of my funds has gone down and now I have to pay capital gains taxes even though the value is down. I wish there were something else I could invest in."

"Why don't you invest in real estate?" I asked.

"Why? What is the difference?" he asked.

"There are many differences," I replied. "Let me tell you about one difference that is really quite interesting."

The retired pilot took a sip of coffee and said, "Tell me. I'm all ears."

"In real estate, I can make money, and the government will let me count it as a loss of money," I said.

"You mean you make money and you get a tax break instead of having to pay taxes on the money you made?" asked the pilot.

"The government gives me a tax break on my gains rather than making me pay taxes on my capital gains," I said. "The government lets me keep more money rather than pay more taxes. One way is through depreciation or what my rich dad called *phantom cash flow,* which is cash flow the average investor cannot see."

The retired pilot listened silently for a long moment and finally said, "Is there more?"

"A lot more," I said. "They'll even give me money."

"How?" asked the pilot.

"If a building is a historical building, the government may give you a tax credit, which is far better than a tax deduction, to improve your investment," I said. "Do you think the government will give you a tax credit to buy more mutual funds?"

"Not that I know of," said the pilot. "All I have seen lately is a capital gains tax on money I've never made and in fact have lost. It sounds like I pay taxes on money I've lost and you get a tax break on money you made. Anything else I should know about?"

"There is," I said. "You can receive a tax credit for 50 percent of the cost of improvement related to the Americans with Disabilites Act. For instance, if you pay $10,000 putting a wheelchair ramp in for handicapped people to have access to your commercial building, you could receive the maximum credit of $5,000."

"You get a $5,000 tax credit?" asked the pilot. "What if the wheelchair ramp doesn't cost you $10,000 to put in? What if the ramp only costs you $1,000 to build?"

"You still get a tax credit for 50 percent of the cost of the improvement," I said. "But of course, I strongly advise you to check with your CPA before doing anything like this. You want to make sure you know the current regulations and benefits before doing anything."

The pilot sat there quietly thinking. "Anything else?"

"Much more. Really too much to discuss just over dinner," I said. "But let me give you three more advantages of real estate over mutual funds."

"Just three more?" said the pilot with a sarcastic smile.

"One more advantage is that the bank will lend you the money to buy your real estate. As far as I know, I doubt if banks will lend you money to invest in mutual funds or stocks. They may use such assets as collateral, but only after you have invested your money to acquire them."

The pilot nodded his head and said, "And number two?"

"Number two is no capital gains tax," I said, "if you know what you are doing."

"You mean I must pay capital gains tax on money I did not make, in fact lost, and with real estate you can avoid capital gains tax?"

I nodded my head. "It's done all the time. It's done via an exchange called the 1031 exchange. For example, let's say I buy a house for $50,000, putting only $5,000 down, borrowing the remaining $45,000 from the bank. And let's say the rent more than covers my monthly expenses so I have cash flow from my investment."

"So your money is working for you," said the pilot.

"Yes," I said, "and that income is passive income so it is taxed at a lower rate than earned income such as paycheck income and income from savings and your 401(k)."

The pilot shook his head in silence. Earlier in the evening we had already had the discussion on the differences between earned, portfolio, and passive income.

Continuing, I said, "After a few years, you find out your $50,000 rental house is now worth $85,000. You sell it for a $35,000 gain but you do not have to pay the capital gains if you want to put it into a bigger investment."

Again the pilot shook his head silently, saying, "In this example, you make $35,000 in capital gains and pay no capital gains tax. I lose money in my mutual funds and I pay capital gains tax. You receive cash flow and have that income offset by phantom losses and expenses, and you pay less in taxes on the income that you do pay taxes on, because it's passive income, not earned income."

"And don't forget the tax credits for improvements made for ADA in a commercial property or if the property is historical," I added.

"Oh no," said the pilot. "How could I forget the tax credits? Everyone knows about tax credits. So what is the third point?"

"The third point is that the bigger the real estate investment, the more the banks and the government want to lend you money," I said.

"Why is that?" asked the pilot.

"When you go to your banker with a real estate investment over, let's say, a million dollars, the banker is not lending money to you. The banker is lending money on the property."

"What is the difference?" asked the pilot.

"When the average person goes to the bank to ask for a loan, the bank evaluates the credit-worthiness of the individual. When this same person wants to buy, let's say a small rental property, a property such as a single condominium, or house, or duplex, the banker still evaluates primarily the person. As long as you have a steady job and enough income to pay for these smaller properties, the bank will often lend you, not the property, the money."

"But on bigger properties, when the price of the property is far beyond the income of the individual to pay for, the bank then looks at the income and expenses of the property itself," said the pilot. "Is that the difference?"

"Pretty close," I said. "On larger properties the asset really is the property and its income stream, not the individual borrower's income stream."

"So it can be easier to buy a bigger property rather than a smaller property," said the pilot.

"If you know what you're doing," I said. "The same is true with borrowing from the government. If you go to the government with a $150,000 property, in many cases the government agency is not interested. But if you want to acquire a property that is a slum and you want to convert it to safe low-income housing, the government has millions of dollars to lend. In fact, if your investment is not over $5 million, it's hard to get anyone in the government to become interested in your property."

"Anything else?" asked the pilot.

"The list goes on," I replied. "But let me give you the downside to real estate."

"Such as?" asked the pilot.

"Real estate is in most cases not as liquid as paper assets. That means it can take longer to buy and sell real estate. The real estate market is also not as efficient as the paper market. And real estate can be management-intensive," I said with a smile.

"Why are you smiling?" asked the pilot.

"Because the disadvantages are often the biggest advantages to the professional real estate investor," I said. "The disadvantages are often only disadvantages to new or unsophisticated investors."

"Give me an example," said the pilot.

"Very briefly," I replied. "Because real estate is not as liquid, and it can be harder to find a buyer or seller, the professional investor can often take his time to make a deal."

"You mean you can do a little one-on-one negotiation with the seller," said the pilot.

"Or the buyer," I replied. "In the stock market, it's often just buy or sell. Very seldom is there any kind of one-to-one negotiation between buyer and seller . . . at least not for most investors."

"You mean there can be one-to-one negotiations between buyers and sellers in the stock market?" asked the pilot.

"Yes," I replied. "But that goes into the gray area of insiders and professional players. It can be done legally, but it is not usually done by the average investor."

"Oh," said the pilot. "But it is done all the time in real estate."

"That's the fun of real estate," I replied. "That is where you can become creative, negotiate terms, cut a better deal, lower the price, or raise the price. Ask the seller to throw in a boat or pay your down payment for you. It becomes fun, once you learn the game."

"What else?" said the pilot.

"You can reduce expenses, improve the value of the property, add an extra bedroom, paint the place, sell off some extra land, and on and on. Real estate is great for the creative investor who is a good negotiator. If you are creative and a good negotiator, you can make a fortune in real estate, as well as have a good time."

"I never saw it that way," said the pilot. "All I've ever done is buy and sell the houses my family has lived in. But come to think of it, that was kind of fun and I have made a better return on my houses than I have made on my mutual funds."

I could see the light was going on in his head. He could now see that there was something else he could invest in besides de-worsifying his portfolio with mutual funds. While the lights were coming on in his head, it was getting late and time to head home . . . and the evening soon ended. A few weeks later, he called to tell me he was out looking for his first rental property and he was having fun, instead of worrying. He said, "Even though my rental income breaks even with my expenses, I can still make money in real estate. Understanding phantom cash flow and the tax laws is like winning financially without making any money."

All I said was, "You're beginning to understand."

Bad Advice from Advisors

Financial advisors are important. The problem is, many financial advisors are not rich nor are they successful investors. In a major U.S. publication, a certified financial planner had this to say about my advice on real estate: "Lots of people have made lots of money in real estate, but primarily in places like California, Connecticut. Our clients who are here in the Midwest haven't experienced that kind of thing."

Her clients should fire her. The reason her clients in the Midwest have not made any money in real estate is because they had her as an advisor. If you understand real estate, tax laws, and corporate laws, and have a good broker and accountant, you can make money in real estate even though the property does not increase in value or turn a profit from rental income. Her report about property increasing in value only in California and Connecticut is also wrong. If she knew her property market, she would know that the fastest growing real estate markets in America were Las Vegas, Nevada, for small cities, and Phoenix, Arizona, for large city growth. She only heard about California and Connecticut because she only knows what is in the news, and most investment news is about paper assets. She does not know what professional real estate investors know, yet she gives advice as if she does know.

As rich dad often said, "Never ask an insurance salesperson if you should buy insurance." Most financial planners are primarily insurance salespeople, not investors. Insurance is a very important investment product, but it is not the only investment product.

How to Find a Great Investment

As with any investment, I am often asked, "How do I find a good real estate investment?" My answer is, "You must train your brain to see what others cannot see."

The next question is, "How do I do that?"

The answer is, "The same way any shopper finds a good deal." At the start of this book I wrote about people who focused on saving driving from store to store shopping for food bargains. The same is true for real estate, or for any investment . . . you need to become a professional shopper.

100:10:3:1

Dr. Dolf DeRoos, who is a longtime friend, has written a book for the Rich Dad's Advisors series, *Real Estate Riches: How to Become Rich Using Your Banker's Money.* Obviously, we colluded on the title. In his book, he details how to find real estate bargains that most people miss. He also discusses how to improve your property to improve the property's value. The basic point he makes is how to shop for property. He calls it the 100:10:3:1 method of buying a property. That means he analyzes 100 properties, makes offers on ten of them, has three sellers say yes, and will buy one. In other words, it takes shopping and looking at over 100 properties to buy one property.

Kiss Many Frogs

As you know, rich dad loved fairy tales as teaching tools. He loved the story of the princess who had to kiss a frog in order to find her handsome prince. Rich dad often said, "You have to kiss a lot of frogs in order to know which one is a prince." In investing, and in many aspects of life, that statement holds true. Today, I am always amazed when I hear that someone took a job at age twenty-five and stayed there all their life. I wonder how they know the difference between a good job and a bad job. When I meet a person who decided to be a doctor at age fifteen, I wonder if they really used reality in making their decision. The same is true in relationships and in investing.

Rich dad said, "Most people avoid kissing frogs so they marry them instead." What rich dad meant was that when it comes to investing and their future, most people do not take enough time kissing. Instead of taking the time to look for good investments, most people act on impulse, hot tips, or let a friend or relative manage their financial investments.

Marrying a Toad

A friend of mine recently came to me and said, "I took your advice and invested in a rental property."

Curious, I asked, "What did you buy?"

"I bought a nice condo near the beach in San Diego."

"How many properties did you look at?" I asked.

"Two," she said. "The broker showed me two units in the same complex and I bought one."

About a year later, I asked how her real estate investment was doing. "I'm losing about $460 a month," she replied.

"Why so much?"

"One reason is because the board that runs the homeowners association raised the monthly maintenance fee. The other reason is that I did not know how much rent per month I could collect. It was a lot lower than I thought," she said a little sheepishly. "I've tried to sell it but I found out that I paid $25,000 more than the market is willing to pay. So I don't want to lose money every month, and I can't afford to lose $25,000 by selling it for less than I paid for it."

As rich dad would say, "That is the price of not kissing enough frogs. If you don't kiss enough frogs, you can wind up marrying a toad." Because my friend did not do her homework, she wound up marrying a toad, an expensive one.

How do you evaluate a good real estate investment? Experience is the greatest teacher. Outlined below are ten very important lessons my friends and I have learned along the way. In addition, I will outline several other resources which may be helpful to you.

The Price of Not Going Shopping

When people ask me how I learned to find a great real estate investment, I simply say, "You need to go shopping."

I agree with Dolf DeRoos's 100:10:3:1 formula for finding a great investment. Over the years, Kim and I have looked at and analyzed literally thousands of properties. When we are asked, "How did you learn so much about real estate?" we simply say, "We have looked at thousands and thousands of investment opportunities." We have also made hundreds of offers to buy property, many offers that were laughed at. The point is, with each property we looked at and each offer we made, our knowledge and experience about the property market and human nature grew.

When we are asked, "What do you do when you don't have any money?" The answer is the same: "Go shopping." In my investment seminars, I often say, "When you go to a shopping center, no one asks you if you have any money. The retailers want you to shop and browse. The same is true with most investments. Shopping, asking questions, analyzing deals is how I got my education. What I learned about investing cannot be found in a book. Just as you cannot learn to play golf from a book, you cannot train your brain to see investments others cannot see from a book. You must get out and go shopping."

Hindsight Is 20/20

My friend who married the toad could have learned a few valuable lessons, if she hadn't decided to say, "Real estate is a lousy investment. You can't make any money in real estate." When I asked her what she had learned, she angrily said, "I should never have listened to you. The market has changed and you cannot make money in real estate today."

There is a saying that "Hindsight is 20/20." The problem is, you do have to turn and look behind you. My friend did not look and learn. Even after I complimented her for taking action, she was still convinced that real estate is a lousy investment, which means her foray into real estate is extra-expensive because she failed to learn from her priceless mistakes . . . mistakes and lessons that could make her smarter and richer in the future. That is the price for having a context that says, "Mistakes are bad." If she had a context that said, "I've taken action, I've made some mistakes, and now I can learn from those mistakes," she would be a much richer person. People who must be perfect, or cannot allow themselves to make mistakes, are often people without much 20/20 vision, and are often people who make the same mistake, which is to fail to learn from their mistakes.

The lessons my friend overlooked from this one simple investment are:

1. Look at more properties.

2. Take your time. There is more than one good deal. Too many people buy because they believe the deal they have found is the only deal in the world.

3. Analyze the rental market as well as the purchase market.

4. Talk to more than one real estate salesperson.

5. Be careful of investing in condominiums. Condominiums most often have a board of directors, made up of homeowners. Homeowners and investors do not always see eye to eye. Most homeowners want to keep their property nice so they spend excessively on maintenance. While it is good to keep up your property, an investor loses control over that very important area of investing, the area of expense control.

6. If expenses are out of control, that also affects the future sales price of the property.

7. Never buy expecting the price of the property to go up. The property should be a good investment in a good economy and in a bad economy. As rich dad always said, "Your profit is made when you buy, not when you sell."

8. Don't invest emotionally. When you buy your own personal investment, it is okay to get emotional. When you buy a property for investment purposes, emotions can blind you. My friend was more excited about the beach being near the property than by the return on investment. She looked at the beach rather than the financial statements.

9. There was not much she could do to improve the property. One of the ways you can make a lot of money is by having control over changing, modifying, or improving the value of the property . . . something you cannot do with stocks or mutual funds. Many times, just adding a garage or an extra room can greatly multiply your return on investment.

10. She did not learn from this experience. Although a relatively expensive lesson, she could have turned the cost of this lesson into millions of dollars if she had been willing to be humble, learn, and try again. Instead, she would rather say, "You can't make money in real estate."

Mistakes Improve Your Vision

By investing the time to analyze thousands of investments, my vision slowly improved. Each time I made an offer to buy a property, I learned something, even if the offers were laughed at or flatly rejected. Each time I had arranged financing with a banker I learned something. Each time I bought a property, I learned something new and valuable, even if I lost money on the property. Today, the accumulation of all those lessons, good and bad, is the education and experience that makes me rich, and allows my wife and me to make more and more money in real estate.

Great investments are seen in your mind's eye, and nowhere else. In the real world, there aren't "For Sale" signs that say, "Here is a great deal." All the signs say is "For Sale." It is your job to train your brain to see a great deal and also negotiate a great deal. That takes dedication and practice.

What Everyone Can Do

As promised, I stated that everyone can do what it takes to become rich. The thing that everyone can do is go shopping for real estate. If you and a partner will agree to look at five, ten, twenty, or twenty-five properties a week, even if you have no money, I promise you that your vision will improve. After analyzing 100 deals, I know that you will find one or two investments that will excite you. When you are excited about becoming rich, your brain shifts into another context and you begin to seek new content, content that can answer the question, "How do I raise the money so I can get rich?"

Everyone can do this, even if they do not have any money. This is all Kim and I do on a regular basis. Now that we have a little more experience, the process of analyzing properties goes faster. In the best and worst of economies, we have always managed to find a great deal. We don't always buy them or put offers on them, but the process of looking for investments and analyzing them keeps our minds sharp and it keeps us in touch with the abundance of opportunities to be found, if only you would just go looking for them.

A product that can assist you in your real estate investing career is an audiotape product entitled *Financial Literacy.* On this tape are samples of different financial forms one must know how to read. One form is a "Due Diligence Checklist." A due diligence checklist is vital for examining the physical condition of a building. While financial statements and proforma statements give you the financial points to analyze, this due diligence checklist guides you in examining the actual property. This checklist can save you money as well as make you a lot of money. It too can be used as an analyzing tool as well as a negotiating tool. As rich dad said, "Financial literacy is more than numbers. Financial literacy is knowing the words that point out to your brain the strengths and weaknesses of your investment. Financial literacy is knowing what to look at, things that average investors miss." This product can also be ordered from the richdad.com Web site.

One last point. Investing in real estate, or any investment product for that matter, requires more than buying one thing and expecting that one product to make you rich. In real estate, Kim and I have a plan on buying ten properties, which means we need to look at 1,000 properties. Of those ten properties, we expect two to be great investments and two to be dogs, investments that we could lose money on. These are generally sold immediately. That leaves six investments that we either have to improve or sell. Regardless if it is real estate, stocks, mutual funds, or building businesses, the ratios tend to remain the same. A professional investor knows this.

Rewards That Others Missed

Every fisherman has a story of the "one that got away." Every real estate investor has a story of the one he or she found, the one that others missed. The following are two stories that are written for the purpose of inspiring you to begin looking at your first 100 investments.

Turning Problems into Opportunities

Story number one: A few years ago, Kim and I were traveling in the mountains, a few hours away from our home. We had decided to take a few days off and enjoy the peace and solitude of the forests. As we always do, we stopped at a real estate office and looked at what they had for sale. The agent showed us the usual overpriced properties that we passed on. Then in her sales book, she had a run-down little cabin with fifteen acres of land listed at only $43,000. I asked her why it was so underpriced.

Her reply was, "It has a water problem."

"What kind of water problem?" I asked.

"The well does not always provide enough water. It is intermittent. That is why it has been for sale for years. Everyone loves it, but it just doesn't have enough water."

"Take me to see it," I said.

"Oh, you won't like it," she replied. "But I will take you there."

About half an hour later, we were walking this lovely piece of forested land, with a lovely old cabin sitting on it. "This is the problem," the real estate agent said as she took us to the well. "This well and land does not have enough water."

Nodding, I said, "Yes, this water problem is serious."

The next day, I went back to the property with a well expert from the area. He looked at the well and said, "This problem can easily be solved. The well produces enough water, but it produces it at different times. All you need to do is add an extra holding tank and the problem is solved."

"How much is a holding tank?" I asked.

"A 3,000 gallon tank will cost you $2,300 installed," he said.

Nodding, I went back to the real estate office and made my offer. "I'll offer the seller $24,000 for the property."

"That's really low," she said, "even with a water problem."

"That is my offer," I replied. "By the way, when was the last time an offer was presented?"

"It's been a long time," she said. "I believe it's been more than a year."

That night, the agent called and said, "I can't believe it. Your offer has been accepted. I can't believe they accepted your price and your terms."

"Thanks," is all I said. In my head and heart, I was jumping up and down with excitement. The seller had not had an offer in more than a year and was sick and tired of paying to make repairs to the house. The seller had accepted my price, my down payment of only $2,000, and the terms of only paying him the balance in a year. In other words, I got the property for a small down payment and no payments for a year.

The next morning, I met with the well expert and asked him to install two 3,000 gallon tanks. The water problem was solved for less than $5,000. A month later, Kim and I went to stay in our new cabin, with lots of fresh water. As we left town, we put the property up for sale. We listed it for $66,000 and it was sold two weeks later. The problem was solved and the property is in the hands of a young couple who now have their dream home in the mountains.

A Change of Context

Story number two: I have a friend, Jeff, who is a landscape architect. He told me a great real estate investment story that I will pass on to you.

Jeff said, "About a year ago, a woman called and said, 'I have forty acres of land I want you to look at.' She had purchased this piece of land for $275,000 on an option. The small town the land was in was against any kind of development."

"Why did she call you?" I asked.

"She wanted me to draw a vision of the future, for the town and the property. She had also hired a former city planner to be part of the team."

"So what happened?" I asked.

"Well, we did our drawings, wrote our proposal for the future, and went before the city council. We were turned down three times," he said.

"Why?" I asked.

"The city council had concerns and kept asking us to revise our drawings and our proposal."

"They kept asking you back?"

"More or less. In reality, we kept asking for their concerns and we kept coming back with plans and drawings that addressed their concerns. Finally the council approved our plan, and then rezoned the property from agriculture to commercial."

"They rezoned your property?" I said. "From agriculture to commercial? How much did that change increase the value of the property?" I asked.

"After her plans were approved, she sold the property to a national insurance company for $6.5 million. They're going to put a large hotel on the property."

"How long did the process take?" I asked.

"A total of nine months," said Jeff. "She paid the city planner and me $25,000 each, as agreed."

"So she spent $50,000 and made nearly $6 million?" I gasped.

My friend Jeff smiled and nodded his head. "That property had sat there for years. Everyone looked at it and said it was too expensive. But she could see what we could not see and she professionally went about showing all of us what was right beneath our noses."

"Are you upset that you only made $25,000?" I asked.

"No. It was a fair return for the work I put in. Besides, I agreed to that amount and she took the risk. If we had not had the property rezoned, she would have lost money. But what I will forever be grateful for is that she gave me vision. She taught me to see what I could never have seen. She taught me to see the abundance that sits in front of each and every one of us, if we will only invest the time to train our brain and eyes to see."

Congratulating him for his new reality, I said, "You gained something much more valuable than your $25,000 fee, didn't you?"

Jeff said, nodding, "Something much more valuable. The city planner feels ripped off, but I don't. I've always heard you talk about your rich dad's context and reality but those words never made much sense to me. Now they do. I realized that, from my context, I thought in terms of thousands of dollars. I realized that she is richer because her context is bigger and she thinks in terms of millions. I also realized that I still think from the S quadrant and she thinks from the B and I quadrants. Even if she had not paid me anything, what I learned is priceless because it has changed my life forever. She has taught me how to be a rich man."

Rezoning a piece of real estate is simply a change of context. The transition from poor to rich is also simply a change of context. Everyone can do it, if they want to.

Where to Keep Your Money

As a teenager, Dolf DeRoos did a comprehensive study of rich people. At the age of seventeen, his research found that most rich people either made their money in real estate, or they held much of their wealth in real estate, after they had made it. Rich dad did too. Although he made a lot of money in his businesses and from playing the stock market, it was in real estate that he parked his wealth.

There are many reasons the rich do this:

1. Tax laws encourage the rich to invest in real estate.

2. There is greater leverage in real estate. A rich person can become even richer by investing with their banker's money.

3. The income from real estate is passive income, the least taxed of all incomes. If there are capital gains from the sale of a property, the capital gains can be deferred for years, allowing the investor to reinvest with what should have been the government's money.

4. Real estate gives the investor much more hands-on control over their assets.

5. It is a much safer place to park money, again if the investor knows how to manage money and property.

The average investor is at tremendous risk by holding the bulk of their wealth in paper assets. As stated all throughout this book, what happens if a retiree's paper portfolio is wiped out in a market crash? Is it all lost? The answer is no, not if the person knows how to protect their paper assets from loss in a bear market. If you only want to hold your wealth in paper assets, however, the following chapter is very important.

Chapter 17

The Leverage of Paper Assets

How to Invest with Less Risk and More Returns

A few months ago, a friend of mine told me he lost over a million dollars in the market. He now has to go back to work. When I asked him why he lost so much, he said, "What else could I do? I did as my advisors advised me to do, which was to 'buy the dips.' So I bought the dips and I kept losing. Now that I have lost over a million dollars, those same advisors are telling me to sit tight and invest for the long term. I don't have many years left to wait."

Investing does not have to be risky. As rich dad said, "While there is risk, investing does not have to be risky." Nor do you have to lose if the market changes direction. In fact, if the market starts to go down, many sophisticated investors make a lot of money. The following are my rich dad's lessons on how to invest in the stock market and make money, regardless if the market is going up or going down.

Keep an Open Context

It is in this section of the book that an open mind and a flexible context are important. If you hear your context saying, "That's impossible," or "You can't do that," or "That's illegal," or "That's too risky," or "That would be too hard for me to learn," simply remind yourself to keep your context open so you can hear the content that is being delivered.

Investing with Insurance in Paper Assets

"Would you drive a car without insurance?" rich dad asked me.

"No," I replied. "That would be foolish. Why do you ask me this question?"

Rich dad smiled and asked, "Would you invest without insurance?"

"No," I replied. "But I'm investing in real estate. I always insure my property from losses. In fact, the bank requires I carry insurance on all property I own."

"Good answer," rich dad replied.

"Why are you asking me these questions about insurance?" I asked again.

"Because it's time for you to learn how to invest in paper assets. Assets such as stocks, bonds, and mutual funds."

"You can invest with insurance in paper assets?" I asked. "You mean you can insure against loss, or minimize your losses?"

Rich dad nodded.

"So investing in paper assets doesn't have to be risky?" I asked.

"No it doesn't," said rich dad. "Investing doesn't have to be risky at all, if you know what you're doing."

"But isn't investing risky for the average paper asset investor?" I asked. "Isn't the average investor investing without insurance?"

Rich dad again nodded, looking me in the eye, and said, "That's why I'm teaching you this. I don't want you to be an average investor. The average investor is interested in averages, which is why he or she is average. That is why there is a Dow Jones Industrial Average. Averages are for average people. That is why there are so many people who listen to their financial advisor and get excited when he or she says, 'The market has averaged a 12 percent return for forty years.' Or 'This mutual fund has an average return of 16 percent over the past five years.' Average investors like averages."

"What is wrong with averages?" I asked.

"Nothing really," said rich dad. "But if you want to be rich, you need to be far better than average."

"So why do averages prevent you from being rich?" I asked.

"Because averages are the summation of wins and losses," said rich dad.

"For example while it is true that the stock market has gone up on average over the past forty years, in reality, it has gone up and down."

"So what?" I said. "Don't most people know that?"

"Yes, most people do know that," said rich dad. "But why lose when you don't have to? Average investors make money when the market goes up and lose money when the market goes down. That is why they are average. What would your averages be if you made money when the market went up and made money when the market went down?"

"That would be good," I replied. "But what do sophisticated investors do?" I asked. "Don't they use averages?"

"Yes they do use averages, but they use different averages. The point I am making here is that the average investor only knows how to make money in an up market and is hence happy to hear that the market has generally averaged up over the years. The sophisticated investor is not looking for average information. The sophisticated investor does not really care if the market averages up or down because they make money in either market condition."

"You mean they never lose?" I asked.

"No. I did not say that. All investors lose at one time or another. But what I mean is that the sophisticated investor is *capable* of winning in up markets and down markets. The average investor only has a strategy for winning in an up market and takes a beating in a down market. Sophisticated investors don't like to take the financial beatings the average investor takes. The sophisticated investor is not always right, and is capable of losing . . . but the difference is, because of their training, skills, tools, and strategies, their losses are generally far less and gains are far greater than the average investor."

Over the years, it seemed strange to me that people would invest their hard-earned money, but not invest much time in learning how to invest. After all my years with rich dad, I could never understand why so many people would rather work hard all their lives than learn to have their money work hard for them. And when they did invest their hard-earned money in the stock market, they were willing to risk it without any insurance from losses. I thought about my poor dad, who worked hard and always said, "Investing is risky." He said that without ever doing any research or taking any classes on investing. Rich dad had taught me how to invest safely with real estate and now he was teaching me how to invest safely in paper assets.

"So investing in the stock market does not have to be risky?" I asked for further clarification.

"No. Absolutely not," said rich dad.

"Yet millions of people invest without protection from loss, without much education, and that makes them risky investors."

"Extremely risky," said rich dad. "That is why I asked if your real estate investments had insurance. I knew they did because your banker requires it. But the average person in the stock market has no insurance. Millions and millions of people are investing for their future retirement without any catastrophic loss insurance. That is risky. Very risky."

"So why don't financial advisors, stockbrokers, and mutual fund salespeople tell them?" I asked.

"I don't know," said rich dad. "I've often wondered that myself. I think the reason is because most financial advisors, stockbrokers, and mutual fund advisors are themselves not really investors, much less sophisticated investors. Most financial services people are salaried or commissioned salespeople, working for a paycheck just as their clients are working for paychecks."

"And they give advice to other people, average investors," I said. "People just like themselves."

Rich dad nodded. "A sophisticated investor can make money in an up market and a down market. The average investor occasionally makes money in an up market and loses money in a down market. Then after losing a lot of money, the average investor calls his or her advisor and asks, "What do I do now?"

"And what does their broker say?" I asked.

"They often say, 'Sit tight, the market will come back in a few months.' Or they say, 'Buy more and dollar-cost-average down.'"

"You wouldn't do that," I said.

"No," said rich dad. "I would not do that. But the average investor does."

"You're telling me I can invest with less risk and make more money in the stock market."

"That is correct," said rich dad. "All you have to do is not be an average investor."

Words That Make You Rich

In book number four, *Rich Dad's Guide to Investing,* I wrote that the poor and middle class were primarily invested in mutual funds. I then wrote that the rich preferred hedge funds. Again, the power of words comes into play. The very word *hedge* is an important word for the sophisticated investor, and there is a world of difference between a mutual fund and a hedge fund. Most of us have heard the term "hedge our bets." The term *hedge* in this context is another word for *insurance*. Just as a gardener might grow a *hedge* to protect their garden from grazing animals, a sophisticated investor will put up a *hedge* to protect their assets.

Simply put, the word *hedge* in this context means protection from loss. Just as you would or should not drive a car without insurance, you as an investor should not invest without insurance or a hedge against catastrophic loss. As common sense as this is, the average investor invests *naked,* which is another term used by sophisticated investors. *Naked* in this term does not refer to the human body, it refers to an asset that is exposed without some form of protection from losses. A sophisticated investor does not like to invest naked, which means being exposed to unnecessary risk. A sophisticated investor will invest with his or her financial positions covered. Just as an insurance salesperson would ask "Are you covered?" . . . sophisticated investors will also ask themselves the same question. In general, the average investor and mutual fund investor is investing *naked* because they are not *covered* against losses.

Not Protecting Your Assets Is Risky

A few days ago, I was one of the keynote speakers at a conference for investors. The main speaker is a very famous television personality, who reports on one of the bigger financial television networks. Her talk was informative and I learned a lot. Yet I found it interesting to hear her say that she only invests in mutual funds.

Suddenly, a participant raised his hand and said, "Don't you feel guilty that you are responsible for the billions of dollars your viewers have lost in the stock market?" His tone was angry, and as he spoke, I could sense that many investors were in agreement with him. It seemed that many investors had come to this conference not to learn about what to invest their money in, but to find out what happened to the money they had lost.

"Why should I feel guilty?" she replied. "My job is to give you information and I do give you a lot of information. I did not give you investment advice. I only gave you market information. Why do you say I should feel guilty?"

"Because you were a cheerleader during this bull market boom," said the angry participant. "Because of you I kept investing and now I've lost everything."

"I wasn't cheerleading," she said. "I was just giving you information in a good market just as I am giving you information in a bad market today."

For the next five minutes, the anger in the room flared. Some people agreed with the angry participant and others were taking the side of the female reporter. Finally things calmed down. The television reporter asked for more questions. A hand shot up and asked her, "Why didn't you tell your audience about minimizing their risk with options?" he asked. This participant was not angry. He sounded more curious and wanted to let the audience know that they could minimize their risk exposure by using options.

"Options?" she said. "Why would I tell them about options?"

"As a hedge against loss in a bear market," he said.

"Oh I would never do that," she replied. "Options are too risky. Any other questions?" she asked, signaling the person who asked about options to sit down.

I could not believe what I was hearing. This TV personality is one of the most respected people in financial journalism. She influences millions of people's lives. Many people look to her for investment advice and now she was saying, "Options are risky." To me, *not* protecting your assets is risky. To me, being financially ignorant is risky. Knowing how to use options to protect your paper assets is easy and not that hard to do. In fact, if you have a good stockbroker, the process is pretty easy. A kid could do it. All you have to do is learn the definitions of a few new words, find a good broker, and start small to gain some experience. Instead, I watched many of the thousand people in the room nod, agreeing that investing with options is risky.

As I sat there, watching her faithful followers nodding in agreement with her idea that options are risky, my mind drifted back to rich dad's earlier lessons on investing in paper assets. I could hear him saying, "Hundreds of years ago, in ancient Japan, Japanese farmers began using options to protect the price of their rice crops."

"Hundreds of years ago?" I asked. "Hundreds of years ago they were using options as hedges against loss?"

Rich dad nodded, "Yes, hundreds of years ago. Beginning in the Agrarian

Age, smart businesspeople have been using options to protect their businesses from losses. Smart businesspeople continue to do so today."

My mind returned to the room in Chicago where this TV journalist was speaking. I wondered to myself, "If smart businesspeople have been using options for years, why is this very influential person misinforming her viewers?" I then asked myself, "What is more risky? Buying a stock or mutual fund and watching it drop 40 percent to 60 percent, even to 90 percent in value and not protect yourself? My banker requires me to have insurance on my real estate. Why doesn't the paper asset industry require all investors to buy insurance on their paper assets . . . assets that millions of people are counting on for their old age?" To this day, I do not have an answer to those questions. As stated earlier, if your house burns down, it can be replaced in less than a year and paid for by your insurance company. But if your retirement plan crashes with the stock market after you have retired, what will you do then? Buy, hold, and pray again? Hope for another bull market? So I continue to wonder why bankers require investors to invest with insurance, yet the paper asset industry doesn't. I continue to wonder why professional investors invest with insurance, yet the average investor, the average investor who is counting on the stock market for their financial security once their working days are over, invests naked and uncovered?

Vocabulary of Insurance

If you want to retire young and retire rich, it is important that you invest some time learning how to protect your assets, especially if you plan on holding your wealth in paper assets. You do that by learning and understanding what my rich dad called "the language of a sophisticated investor." In my investment seminars, I call it the vocabulary of insurance.

Before getting into those words, I believe it important to review a few other words. The following are other words that need to be defined before getting into the words of insurance:

1. Investor vs. trader: Most people who think they are investors are really traders. Just as most people think their liabilities are assets, many investors are traders rather than investors. One more point. Many people who think they are *investors* are really *savers*. That is why most people who have 401(k) retirement plans, or IRA, Keogh plans, often say, "I am saving for retirement." A

saver simply puts money into an account and does nothing else. An investor is a person who actively manages his or her own portfolio or account.

So what is the difference between an investor and a trader? An investor buys to hold and a trader buys to sell. When a person says, "I bought this stock or piece of real estate because I know the price is going up," I know this person is really a trader . . . in other words, they are buying only to trade, not to use. That is why I say most people are traders rather than investors. A trader generally wants the price of their asset to move up so they can sell it for a profit. An investor wants the investment to return their money as quickly as possible, all the while holding on to the asset. Rich dad said, "An investor buys a cow for milk and for calves. A trader buys a cow to slaughter."

If you want to be successful in the world of investing, regardless if it is in paper assets, businesses, or real estate, you need to be both an investor and a trader. An investor knows what to analyze and how to manage investments and a trader knows how and when to buy and sell. An investor usually wants cash flow from the asset and the trader wants to realize a capital gain from buying low and selling high.

2. Fundamental investor vs. technical investor: A fundamental investor looks at the financial statement of a company or property. A fundamental investor is often concerned with earnings, the management team, and the long-term potential of the business. A pure technical investor does not care about the company's fundamentals. They don't even care if the company is profitable or well run. The technical investor only cares about the market's sentiment at that moment. While a fundamental investor looks at financial statements, a technical investor would rather look at historic charts that reflect the market's sentiment. Later in this chapter there will be some charts to look at.

A technical investor can be a good technical investor and lose money simply because he lacks proper fundamentals. Many "day traders" eventually lose or go broke because they have poor personal money management fundamentals. The same is true for fundamental investors. Many fundamental investors wonder why they do not make money, or lose money, even though they are investing in good, solid, profitable companies. Many fundamental investors lose even though they invest with good fundamentals because they lack the knowledge of technical trading.

This reality is why rich dad wanted his son and me to be qualified or sophisticated investors, investors with both good fundamental skills and good technical skills.

3. Average investor vs. sophisticated investor: The average investor barely knows what a financial statement is. The average investor is better off investing for the long term, de-worsifying their portfolio, investing in mutual funds, and then buying, holding, and praying. The sophisticated investor is someone who has money and understands both fundamental investment techniques as well as technical trading techniques.

Words That Help You Win in Any Market

If you want to retire young and retire rich, protecting or insuring your assets from catastrophic loss is vital. The average investor in paper assets never feels secure. That is why the average investor feels that investing is risky and, for them, it is. Because they feel insecure, they entrust their money to a fund manager, or their brother who is a stockbroker, or a financial planner, hoping and praying that this person will protect them from market disasters. The problem is, the average mutual fund manager or stockbroker cannot protect them from a crash nor can they help them make money in a flat market that is moving sideways.

The way to win and protect your assets in any market is to learn and truly understand the vocabulary of the fundamental and technical investor, especially in paper assets. It is easy to do if you will invest a little time. Just as a banker will ask to see your financial statement before giving you a loan, which is fundamental, and require you to have property, title, and mortgage insurance on a real estate investment, which is to insure the technical or catastrophic risk, you too should require the same of yourself if you want to invest in paper assets. The way you do that is to begin understanding the words of insurance when investing in paper assets. A few of these words are:

1. Trends
2. Moving averages
3. Stop orders
4. Call options
5. Put options

6. Straddles or collars
7. Shorts
8. And many more

The average investor may have heard some of these terms but probably does not understand them or has never used them. Many average investors simply discount these very important words by saying, "It's too risky." Saying something is risky may also be saying, "I'm just too lazy to study the subject."

What You must Know

If you want to retain your wealth in paper assets, you must know how to insure your paper assets against market crashes. The following is a sampling of what you must know. Again, it begins with words.

TRENDS

Every sophisticated investor must understand trends. There is a saying that all sophisticated investors say and that is, "The trend is your friend." Please remember and use that saying.

So what is a trend? The best way to explain it is by telling you a story. When I was a teenager, growing up in Hawaii, most of my friends were training to be big wave surfers. Every winter, when the large swells rolled in from the north, we would enter the water to prove our courage and improve our skills. One year, a new student arrived from the mainland. He was a pretty good surfer in the small summer swells. When winter arrived, he ventured into the water thinking nothing had changed, except the height of the waves. On his first ride on a large wave, he lost control and wiped out at the bottom of the wave. The huge wave curled over him and we did not see him for a long time. Finally, he popped up some distance from us, coughing and swimming as hard as he could. Those of us that were surfing with him could not believe what we saw. We could not believe he was trying to swim against the current. One of us finally said, "Oh no. I can't believe he's trying to swim against the current. No one is that strong a swimmer."

When large waves hit the shore, all that water must find a way back out to sea. It is this movement of water out to sea that causes a rip current. It is like a river of water moving parallel to the beach and then out to sea. For those of us raised in the islands, we know to simply relax and let the current take us out to deeper water. Once the current has dissipated, we know to simply swim or body surf in through a safer channel. This new friend did not know how powerful a rip current could be. Instead of going with the flow, he tried to fight it, became exhausted, and nearly drowned. The same thing happens with new investors.

Investment cycles come in waves, as do ocean waves. They also change with the seasons. Surfers learn to respect the change in the power of the waves and water with each change of season. Sophisticated investors do the same thing. That is why sophisticated investors say, "The trend is your friend." Just as experienced surfers learn not to fight the waves or currents, sophisticated investors go with the trends, changing strategies when appropriate, or standing on the sideline if things are too choppy. Average investors continue to buy and hold, buy the dips, or call and ask their brokers, "Is this the bottom?" as they get pounded.

Three Basic Trends

There are three basic trends that affect paper assets as well as all other investment products. One is an up-trending market, often called a bull market. The second trend is a market heading down, and that is called a bear market. The third trend is a sideways-trending market, which is a market that is not going up or not going down. The sophisticated investor uses different strategies for the different trends. The average investor has only one strategy and tries to use it on three different trends. That is why they ultimately lose. The idea of investing for the long term is basically a good idea, but investing for the long term with only one strategy is a loser's way of investing.

Even animals are aware that there are changes of seasons. When the first chills of winter arrive with the fall season, most animals know they need to prepare for the change that winter brings. The same is true for sophisticated investors. It is only the average investor who believes the words of their financial advisors, "Invest for the long term. Buy and hold even though the market goes down." If animals are smart enough to know that things change, why aren't humans?

MOVING AVERAGES

Trends are caused by buyers and sellers. If there are more buyers, then the trend is up. If there are more sellers, then the trend is down. An average investor takes comfort when their financial advisor says to him, "The market has gone up over the last forty years." The sophisticated investor is not watching a long-term average but a moving average. Just as a surfer watches the daily rise and fall of the tides, the sophisticated investor watches the ebb and flow of money in and out of the market. The sophisticated investor watches these charts because these charts tell them when to change strategy.

The diagram below is a chart of a moving average. As said earlier, fundamental investors look at financial statements and management teams, a technical investor looks at charts, and this diagram below is one of the charts they look at.

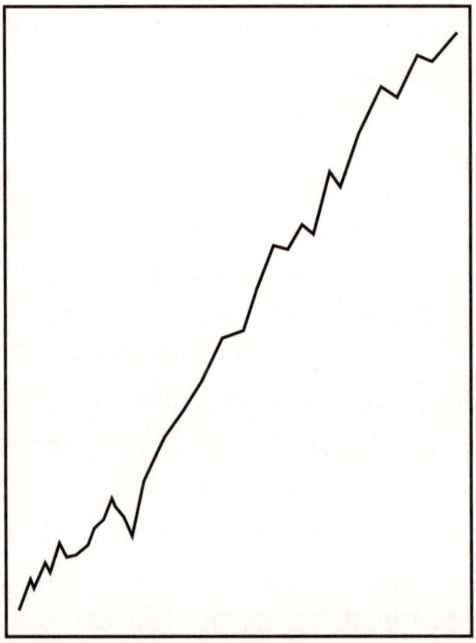

Point one is an up trend.

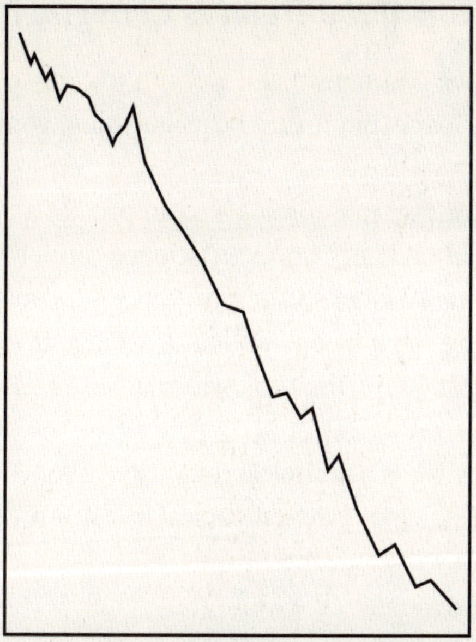

Point two is a down trend.

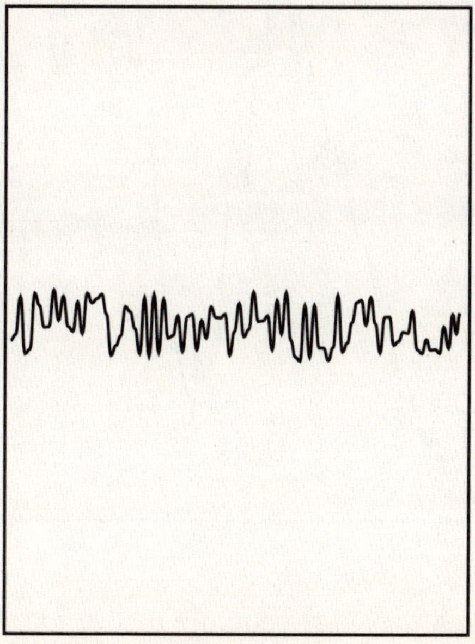

Point three is a sideways-moving trend.

How Do You Know If the Trend Is Changing?

Does the market give you signs that it is about to change? The answer is yes. It is not an exact science, but it sure beats guessing, going on hunches, and investing on hot tips.

Most of us know that meteorologists can predict a hurricane. Although predicting the weather is not an exact science, nonetheless today we are given ample warning if a large storm is brewing. A technical trader can do almost the same thing. That means while the average investor is holding and praying the market stays up, the professional investors are selling before the storm hits.

There are many signs a technical trader looks for. The following charts show one of the telltale patterns a technical investor watches for.

DOUBLE TOP

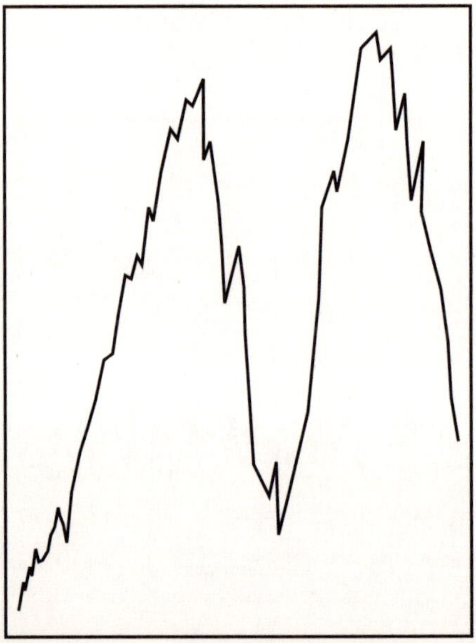

Technical traders call this chart pattern a double top. When technical investors see this pattern they become cautious and begin to change investment strategies, or get out of the market entirely. If you notice, the price of the stock tumbled down sharply right after a double top.

DOUBLE BOTTOM

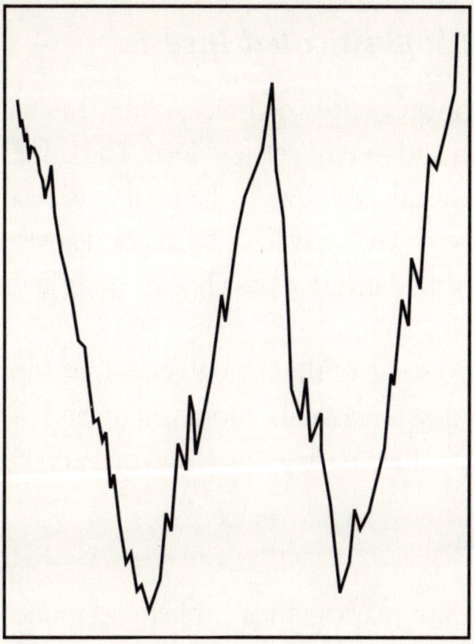

A similar pattern occurs at the bottom of the market. This pattern is called a double bottom. When technical investors see this pattern emerging, they again change strategies or begin to buy stocks while average investors have given up hope and are selling.

There are many different types of patterns that technical investors look for. Nor are these patterns absolutes or guarantees. Yet they do give the sophisticated investor a significant advantage over the average investor, who is clueless about these market signals. One big advantage a technical investor has is that they have the time to protect their asset prices with insurance. The average investor sits there fully exposed, uninsured and unprotected. Millions of investors have their financial future sitting at risk, hoping and praying their financial advisor's advice will protect them from the storms that return on a regular basis to any financial market.

Every time I hear the so-called financial experts advising, "Invest for the long term. Don't panic. Just sit tight. Always remember the market on average has gone up over the past forty years," I cringe. When I hear these experts saying such words, I shake my head and feel badly for those millions of people who listen to such experts and entrust their financial future to them. Investing does not have to be risky, if you know what you're doing.

The Tools of the Sophisticated Investor

The average investor only has two choices once the market changes directions. They can hold and lose or sell and lose. The other day, I heard a well-respected investment advisor say, "In February of 2000 I told you to sell everything you owned." That may have been good advice for the average investor but a sophisticated investor has choices other than buying and losing or selling and losing.

The following are some of the mental tools that sophisticated investors use to protect their assets and make money in up and down markets. These are the tools that help them make money, and protect their money when the market goes down.

STOP ORDERS

A sophisticated investor may call their broker and request a stop order if he or she suspects the price of their stock may go down, especially if the market trend is down. The average investor does nothing and if the price of their stock goes down, they just watch it go down. Not knowing what to do, their buy, hold, and pray strategy turns to a buy, hold, and lose strategy.

This is how a stop order works. Let's say your stock is at $50 today and the charts tell you that the market is trending down. All you have to do is call your broker and put in a stop order at, let's say, $48. If the stock price begins to drop to, let's say, $30 because more sellers have entered the market, your stop order becomes a market order and the stock is sold at $48 and your losses are limited to $2. The average investor would lose $18 and still be clinging to the stock.

Although stop orders are often used as "insurance" by investors, they are not always used by very sophisticated investors. Often the share prices tend to gap on the opening transaction and sophisticated investors already have the news and have decided whether to sell their shares or cancel the stop limit order. The following are two reasons why stop orders might not succeed in a falling or volatile market.

The first reason a professional investor might not use a stop order is because the trend is heading down too fast. Sometimes in a rapidly falling market, the stop order can be passed by without being executed. For example, let's say the price of the stock is at $50. Since the trend is down the investor puts in a stop order at $48. That means if the price drops to $48, the stock is automatically sold. But if the market should drop rapidly, it is possible that the $48 price can be "gapped" or skipped. That means there are so many people selling that there are no buyers at $48, so the stop is passed, or gapped. If the price stops at $40 because a few buyers step forward, the best the investor can do is hold on at $40 or sell at $40. Their stop was passed over.

Another reason a stop may not be used by a professional investor is because they are not certain of the trend of the market. For example, again the stock is at $50 and a stop is put in at $48. As expected the stock drops to $47, the stock is sold at $48. The investor feels relieved until he or she realizes the market has suddenly trended up and the price of their stock is now $65. Not only have they lost $2 a share, they have lost out on a $17 move up.

Making a Killing or Being Killed

We have often heard someone say, "I am making a killing in the market." During the dot-com boom and bust, there were many people who went into the mania with the idea of making a killing and, instead, they were the ones that were killed. In the news today, many people laugh and chuckle at the dot-com mania, saying, "How could people have been so foolish?" What many people do not hear about are the people that did make a killing on the way up and on the way down.

A friend of mine made a fortune buying early in the dot-com IPO craze. He made a killing, as they say. He also made a killing on the way down. Just before the top, in late 1999, he sold every share of dot-com stock he owned. Then as the top neared, he began selectively shorting (explained below) some of the same dot-com company stocks that made him rich on the way up. Three of those companies fell so far that they went into bankruptcy. So he made a fortune on the way up and made an even bigger fortune on the way down. Why? The reason he made more of a fortune on the way down was because he did not use any of his own money and he has not paid taxes on the money he got from shorting the stocks of companies that went bankrupt.

When I asked him why, he said, "I shorted shares at the top, which means I borrowed them. Then the companies went down and went bankrupt. I have yet to pay taxes because there has been no closing transaction, so I owe no tax. All I did was sell shares of stock I did not own or I borrowed, and now I await the time when I can buy them back and return them to the person I borrowed them from." Today, he has nearly $875,000 in money he made by shorting a few stocks, sitting in a tax free municipal bond fund, collecting tax-free interest. Interest from money he received by selling stocks he did not own. He says, "I'm waiting for the opportunity to buy those shares back, but until then I collect the interest on tax free capital gains money."

If you do not understand this transaction, do not worry. Most people do not. If you would like to understand it better, contact a stockbroker or your accountant and ask them if they can better explain it to you.

The point is, if you want to make a killing on the way up you also need to know how to make a killing on the way down. If you don't, then you are often the one being killed by the people making a killing.

There is a lot more to learn about using professional trading tools such as stops. There is also a lot more to investing with these tools than just asking your broker to put in a sell stop or a buy stop, which is a stop in the other direction. Sophisticated investors need to have many more tools than average investors. If they don't they too will get killed while their peers are making a killing.

This unfair advantage that sophisticated investors have is the reason why when I am asked, "What advice would you give to the average investor?" my answer is, "Don't be average." I say that because your financial future and your financial security are too important to just be average.

A word of caution and warning: This is not a book on technical trading. The above example on a stop is a very simple explanation. A sophisticated investor knows how and when to use a short because there are times when stops work well and times when they do not work at all. Before running out to use any of these technical processes, please read, ask, attend classes, and gain experience before attempting to use any of the techniques I have described and will be describing.

The primary reason I list a few of these techniques is to let people who think that investing is risky know that investing does not have to be risky. It is still up to the individual to seek further knowledge if they want to use these techniques.

CALL OPTIONS

Another word for options is insurance. Simply put, a call option gives the owner of the option the right to buy shares of stock at a certain price per share over a predetermined period of time. A call option is an insurance policy, protecting the investor from missing out on a sudden *increase* in the price of a stock. For example, let's say the trends and moving average charts indicate that more buyers are entering the market, so prices are moving up and the investor wants to insure he or she can buy the stock at a better price in case the stock goes up in value. Let's use as an example a stock with a price of $50 per share today. The investor calls his broker and says I want to buy a call option to buy 100 shares of stock at $50 per share. He might pay $1 per share for that call option, costing him $100 (each option covers 100 shares). He's protecting himself from a sudden upside move.

Three weeks later, the investor returns from a fishing trip and finds out that the stock has risen to $60 per share. The call option technically allows the investor to buy 100 shares of the stock at $50 per share. He could then, if he chooses, sell the same 100 shares at $60 per share.

Otherwise, if the stock had stayed at a market price of $50 per share or below, the option would expire worthless, or as sophisticated investors say, "out of the money."

In the example of the stock rising to $60 per share, the average investor might then exercise his right to buy 100 shares at $50 per share for $5,000 and simultaneously sell 100 shares for $6,000, realizing a gain of $900 ($6,000 less the $5,000 less the cost of the option, $100). On the other hand, a sophisticated investor would just choose to sell his option for $10 per share, or $1,000 for the unit of 100 shares, realizing a gain of $900 ($1,000 less the cost of the option, $100).

When you examine the transaction, the average investor put up $5,000 to make $900. The sophisticated investor put up $100 to make the same $900 gain. In this oversimplified example, which investor made more money with his money?

The answer I would give is the investor who bought and sold options, or the sophisticated investor. The average investor put up $5,000 to make $900, or an 18 percent return in a month. The sophisticated investor put up $100 and made $900 in less than a month for a 900 percent return.

Again, this is an oversimplified example and I strongly recommend you study more, gain some experience, and find a competent stockbroker to assist you through this learning process.

This example illustrates why rich dad did not want to own much, but instead why he sought only to control. Options give you control over the buy and sell process. It also illustrates one example on how leverage can be created in paper assets and how leverage can be used with less risk and higher returns if you know what you are doing. In this example, the sophisticated investor only put at risk $1 per option and the average investor put up $50 per share. When you go back to the discussion on the velocity of money, which investor's money is moving faster? Which investor can become richer faster?

Rich People Don't Like to Own Things

You may have noticed something with this last example. You may have noticed that you do not necessarily have to own the stock in order to own an option. This often overlooked detail can have large financial consequences if you understand it.

The point is, my rich dad never wanted to own anything and my poor dad did. My poor dad often said, "This house is in my name." "My car is in my name." My rich dad said, "You don't want to own anything. All you want to do is control it." Options are another example of this way of thinking. My poor dad wanted to own the stock and my rich dad only wanted to own the option to buy or sell the stock. Today, I notice many people take pride in owning stock when, in many ways, there is far better leverage in buying and selling options. In other words, it may take far less money to make a lot of money trading options rather than buying shares of stocks.

PUT OPTIONS

In the previous example, you saw how call options are used to make money in an up-trending or bull market. When the trend of the market is down, the sophisticated investor will use put options not only to make money, but also to protect the value of her stock in case prices begin to fall.

For example, the stock price is $50. The market moves down and the price of the stock falls to $40. The average investor has lost $10 per share. If she had 100 shares, she lost $1,000, on paper. The point here is that the investor has only lost on paper, but not in reality. If she sold at $40 per share, then she would have lost. It is this idea that the loss is only a paper loss is why so many losing investors suddenly say, "I'm in for the long haul." Those words usually mean this investor will now wait until that stock goes back up to $50, which may happen overnight, over years, or never. This is the buy, hold, and lose strategy of someone who is the eternal optimist or someone who hates to admit they made a mistake and lost.

The sophisticated investor would invest differently. Instead of sitting there worrying about the price of her stock falling, this investor would have her broker put in a stop order or buy a put option. Again, there are different reasons for using a stop and for using a put option, and those reasons are beyond the scope of this book. The point here is that the sophisticated investor will do something in case the market changes directions and begins to trend down.

Instead of praying the market does not go down, let's say the sophisticated investor buys a put option for $1 per share for the right to sell her shares at $50 per share. The put would cost her $100, or $1 per share for 100 shares. The market goes down as more sellers enter the market and the price of the stock drops to $40 per share. The sophisticated investor is happy because she has just protected her position at the share price of $50. What she continues to lose in the long stock position as the shares drop under $50 she recaptures in the increasing value of the put. The investor without a put loses dollar for dollar as the share price drops. The sophisticated, or hedged, investor is really flat. The loss on the stock has been recaptured with a gain in the put.

How does the sophisticated investor make money with a put when the average investor lost? The sophisticated investor could exercise her put, or right to sell 100 shares at $50 per share, and receive $5,000. If she chooses, she could then go to the market and buy 100 shares at $40 a share for $4,000. The net result is, she has her 100 shares of stock and an extra $900 ($1,000 less the cost of the put). (There are many security rules and regulations that must be followed and considered.)

The average investor, with no put option, only has his or her shares, which are now worth less and still has *not* gotten any of his or her money back.

If this is confusing to you, do not worry, it is confusing to most people the first time. It is important to remember what was written earlier in this book about the need to think in opposites. For many people learning to use options is much like learning how to eat with your left hand after you have spent years eating with your right hand. It can be done. It just takes a little practice. The point to remember is that the process of using options to protect your assets as well as make money in up or down markets is not a complex process. Most people can learn it if they give themselves a little time to understand it. Saying it one more time because it is important, investing does not have to be risky, if you have the right advice and right advisors. You don't have to spend your life worrying about your paper asset portfolio being wiped out by a market crash. Instead of worrying about market crashes, you can prepare to become richer and richer the more the market goes up, down, and sideways.

What is important to note is that the average investor who lost money is often sitting, waiting, and listening to their financial advisor's advice of "Hold on and invest for the long term." They do that because they only have a strategy for only one market trend, and as you now know, there are three different market trends.

A Sophisticated Investor May Not Buy Stocks

There are sophisticated investors who never buy or sell stocks. They trade only in options. When I asked one of my option trader friends why he only invested in options rather than stocks, he said, "Investing in stocks is too slow. I can make much more money with less money investing in options. I can also make more money in less time. Investing in stocks and hoping to make money is like sitting around waiting for the paint to dry."

STRADDLES OR COLLARS

Straddles or collars are the ultimate insurance protection. In overly simple terms, a straddle or collar is placing a put and a call around a price position. For example, if the price of the investor's stock is $50 per share, a sophisticated investor may have a call option placed at $52 per share and a put option in place at $48 per share. If the market suddenly goes up to $62 per share, the investor has the right to still buy his or her shares at $52. If the market goes down to $42, the investor has the right to sell his or her shares at $48, minimizing the loss. If the stock's market price is at $42 and the investor has a put option, which is the option to sell a stock at $48, that option suddenly becomes very valuable, in some cases, much more valuable than the stock itself. The point is, collars or straddles are used to protect both the up- and the downside risks and opportunities. It can be an ultra-conservative strategy, if you know what you are doing.

Again, this is not meant to be a book on options trading. Obviously I have oversimplified the process for the sole purpose of promoting a basic understanding of options. Also, there are much more sophisticated strategies that can and are used to protect assets and increase returns.

SHORTS

When I was a kid, I was told not to touch or use things that did not belong to me. That is not true in the stock market. When someone shorts a stock, that literally means they are selling something they do not own. If my mom knew I was doing this, she would have a strong and long discussion with me. But then again, my mom was not an investor.

First of all, a *short* is not an option. When someone says, "I am shorting this stock," they are trading in stocks not options. A sophisticated investor knows the differences between a short and options and knows when and when not to use them. Again, knowing when and when not to use them is beyond the scope of this book.

Why short a stock? Generally, if the investor feels the price of a stock is too high, and the market is trending down, a sophisticated investor may find it profitable to begin to use shorts to make money. Shorting a stock is simply borrowing someone else's stocks, selling them into the market, and putting the money into your pocket. If and when the market price of the stock comes down, the investor buys the stock back and returns it to the person they borrowed the stocks from.

For example, let's say XYZ Corporation's stock price is $50 and the market is trending down. The following is a sequence of events involved in shorting a stock:

1. The investor calls his or her stockbroker and asks to short 100 shares of XYZ stock.

2. The broker then borrows 100 shares from another client's account and sells the 100 shares for $5,000.

3. The broker then deposits the $5,000 into the account of the investor . . . the investor who did not own the stock.

4. In his client's account, the account where the stock was borrowed from, there is an IOU for 100 shares of stock, not $5,000.

5. Over time, the stock price of XYZ drops to $40 a share.

6. The investor who borrowed the shares calls the stockbroker up and says, "Buy me 100 shares of XYZ at $40."

7. The broker buys the 100 shares of stock at $40 and returns the 100 shares to the account of the client, the client who loaned the shares to the investor.

8. The stockbroker pays for the 100 shares from the $5,000 in the investor's account. The $5,000 has come from the original sale of the 100 shares of stock at $50.

9. The investor has realized a $1,000 profit, less fees, commissions, and taxes, by selling shares of stock he or she did not own. The investor made money without any money. That is, in simplified terms, the process of shorting a stock.

A few more points:

Point #1: The moment the investor bought the shares at $40 and returned the 100 shares to the original investor, the shorting investor is said to have "covered their short position." Those are very important words to remember.

Point #2: As you can tell, there is tremendous risk in shorting a stock. A person can lose a lot of money shorting a stock if the market trends up and the stock price goes up. In this example, this same investor would lose $1,000 if the stock price went to $60. But as rich dad often said, "Just because there is risk, does not mean it has to be risky." There are sophisticated investors who will *straddle* a short by buying a call option for $51. If the trend did turn up and the stock price went to $60, the investor would pay $51 per share instead of $60 a share, again minimizing their exposure.

Point #3: You may have noticed that I made reference to the market trends. Remember the saying, "The trend is your friend." Don't be like my friend who tried to swim against the rip current. More than knowing the definition of words such as shorts, straddles, call options, and so on, it is important to know how they are related to one another. In other words, using a short is pretty safe in a down-trending market, and much more risky in an up-trending or sideways-moving market.

Point #4: If you have no idea what has just been covered, do not worry.

It only takes a little time and a little practice to make these words a part of your vocabulary if you want to. The main point of all this is that investing does not have to be risky, if you are willing to invest a little time to increase your education, as you are doing now. Once you learn to minimize risk, you can greatly increase your returns because you are not doing what average investors do.

Why It Does Not Take Money to Make Money

People often ask me, "Doesn't it take money to make money?" If you understood the process of shorting a stock, you will know the answer to that question. When a person shorts a stock, they receive money for selling something they did not own. So it really does not take money to make money. Yet, the real answer to the question, "Doesn't it take money to make money?" is "It depends upon who is doing the investing."

Rich dad said, "The less financially intelligent you are, the more money it takes to make a little money. If you are financially intelligent, it doesn't take any money to make a lot of money." The following example further illustrates this point and also illustrates the value of having a strong and rich financial vocabulary.

A few months ago, I called my stockbroker and said, "Write a naked put option on XYZ. Write it for ten contracts."

My broker, Tom, asked me a few more questions and then said, "It's done." What he asked me was the time horizon for the option and other questions that are again outside the realm of this book.

What I had just done was sell put options, not buy them. This is an important point. The reason it is important is because up to now, options have been used as insurance policies, which is why most people buy options. When you use the words "write an option" it means you are selling the option, not buying it. The very rich sell options just as the very rich sell shares of stock, not buy them. Bill Gates became the richest man in the world by selling shares of Microsoft, not buying shares of Microsoft. The same is true in the world of options . . . only it is much faster, easier, and can be more profitable, again, if you know what you are doing.

When I said to my broker, "Write a naked put option," I was saying, "I want to sell options on stock I do not own." In this case they are put options and I wanted ten contracts, which means 1,000 shares, since a contract is 100 options.

Tom called back later that day and said, "You got $5."

I said, "Thank you," and the transaction was over for the time being. I did not have to watch the stock or the market and was free to go about doing what I wanted to do. When Tom said he "got" me $5, that meant he put $5,000 into my account that day. In other words, it took me less than five minutes to make $5,000. On top of that, I did not put up any money nor did I sell anything tangible. In many ways, I sold nothing and made $5,000 in less than five minutes. (As a point of clarification, while I did not put up any money or sell anything tangible, I have other assets in my brokerage account that act as collateral on the transaction, which allows me to work with my broker in this way.)

A few weeks later, Tom called back and said, "It expired out of the money."

"That's great," I replied. "By the way, when are we going to play golf?"

Translation

First of all, I do not write about this transaction to brag. I write about this one actual transaction only to illustrate the power of words. Those words are more than words to me. They are real and alive in my brain. Those words are tools, tools that make me rich . . . tools that allow me to make money without any money. As rich dad always said, "There are words that make you rich and words that make you poor."

When I said to Tom, "Write a naked put option on XYZ," I was saying, "Sell to someone the right to sell me the stock they own for a certain price." On that day, XYZ was selling for around $45 per share. My put option assured the person buying the put option that I would buy his stock at $40 per share. In other words, I was selling insurance to the owner of XYZ stock. If the stock price had fallen to $40 per share and the put exercised I would have bought it at that price, protecting him from further losses.

When Tom called me back and said, "You got $5," he meant I got $5 per share covered by the put option. In the vocabulary of options traders, "writing" means selling. It is also the same word used in the insurance industry. Many of us have had an insurance salesperson say, "I am writing you a life insurance policy with a death benefit of $100,000." Another word the insurance industry uses is "underwriting," which means they are guaranteeing you something for a price. In other words, writing means selling in the world of insurance and in the world of options. In this case, I was underwriting the investor's $45 risk exposure for $5 a share. I was guaranteeing the investor that I would buy their stock for $40 if the price went down that low. In this case, I became the insurance company, which is why I was "writing a naked put option." I was insuring something I did not own, which is what insurance companies do.

A Loser's Context

Now I can hear some of your mind's context saying, "But that is so risky. What if the stock market crashes? What if you have to buy the shares at $40?" As stated all throughout this book, a person needs to keep their context open if they want to learn anything. Or as rich dad said, "Just because there is risk does not mean it has to be risky."

I saved this section for the end of this book because I wanted to make sure your context was somewhat prepared to receive this information. I have never written about this before because I never wrote about the importance of context before. For most people, their context is not able to grasp much less accept what I am about to explain. If you have stuck with me this long I say "congratulations." When I speak to some of my friends or others with a loser's context, which is a context that is driven by the fear of losing, the noise from their fear is so loud, they cannot hear what I am saying or about to say. Their fear of risk and losing kicks in and their minds start chattering away, saying, "That's too risky. Don't tell me any more. I can't do that." So thank you for hanging in for all this time.

In that five-minute transaction, I basically agreed to buy 1,000 shares of XYZ stock for $40 per share if the investor who held the stock would pay me a $5 per share premium. The money, or $5,000, was deposited into my account. A few weeks later, the price of the stock was around $43 and so the option or insurance policy expired worthless, or "out of the money" as they say. The $5,000 was mine to keep, less commissions, fees, and taxes. The point I want to emphasize is that it took less than five minutes, I sold nothing, did nothing after that, meaning I did not have to sit in front of a computer screen watching the ups and downs of the market, and made $5,000.

There are many people who do not make $5,000 a month and if they do, they pay far more in taxes than I did on the same amount of money. A worker would pay self-employment tax on that $5,000 and I would not because it was not the same kind of income. A worker earns $5,000 in earned income and I earned $5,000 in portfolio income.

Making Money out of Thin Air

Before going further, I think it important for you to ponder how the $5,000 was made because it was made out of thin air. When you inspect this transaction, you will begin to realize I made the money by selling something *I did not own*. I also made the money by selling something that *did not exist,* until I decided it existed. The transaction was like making money out of thin air. If you can truly understand what went on in this transaction, physically as well as mentally, you can begin to understand the power of your mind to create money out of nothing. That ability is often called the power of alchemy. Now you may further understand why rich dad had me work for free when I was a kid. He wanted to train me to think about creating money rather than working for money. He wanted me to develop a different context, a context not dependent upon hard work to become rich.

Making Losers Happy

Rarely do I tell people about this process. I have gotten tired of arguing and trying to explain this process to a loser's context. The times I have talked about this option process I often hear comments such as:

1. It takes too much time. I don't want to spend my days watching the market.
2. It's too risky and I can't afford to lose.
3. I have no idea what you're talking about.
4. You can't do that. It's illegal.
5. My stockbroker says it's not that simple.
6. What if you're wrong and you make a mistake?
7. You're lying. You can't do that.

In other words, losers lose because they cannot listen without their context kicking in. This book has been about context and a person's reality. The reason I hesitate giving people content is because most people's context can't handle the content I just discussed. Now that the book is drawing to a close, I am more willing to give you the content that so many people want. I just trust your context will allow you to absorb and allow you to use the content and turn it into action.

In other words, when I am asked to tell what I do and I tell them, in many cases it is their context that fights back. Their context fights back, closes shut, argues, or finds reasons why it can't be done. Now that I have spent time explaining context, I will give you the final content on why this writing of naked puts is a low-risk, high-return investment, even if things do not go your way.

The Price Drops to $35

First of all, I was not really concerned about having to come up with the $40,000 in order to cover my naked position. There are three reasons why I was not concerned about being wrong. The reasons are:

1. I had the money to cover my position in case I did have to buy the stocks.
2. History proves that 85 percent of all options expire without being exercised. An 85 percent chance of winning is far better than the odds offered by the stock market or Las Vegas.
3. I wanted to own the stock anyway. I just wanted to buy it at a deep discount.

So the question is, could the stock price have dropped and could I have been forced to buy the stock at $40 per share? The answer is yes. That is the agreement I sold as a naked put option. The difference is, a person with a winner's context knows that he or she can win even when they lose. That is why they are not afraid of losing. A loser can only think of losing and that is why they rarely win.

Let's say the price of the stock drops to $35 per share. A person with a loser's context would only see the loss and never the win. A loser would say, "I just lost $40,000 because I had to buy 1,000 shares of stock at $40 per share." The loser would see how much risk they had and never do the deal. Their context would slam shut or chatter on about how risky this idea was.

They would not be able to think any further because their emotions have taken over their brain. The loser would see the $40,000 exposure to be a greater risk of loss than the $5,000 in five minutes potential for gain. On top of that, if the stock had dropped to $35 a share, they would have seen an additional $5,000 loss. Their loser's context would be in full control of the person.

The reason I have spent so much time at the start of the book on the leverage of the mind is because of the examples of such transactions. When I tell people what I do, regardless if it is in building a business, investing in real estate, or investing in paper assets, it is most often the person's context that determines the validity of my content. A loser will always, and I do mean always, think that what I do is too risky, even though it is not. A poor person will always, and I do mean always, think that they cannot afford to do what I do. A hardworking person will often say, "I don't have the time to do what you do because I am too busy working." And a person who is not interested in what I do will say, "It sounds too complicated. I just don't understand. Besides, I'm not that interested in money."

Most people will never retire young and retire rich simply because they do not have a context capable of making that idea a reality. That is why I spent so much time at the start of this book on the leverage of your mind and the leverage of your plan. Context is more important than content. What I did and I continue to do in order to have retired young and retired rich is simple, if you have the appropriate context. What I do is not hard, nor is it complicated. As I said, it took me less than five minutes to make $5,000. To many people, that possibility is out of their context, which is the same as saying it is out of their reality. Many people would be willing to work thirty days just to make $5,000. They are willing to work for thirty days because their context allows them to think that $5,000 in thirty days is possible or real. But $5,000 in five minutes is not within their context, so that idea is met with, "He's lying, it's too risky, I can't do that." In other words, their context rejects the possibility. Instead their context comes up with ideas that fit their context. That is why so many people spend their lives working hard physically rather than working hard on expanding their context. They physically work hard for money rather than expand their financial context and increase the financial content they put into their brain.

A Winner's Context

The question a person with a winner's context would ask is, "How do I win if I lose?" "What happens if the price of XYZ goes below $40? How do I win then?" That is the context of a winner. They know they can win even if they lose. Most importantly, they can keep an open mind, even though what they are hearing is beyond their context. In other words, a winner can keep an open mind, even though what they are hearing frightens them or is completely new to them. As rich dad always said, "A loser's mind closes faster than a winner's mind."

Earlier in this book I wrote about the importance of an exit strategy. A winner is always looking for a winning exit strategy even if they are losing. Let's use this naked put option as an example. Before going into the transaction, I already had an exit strategy that would allow me to win, even if things did not go my way. Again, it is the context more than the content. Regardless if it is in stocks, real estate, or business, it is a winning context that allows winners to win, regardless if they are losing. In this example, it is the context of having a winning exit strategy that is part of the winner's context. A loser only sees the risk or the losses and never sees the possibility of winning, even if they do lose. A loser only takes a risk if they are guaranteed that things will go their way. That is why so many people want guaranteed pay and guaranteed benefits. They would rather have guarantees than possibilities. A winner will look for opportunities knowing they will win even if things do not go their way. It is not simply being an optimist. As rich dad said, "There are many people who think positive thoughts, but they think those thoughts inside a loser's context. Having a winning context is knowing you will win, even if you lose."

How to Win If You Lose

On the day I called Tom, I had already done my homework, which took less than a minute. This is what I knew before placing the order:

1. The market was trending down.

2. The price of XYZ had recently been battered, dropping nearly $20, to $45. The investors who held the stock had to be pretty nervous.

3. I knew XYZ was a good company, with good earnings and dividends. It was well managed and it would do well in a good economy and a bad economy.

4. It is a widely followed company, which means it has many investors who are interested in this company.

5. It is a company I wanted to own and hold on to, if the price was right.

6. I had $100,000 in an interest-bearing account if I had to buy the stock. All Tom had to do was transfer the money and he had the authority to do so.

If the stock had fallen to $35 per share, I would have been ecstatic, even if I had to pay the $40,000 to fulfill my put option agreement. Why? Again, the answer is my exit strategy.

Let's say I had to pay $40,000 for 1,000 shares of stock. What is my real price of the stock?

The answer is $35,000 because I had already received $5,000 for the option. So even though the price fell below my put option price of $40 per share, I was still paying only $35 per share, which would have been a great price for that stock anyway, and I would have owned the stock.

The next step would be to immediately *sell ten covered call options (100 shares per call option)* at $5 per share on the 1,000 shares I owned. The reason it is called *covered* is because this time I actually did own the shares I was selling the option for. I used the term *naked* in front of *put option* because I did not own the stock. Again, most people would simply say, "It's too risky to sell something you do not own." And it is, if you do not have the right context and content.

Why sell a covered call? The answer is found in the term *velocity of money,* a term which was discussed earlier. By selling a covered call, I agree to sell my stock for, let's say, $40 per share, in case the price should rapidly shoot up. A person afraid of missing out on a market move up will pay for an option. If the stock price had gone up to, let's say, $50 per share, I would then be obligated to sell my 1,000 shares for $40,000. In this case I would have gotten all my money back plus the money I collected from my options. So I would have won even if I had lost.

If the stock price did not go up, I would still have collected some money, in this case $5,000 for the call options, even if the price of stock did nothing.

The average investor would be holding a losing position in this stock and listening to their financial advisor saying, "Invest for the long term. Be patient. The stock market on average has gone up over the past forty years. So sit tight and wait." That is more of the buy, hold, and pray mentality that most investors and many investment advisors have.

By selling covered call options, I might have put another $5,000 in my pocket, again dropping the basis of my stock down to $30 a share, which would have made me even happier, since I wanted to own the stock anyway. Because of my puts and call selling, instead of paying $40,000 for stock I wanted to own, I was actually paying $30,000, even though in this example the market would have been at $35,000.

It's Like Learning to Eat with Your Other Hand

Again, if you did not fully understand this, do not worry. It is in theory simple and not hard to understand, if you spend a little time studying the subject. It is much like learning to eat with your left hand after spending your life eating with your right. It is simple in theory and simple once you learn to do it. It's learning to think and do things in different ways that is sometimes hard.

What Everyone Can Do

To me buying options to protect your assets makes sense and selling options for cash flow is fun. One of the reasons I do not worry about money is simply because I know I can go to the market and make more money in minutes than most people make in months . . . and pay less in taxes.

Can everyone do what I do? Absolutely . . . but only if they are willing to invest some time in expanding their context and increasing their financial context.

So what can everyone do? The following are some suggestions:

1. Borrow a book from the library on options trading. First learn the definitions of words and then read for greater understanding.
2. Buy a book from your local bookstore or order it online. I recommend physically reviewing the book before buying it because you may want to start with a simple book first.

3. Attend a seminar on options trading. There are many available.

4. Find a stockbroker who will teach you and guide you through the process.

5. Play CASHFLOW 101 at least twelve times so you learn the mind-set of fundamental investing. After you have mastered 101, you can move on to CASHFLOW 202, which is the game that teaches people how to use call options, put options, shorts, and straddles. Most importantly, CASHFLOW 202 teaches you to think in multiple directions depending on changing market trends. I believe the most powerful aspect of CASHFLOW 202 is that it is a physical, mental, and emotional way of learning, a multidimensional subject. In other words, the game will teach you to think in different directions. The reason most investors lose is because they have been trained at home, in school, and in the workplace to think only in one direction. A sophisticated investor needs to think about how to make money in an up-trending market, a down-trending market, and sideways-trending market. CASHFLOW 202 teaches you to think that way, have fun, and learn using play money instead of real money.

Is Investing Risky?

So is investing risky? My answer is absolutely not. In my opinion, being ignorant is risky. If you want to retire young and retire rich, learning how to insure your assets against loss is fundamental. It is the average investor who would rather not study and would rather say that investing is risky . . . that is in the greatest of risks. As I said, "Never in the history of the world have so many people bet their financial future and their financial security on the ups and downs of a stock market." That is risky only because these investors know it's risky and yet they do nothing about the risk. As my rich dad said, "The I in the I quadrant stands for investor, not ignorance." He also said, "Investing in itself is not risky. But being financially ignorant and taking advice from financially ignorant advisors is very risky. Not only is it risky, it is also expensive. It is expensive not only in terms of money, it's more expensive in terms of time. Millions of people spend their lives clinging to job security rather than seeking financial freedom because of financial ignorance. Because of financial ignorance many people cling to a small paycheck rather than seek the abundance of money that is available. Because of financial ignorance, people put money in their retirement accounts and then worry about it being there when they need it. Because of financial ignorance, millions of people spend more time at work, making the rich richer, rather than spend their time enriching the lives of those they love. No, I would not say investing is risky. But I would say that being financially ignorant is risky and it is expensive."

Chapter 18

The Leverage of a B Quadrant Business

The Richest Game in the World

The richest self-made people in the world are entrepreneurs from the B quadrant. They are far richer than movie stars, sports stars, and highly paid professionals. When I made my decision to not follow in my poor dad's footsteps after returning from Vietnam, it was my rich dad who suggested I start by learning to build businesses. He said, "The reason the richest people in the world are from the B quadrant is because it is the hardest quadrant to be successful in. But if you are successful, the floodgates of abundance open up and wealth showers down upon you. If you can build a B quadrant business, you are playing in the richest game in the world."

When you look back upon recent history, it is people like Bill Gates, Michael Dell, Thomas Edison, Henry Ford, Ted Turner, John D. Rockefeller, and others who are at the top of the famous B quadrant list. There are many more who are not as famous. All of them became financial giants because they built a giant asset. They used the biggest leverage of all, the leverage of building a business that served millions of people.

It has been said that the best investment you can make is an investment in your own business . . . and I agree. The returns on your investment defy normal investment calculations, if you know what you are doing. It is possible to take a few hundred dollars and turn it into billions of dollars. It is also possible to not only make yourself rich, you can make your friends, family, business associates, employees, and investors richer beyond their wildest dreams. That is why it is called the richest game in the world.

When I was younger, rich dad constantly reminded me that there were three basic classes of assets. They are:

1. Real estate
2. Paper assets
3. Businesses

While I did dabble in paper assets and real estate, it was building a business asset that rich dad encouraged me to focus on. He said, "Start with the hardest first and the rest will be easy." Today, I tend to agree with him.

Exit Strategy

In this book I wrote about the importance of an exit strategy. They are:

Poor	$25,000 or less per year after they retire
Middle class	$25,000 to $100,000 per year
Affluent	$100,000 to $1 million per year
Rich	$1 million or more per year
Ultra-rich	$1 million or more a month

As this book comes to an end, I ask that you begin to pay some attention to the idea of your own personal exit strategy. Also note your mind-set or your context as you ponder your choice. Is your mind saying, "I can't do that," or "That would be too much trouble," or "I'm not smart enough," or other such context-defining personal realities?

When my rich dad worked with me on my personal exit strategy, I had to go through the doubts and limitations caused by my limited context. After a few months of discussion, I knew my best chances were in the B quadrant. In my opinion, even before choosing your exit level, you may want to assess your personal strengths and weaknesses, and which quadrant offers you the best shot at retiring young and retiring rich.

Recently, someone in my investment class said, "Oprah Winfrey became the richest woman in entertainment through the S quadrant."

I then asked the individual why he thought that. His reply was, "Because she is a self-employed person. If she stopped working, her income would stop."

"How do you know that?" I asked. I then asked him what HARPO Productions was. He did not know.

My answer was, "HARPO Productions, which is Oprah spelled backward, is Oprah's company . . . her B quadrant business. That business is run by other people and invests in other ventures. She may be a star in the S quadrant, but her context is in the B quadrant."

The point of saying all this is that the quadrant you are in has little to do with what your profession is. Michael Jordan may have been an employee of the Chicago Bulls, yet he still had his own B quadrant business on the side. A medical doctor can be in the E, S, B, or I quadrant, depending upon their context. So can a janitor be in all four quadrants. I say all this because too many people have a context in only one context, rather than learning to have more than one context. Those people with tight or rigid context walls often work the hardest, the longest, and often wind up with the least. In today's Information Age, it is imperative that we all have more than one context and be in more than one quadrant. If you can do that, you will find that your possibilities of attaining a higher level exit strategy will become easier and possibly more realistic.

In other words, the reason Kim and I can exit at or above the ultra-rich level is because we operate primarily from the B quadrant. Instead of working for thousands, or millions, we work to have tens of millions, and maybe more, as our exit strategy.

Rich Dad's Guide to Investing

In book number three, *Rich Dad's Guide to Investing,* I wrote about my decision to learn to become an entrepreneur. In all my books, I wrote about the number of times I failed, and what it took to stand back up. In my opinion, it is the context of being successful, regardless of which quadrant you are in. The reason I mention book number three is because the second half of that book is about building a business, the biggest and richest asset of all. If you would like to build a B quadrant business, you may want to read or reread that book, since I will not be going into how to build that asset in this chapter.

Also, the reason I support network marketing so much is because the word *network* is the word that the very rich use. Recently I wrote a book for the network marketing industry entitled, *The Business School for People Who Like Helping People*. That short and simple book is written primarily for anyone who wants to make the switch from the E and S quadrant. The book and audiotape support anyone who wants to invest the time to change their context from the E and S quadrants to the B quadrant, the quadrant that produces the richest people in the world. The book and audiotape explain why people like John D. Rockefeller and Bill Gates built networks. The book and audiotape open with rich dad's statement "The richest people in the world look for and build networks; everyone else looks for work."

If you would like a copy of the book and audiocassette, you can go to our Web site, at richdad.com, and order it.

Last year a friend came to me and said, "I made a 35 percent return on my mutual funds in 1999." I replied with a sincere "Congratulations." When he asked me what my returns were, I said, "I really do not know." It is not that I do not know, I did not know how to tell him that my returns do not fit normal standards of measurement. While my friend's mutual fund investments had returned him 35 percent on his money, which is very good, my personal returns were in the millions of dollars without any of my original money invested. You may recall the previous chapter discussing the velocity of one's money. The reason I had trouble answering his question is because my money had already moved on and my return on investments were technically infinite. That is why I said little about my returns and congratulated him on his success in the 1999 market.

Again, my point in stating this is not to brag about my results. The point I want to make is about the differences in context. My friend is happy to receive a 35 percent return while a person who builds a business would not be. In my opinion, it is the power found in the differences in context. A person from the E and S quadrant often has a different point of view on what is possible financially. A person from the E or S quadrant is often willing to work hard forever, never really asking himself if there is another way to accomplish what they want to accomplish. So the reason I recommend the network marketing industry and its educational programs is primarily to give individuals a chance to open their context to other points of view.

By the way, my friend's 35 percent return turned into a negative return after March of 2000. He is now angry with Fed Chairman Alan Greenspan and is hoping and praying the market comes back. If it doesn't come back, he may have to go back to work.

Why Don't More People Build B Quadrant Businesses?

The question is, If building a B quadrant business is so lucrative, then why don't more people do it? A part of the answer is found in the following lesson from rich dad.

When I was making my decision to start my first real B quadrant business, I asked rich dad, "If building businesses is the richest game in the world, why don't more people play the game? Is it because of lack of money, skills, or talent?"

Rich dad's answer was short and to the point. He said, "The hardest thing about business is working with people."

"People?" I replied. "Working with people is the hardest part of business?"

Rich dad nodded and said, "Most people cannot build a business simply because they lack people skills. People work with people all day long, but just because they work together does not mean they can start a business together. And just because they start a business together does not mean that business will grow into a very large business."

"So if I learn to work with people, I can play the richest game in the world?" I asked. "If I learn to work with people I can become very rich?"

Rich dad nodded.

If You Can Work with Different People You Can Become Rich Beyond Your Wildest Dreams

Over the years, rich dad spent a substantial amount of time teaching his son and me how to work and deal with different types of people. If you read *Rich Kid Smart Kid,* you may recall that rich dad often had his son and me sit with him as he interviewed people. Learning how to hire and fire people was an interesting learning process, especially when the people rich dad was hiring and firing were as old as my mom and dad. To him, teaching his son and me how to deal with different types of people was one of the most important educational head starts he could give us. He would say, "If you can work with different people, you can become rich beyond your wildest dreams."

For those of you who read *Rich Dad's CASHFLOW Quadrant,* you may remember how important this simple diagram was to rich dad:

Rich dad had created this diagram to illustrate his point that the world of business is made up of four different types of people. The E quadrant represents employees, the S small business or self-employed, the B quadrant the business owner, and the I quadrant the investor.

The primary point of this diagram was that people from the different quadrants are at the core different. Rich dad would say, "To be successful in the B quadrant, you need to know how to communicate with and work with people from all four quadrants. It is the only quadrant that absolutely requires that ability." In other words, one of the reasons so many businesses fail is because the entrepreneur is often unable to work and get along with different types of people.

During the 1980s, I was back in Hawaii, and rich dad invited me to sit in on a board meeting where he was one of the directors. The company was in trouble and rich dad wanted me to learn from this unpleasant experience. The company was a small start up company that explored for oil in Canada. Rich dad did not form the company, but now that the company was in trouble, he had been invited to join the board and see if the company could be saved.

The company got into trouble due to a single decision by the CFO. This decision had left the company deeply in debt and about to go bankrupt. After the meeting began, rich dad asked the rest of the board, "Why was he [the CFO] allowed to make such a big financial decision without checking with the board?"

The answer from another board member was, "Because he was a senior vice president of XYZ Giant Oil Company."

Rich dad raised his voice and said, "So what? So what if he was at one time a senior vice president of a large oil company?"

"Well, we thought he knew much more than we did. So we let him act on his own," said another board member.

Rich dad rapped his fingers on the table and then said, "He may have been a senior vice president but he was still an employee for thirty years. He was an employee of a large company. He has not a clue on how to run a small start-up business with a very limited budget. I recommend you replace him, preferably with someone who owned his or her own company, and has had full financial responsibilities, even if it was not an oil company. There is a very big difference between an employee and an entrepreneur regardless of what industry they come from. There is a very big difference between running a small company and a big company. In a big company a mistake of this size doesn't hurt the company. In a small company, a mistake of this size destroys the company."

The company eventually went bankrupt. A year later, I asked rich dad why it finally went down. He said, "The company was grossly mismanaged from the board of directors on down. Although the company had hired great people and paid them a lot of money, those people never became a great team. Successful entrepreneurs create great teams. That is how they compete with big companies with more money and more people."

The Different Skills

In book number three, *Rich Dad's Guide to Investing,* I wrote about rich dad's BI Triangle, which is reproduced on the next page.

The BI Triangle is important for anyone who wants to start a B quadrant business or already owns one. It is also important for anyone who has a million-dollar idea and plans on turning it into a business. In other words,

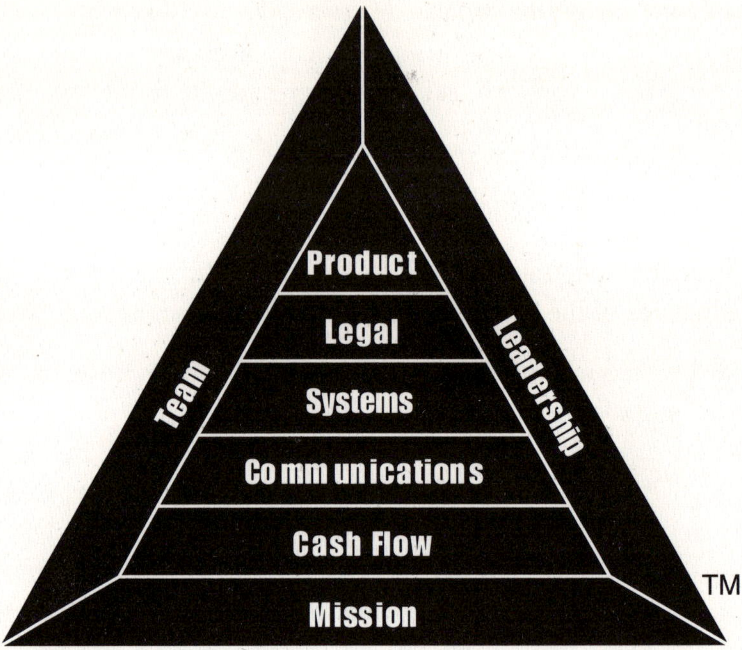

one of the reasons people have a difficult time starting a B quadrant business is because a true business needs more than one skill or specialty.

Our school system produces people with these specialized skills. It takes a true entrepreneur to pull these skills together and have them work as a team in order to build a power company.

The Big Problem

The big problem goes beyond just having all four quadrants in your business and having the different technical skills of the BI Triangle. The problem is finding a leader, an entrepreneur who can get these different people with different skills and different core values to work together as a team. That is why rich dad said, "The hardest thing about business is working with people." He also said, "Business would be easy if it wasn't for people."

In other words, an entrepreneur must first be a great leader, and all of us can work on improving our leadership skills.

What Is an Entrepreneur?

Rich dad taught his son and me to be entrepreneurs. When I asked him what an entrepreneur was he said, "An entrepreneur sees an opportunity, puts together a team, builds a business that profits from the opportunity."

I then asked him, "What if I see an opportunity and I can take advantage of it by myself?"

"Great question," said rich dad. "If you see an opportunity and you can take advantage of the opportunity by yourself, then you are a small businessman or a self-employed person." Rich dad went on to explain the difference between a tradesman and an entrepreneur. He said, "A tradesman or craftsman is someone who can produce a product or provide a service primarily by themselves. For example, an artist can paint a picture by him- or herself, or a dentist can fix your tooth by him- or herself. A true entrepreneur cannot do what he or she needs to do by her- or himself. An entrepreneur must be able to pull together smart people from different disciplines and skills and have them work together to achieve a common goal. In other words, an entrepreneur builds teams that take on products that no one individual can do on her or his own. The reason most people remain small is because they solve problems they can solve themselves."

"So an entrepreneur takes on a task that requires a team," I said. "A B quadrant person does not get paid unless their team can do what needs to be done as a team. Most employees and self-employed people get paid for what they can do as individuals. An entrepreneur does not get paid unless his or her team is successful."

Rich dad nodded and explained further by saying, "Just as a building contractor uses tradespeople such as plumbers, electricians, carpenters, and professional people such as architects and accountants to build the house, an entrepreneur brings in different tradespeople, technicians, and professional people to help him or her build a business."

"So in your mind, an entrepreneur is really a team leader, although he or she may not physically work on the team?" I asked.

"The better you can lead a team of smart qualified people, without having to work as part of the team, the better and bigger entrepreneur you can become," said rich dad. "I own several companies but I do not do any of the work inside the company. That way I can make more money and do more things without having to do the work. That is why leadership is an essential skill required to be a true entrepreneur."

"Can leadership skills be learned?" I asked.

"Yes," said rich dad. "I have noticed that all of us have some leadership skills. The problem with most people is that they devote their lives developing their professional or career skills, which is why there are more people in the E and S quadrants. Very few people devote their lives developing their leadership skills, which is the skill most required for the B quadrant. So, yes, leadership can be learned." Years later rich dad said, "Leaders rise to challenges while others look for job security."

Leadership Lessons from Vietnam

Some of you may know that I went to Vietnam for several reasons. One was because both my dads thought it was the obligation of sons to defend or fight for their country. Another reason was to learn leadership skills. Rich dad said, "Asking soldiers to overcome their fears and perform courageously while under intense pressure and risk of life is a test of anyone's leadership skills." While in Vietnam, I saw men do horrible things, but I also saw men perform feats of bravery I will never forget. One of my commanding officers said, "Inside every soldier is a hero. It is the leader's job to bring out that hero that lives in each of us." Today, I use many of the leadership skills I learned in combat in my business. In combat we did not give young men orders and expect them to follow orders blindly. In combat we learned to ask young men to be heroes, and that skill works in business as well as in combat.

Develop Your Own Leadership Skills

You don't have to go to war to develop your own leadership skills. All you have to do is take on challenges that others run away from. Most of us have heard the saying "Never volunteer for anything." To me, that is the creed of a person who is going to go backward in life. Rich dad often said, "Leaders take on challenges that others are afraid of." He also said, "The size of the leader is measured by the size of the task they undertake." Dwight Eisenhower is famous because he took on the D-Day invasion and the European campaign during World War II. John Kennedy took on the task of putting a man on the moon. Leaders seek challenges that others back away from. Too many people never develop their leadership skills simply because they make it a habit to back away from the challenges placed in front of them. They make it a habit of *never volunteering*.

Every business, every church, every charity, every community needs more leaders. Each organization gives you the opportunity to step forward and be accountable. Each opportunity gives you an opportunity to learn those priceless leadership skills required in the world of entrepreneurship.

Many people are not qualified to participate in the richest game of all, the game of building businesses, simply because they fail to gain the skills of leadership.

If you step forward to be responsible for your church's potluck dinner, you are stepping forward to gain more leadership skills. Even if no one volunteers with you, you will learn something important. You will learn how to reach out and speak to the hero that rests inside each and every one of us. If you learn to do that, the next leadership task you undertake will be easier, more successful, and you will learn more about leadership. If you do not develop your leadership skills, the chances of you building a business and participating in the richest game in the world may never be developed. I have met so many smart people with great business ideas, but they simply lack leadership skills, the skill required to build a business team and have that team turn their ideas into millions, maybe billions of dollars. In the richest game in the world, leadership is the key, because it takes a leader to turn individuals into a team.

Suggested Reading

There are several books I have read that can assist in a person's entrepreneurial development. They are:

1. *The Monk and the Riddle* by Randy Komisar (Harvard Business School Press). This book was given to me by my friend Tom, my stockbroker. Tom is a great options trader but he is better at picking small start-up companies and investing in them as they grow bigger and bigger. He gave me this book at a time when I was ready to sell one of my companies and move on. After reading the book, I stayed with the company and began to build it rather than sell it. It is a great book about one of life's great riddles.
2. *First, Break All the Rules* by Marcus Buckingham and Curt Coffman

(Simon and Schuster). An excellent book for anyone who manages or leads people. This book is based on in-depth interviews by the Gallup Organization of over 80,000 managers in over 400 companies.

In the Industrial Age, managing people was like herding sheep. Today, in the Information Age, managing people is like herding cats. That means each person today needs to be treated as an individual rather than as part of a group. This book delivers great insights into how to deal with different types of people going in different directions and turn them into a team.

3. *Emotional Branding* by Daryl Travis (Prima Publishing). What is a brand worth? I recently read that Coca-Cola's plant, equipment, and other capital assets were worth approximately $8 billion, while the brand is worth $80 billion.

One of the less known benefits of investing the time to build a business is the benefit of also building a brand. In this world of increasing global competition, the better you are at building a business as well as building a brand, the wealthier you become.

Imagine for a moment the power IBM has over XYZ Computers. XYZ might have a better computer but IBM has a better brand. We at richdad.com realize that our value goes far beyond our books, games, and other products. We are very conscious of building a worldwide brand as well as building a business.

4. *Protecting Your #1 Asset* by Michael Lechter (Warner Books). This book is one of the Rich Dad's Advisors series of books. Michael Lechter is my attorney. He is also the husband of my business partner and co-author, Sharon Lechter. Michael is one of the top attorneys in intellectual property such as brands, trademarks, and patents. As you can tell from Coca-Cola's example, a brand or an idea can be worth billions of dollars.

For those of you who have a million-dollar idea for a business or product in your head, this book is a must-read. Your number one asset in the Information Age is your ideas. Before divulging your ideas, it is important that you read this book. Michael's fees are high, so this book is a bargain in priceless information.

5. *SalesDogs* by Blair Singer (Warner Books). This book is also one of the Rich Dad's Advisors series of books. Blair Singer has been one of my best friends for over twenty years. Blair and I started out together as salesmen pounding the streets of Hawaii, looking for business.

One of the most important educational processes I went through was first to learn to sell and second learning to manage a team of over 350 salespeople, spread across America and Canada. It was a tough job but I learned a lot from the process. I started out a horrible salesperson and a horrible sales manager. The process of learning how to be a good salesperson and a good sales manager was priceless although at times painful.

Blair's book is essential for anyone who wants to improve their personal sales skills, a skill essential for anyone who works with people and needs to lead people. This book is also important for sales managers, because learning how to manage a team of salespeople is a task unto itself. If management today is like managing cats, managing a sales team is like managing a team of dogs, dogs with different barks and different habits. That is why this book is entitled *SalesDogs* because a room full of salespeople is really like a kennel, more than an office. This book offers very important management and business insights, swirled around a humorous look at the different dogs that make up a sales team.

SalesDogs is an important book for anyone who wants to improve their number one business skill, which is the skill of being able to sell an idea to other people. In my life, I have met many smart people who struggled financially simply because they could not sell and they could not manage other people.

A Tip from the Marine Corps

As a new Marine lieutenant in Vietnam, I had a commanding officer put up this simple diagram:

Mission

Team

Individual

He said, "The highest priority is the mission. The individual is last."

After returning from Vietnam, I often saw more people with a different ranking of priorities. In business and in the civilian world I often see people with their list in this ranking of priority:

INDIVIDUAL

TEAM

MISSION

In other words, they come first, their group second, and the overall mission of the business or the organization last, if at all.

In Vietnam, my commanding officer explained that as junior officers, our job was to protect the mission and the team from the betrayals of individuals. In other words, we were trained to *take out,* in one way or another, anyone from within our ranks who thought of himself first and, in doing so, jeopardized the team and the mission. Learning and practicing that in combat has greatly affected my way of leading in business.

For those of you who saw Steven Spielberg's *Saving Private Ryan,* in my opinion the most realistic movie on war I have seen, there is a great lesson in the movie. In the movie, Tom Hanks, a schoolteacher who became an Army lieutenant, could not shoot a German prisoner. To me, that was the pivot point of the movie . . . also one of its great lessons. Because Tom Hanks could not do his job, which in this case was to take out an individual, the German prisoner, he put himself, his team, and the mission of the team in grave jeopardy. In the end, not only were many of his men killed because of his inability to shoot a German prisoner, the mission almost fails, and Tom Hanks is ultimately killed by the man he would not kill.

It is fortunate that most people will never have to face the horrors of war and some of the tough heartbreaking decisions that are often required to be made. Nonetheless, we all face such tough decisions in our personal lives and in our business lives. Some examples are:

1. The other night at a party at a friend's home one of the guests got very drunk. When he stood to leave, the host asked him for his car keys and offered to call a cab. The guest became very upset, denying that he was too drunk to drive. An unpleasant scene erupted and the host persisted, finally

wrestling the guest to the ground and forcibly taking his keys. A cab was called and the guest was sent away safe, but very upset. The guest and the host have not talked since. To make matters worse, some of the other guests think the host overreacted and they too have decided not to talk to the host. Personally I think the host was very brave and did the best thing at that time. Could the host have handled it differently? Sure. But he did what he thought was best at that moment. That is what leaders do, even if what they do is not the best thing to do.

2. Years ago, my rich dad found out that one of his top managers was having an affair with one of the secretaries in his company. He immediately called the man in and asked him to leave. The secretary was also asked to leave. When I asked him why, he simply said, "Both are married with children. Anyone who would cheat on their spouse and their children is someone who will cheat on anyone." I am not saying rich dad did the right thing, but again, he did what he thought was best at the moment. Although both employees were very important to him, he felt that their actions were not in keeping with the values he wanted for his company. He said, "When I take a stand, everyone else knows where they stand."

Both stories are examples of leadership. It has been said that "leaders do the right things and managers do things right." Rich dad agreed with that statement. He said, "Leadership is not a popularity contest. Leaders inspire others to be leaders."

A Final Lesson from Vietnam

At the end of his talk to his junior officers, my commanding officer added the following words to his talk and his diagram:

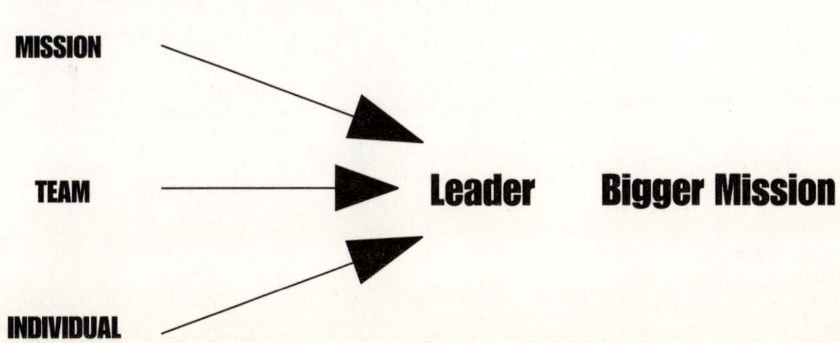

The CO then said, "A leader is responsible to the mission, the team, and the individuals. But as you can see, a good leader must also be a good follower . . . realizing that his team's mission is important because it is a part of a bigger mission and answering to a higher calling."

Rich dad said, "A slingshot is just a slingshot. When David stepped forward to take on Goliath, the greatest forces in the world stepped forward with him." He also said, "Always remember that the richest game in the world is just a game with a mission and a higher calling."

So in closing, I leave you with this thought. Each and every day, new Goliaths are born and new Goliaths step forward. What the world needs are more and more new Davids, armed with just a slingshot, but backed by the most powerful forces in the world. Regardless if you choose to play the richest game in the world or not, just know that you too can access the power that powered David's slingshot. All you have to know is who your Goliath is and then find the courage to step forward bravely. The moment you do that, you begin playing the richest game in the world, a game where the rewards are far more important than money. When you step forward you tap into the power that was behind David's slingshot. When you find that power, your life will never be the same. As they said in *Star Wars,* the modern version of David and Goliath, "May the force be with you." This invisible force is the greatest of all leverage and it is a leverage that is available to all of us. All you have to do is step forward and take on something bigger than yourself.

The conclusion of this book is about the rewards from building or acquiring assets that work hard so you do not have to.

Chapter 19

Hot Tips

Things That Most People Can Do to Get Rich Quickly and Stay Rich Forever

The process of retiring young and retiring rich is a mental and emotional process, more than a physical process. If you are prepared mentally and emotionally, what you physically have to do is very little. The following are some additional mental and emotional processes you may want to incorporate into your life. If you do these suggested simple processes regularly and they become a part of your life, I trust that you will find retiring young and retiring rich will become more of a possibility for you.

Why Do You Need a Paycheck?

When I was in high school, rich dad often had me sit next to him when people came in to apply for a job. During one of these interviews, a man a few years older than rich dad came in to apply for a management position in one of rich dad's companies. This applicant was about forty-five years old, was well educated, had a very impressive résumé, a great employment record, was well dressed, and seemed confident and competent. As the interview progressed, this gentleman continually reminded rich dad that he had gone to a great state college and had received his MBA from a prestigious university on the East Coast, with honors.

"I'm interested in hiring you," said rich dad, after interviewing him for about an hour, "but why do you want such a high salary?"

Again, the applicant referred back to his impressive education and his work record, saying, "I'm well educated, I have the right job experience, which makes me highly qualified for the job and deserving of the salary."

"I don't disagree," said rich dad. "But let me ask you this. If you're so well educated and so experienced, why do you need a job? If you're so smart, why do you need a paycheck?"

The applicant was taken aback by that question. He stammered a little and then said, "Well everyone needs a job. We all need a paycheck."

The room became very quiet as rich dad let his answer echo in the room. It was obvious that the applicant came from a different reality, a different context, a different mind-set from rich dad. He was becoming argumentative and beginning to defend his reality, instead of trying to understand rich dad's reality. Looking up at the applicant, rich dad quietly said, "I don't. If this business folded, I still would never need a paycheck." He then turned to his son and me and said, "These boys don't. They work for me for free. That is why they're going to be far richer than you someday, even if they don't go to as good a school as you did or receive the academic honors you have. I don't want these boys to ever want or need a paycheck." With that, rich dad picked up the applicant's résumé, placed it on top of a pile of other résumés, and said, "I'll call you if I'm interested in hiring you." The interview was over.

Tips on How to Get Rich Quickly

In *Rich Dad Poor Dad,* I wrote about how rich dad took my 10 cents an hour job away and offered me his reality, the reality that I could become richer faster if I worked for free. People often say, "You didn't really work for free," or "My house is an asset." Little do they know that they may have read the book, yet they continue to see the world from their same reality, context, or mind-set.

When rich dad asked that applicant, "If you're so well educated and so experienced, why do you need a job? If you're so smart, why do you need a paycheck?" he was asking the applicant to expand his reality. But instead of doing his best to expand his reality, the applicant argued and defended his reality, closed his mind, and for all practical purposes ended his chances of being employed by rich dad.

A World Without Paychecks

I created the game of CASHFLOW to teach people how to live in a world without paychecks. People who play the game repeatedly often find the possibility of such a world to be far more exciting than working hard all their life for a paycheck. If you want to retire as young and as rich as possible, you will need to consider a world without a paycheck. If in your reality, context, or mind-set, you need a paycheck, the chances of you retiring young and retiring rich are slim. Rich dad often said, "People who need a paycheck are slaves to money. If you want to be set free, you must never need a paycheck or a job." So if you are serious about retiring young and rich, you too will need to change your reality to the possibility of a world without a steady paycheck or a job. When I state this context to most people, you can almost feel their blood pressure rise, their chest and stomach tighten, and hear their subconscious mind take over their conscious thought. The fear of not having a steady paycheck to cover one's financial survival is a fear most of us know well. If you have difficulty seeing yourself in a world of not needing a paycheck or a steady job, then your first step is to begin asking yourself, "How can I get rich without a paycheck or steady job?" The moment you begin asking yourself that question, you open your mind and begin your journey into another reality.

When rich dad asked the person applying for the job, "If you're so well educated and so experienced, why do you need a job? If you're so smart, why do you need a paycheck?" he was asking him to stretch his reality and see another reality. Instead, the applicant argued and defended his reality, thinking his reality was the only reality. I have seen rich dad ask that question of other applicants. It was his way of actually trying to help the applicant. It was his way of trying to teach the applicant a very important and basic financial lesson, the lesson that money will not make you rich . . . that a high-paying job alone will not solve a person's financial needs. When rich dad asked anyone that question, he was trying to have that person understand that academic success does not necessarily equate to financial success. As rich dad often said, "A high academic IQ does not necessarily mean you have a high financial IQ." During the interview with the person who was so proud of his academic achievements, rich dad was really doing his best to find out if this person was interested in learning how to increase his financial IQ. As I said, I have seen rich dad ask that same question of other applicants. Those that listened to his reality and studied with rich dad as they worked for him became very wealthy, retired early, and went on to live lives of financial freedom . . . even though they were not paid the high salaries they initially wanted.

The point is this: If you want to retire young and retire rich, financial IQ is more important than academic IQ. The following are really tips on how to increase your financial IQ so you can begin to live in a world without needing a paycheck. The sooner you can see a world without paychecks, the better chance you have of becoming rich quicker.

HOT TIP #1

So hot tip number one is begin to see yourself in a world or reality where you will never ever need a paycheck or job again. It does not mean you will never work again, it simply means that you will stop being so financially needy or even desperate, selling your precious life for a few dollars, living in fear of losing your paycheck or being destitute.

Once you can entertain a world of never needing a paycheck again, you can begin to see the other world . . . the world without jobs or paychecks.

Bill Gates Is Low Paid

A number of years ago, I saw a headline that read, "Bill Gates is Not the Highest Paid Man in the World." The article went on to say that there are many executives in the world of business who are paid much more than Bill Gates, yet Gates was the richest man in the world. The article stated that at that time, Gates was only paid about $500,000 a year but his asset base was in the billions and growing.

HOT TIP #2

If you let go of the idea of needing a steady paycheck from earned income, the next question to ask yourself is what kind of income you want. For example, earlier in this book I stated that there were three basic kinds of income. They are:

1. Earned—50 percent money.
2. Portfolio—20 percent money.
3. Passive—0 percent money.

These are the three main categories, yet there are many other types of income. Most people have spent their lives studying and working hard for earned income, which is why so few people can retire young or retire rich. If you are serious about retiring young, begin studying the different types of income, which will allow you to become rich without working forever. Some of the other types of income are:

4. Residual income, which is income from a business, such as a network marketing business or a franchise business you own but someone else runs.
5. Dividend income, which can be income from stocks.
6. Interest income, which is income from savings or bonds.
7. Royalty income, which can be income from songs or books you have written, and trademarks and inventions (whether or not patentable) that you have created.
8. Financial instrument income, such as income from trust deeds from real estate.

So the hot tip is, once you get used to the idea of not having income from a job or your labor, then you can begin researching different types of income that come from different types of assets. Rich dad had Mike and me study and research the different types of income and then decide which type we wanted to study further.

You can go to a library or ask your accountant about the different types of income there are . . . income that is derived from things other than your labor. The moment you begin to study and find the different kinds of income that interest you, they begin to grow to become a part of your new and expanding reality.

The point is, don't do too much. Just let other types of income and assets come into your reality. The more the idea of different types of income settles in, the more you think about such income, without the pressure of having to do anything, the more the idea takes root in your brain and begins to grow. Most people think they must do something immediately, but that is not my experience. I simply let the idea of investing in real estate for passive income rattle around in my brain years before I bought my first property. One day I woke up and I knew it was time to begin taking classes and begin investing. It was relatively effortless . . . but only after I let the idea become a part of my new reality.

When you look at a financial statement, it is understandable why my poor dad insisted on job security.

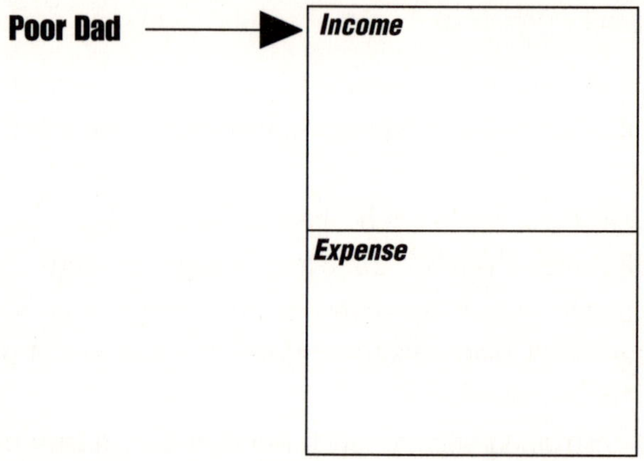

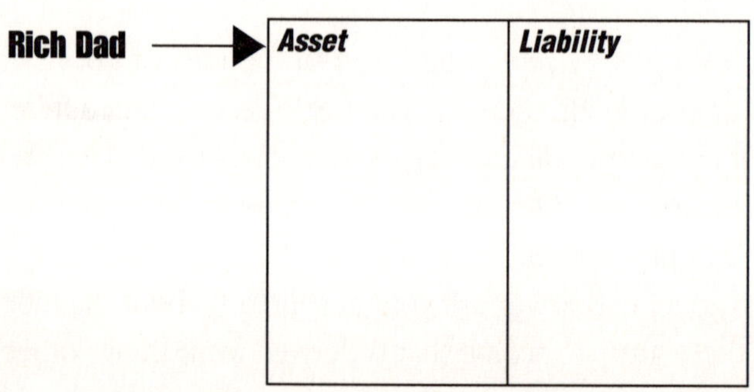

Since my poor dad had no assets, and always said "Investing is risky," he naturally clung desperately to his job. After all, that is all he had and the only income he knew of was earned income.

My rich dad had his son and me focus our attention on acquiring assets and developing our financial IQ via which to acquire those assets. Because we had learned the importance of financial IQ, his son and I worked diligently ever increasing our skills to acquire those assets. Although we were nervous at the start, today, acquiring assets is fun, easy, and exciting. When I say it is easy to get rich quickly and stay rich forever, it is true, if you give yourself the time to allow that reality to grow into your reality.

While on a trip through Australia, a young baggage handler took my bags at the airport and said, "I love your books."

I thanked him for telling me and asked him what he had learned.

"Well, the first thing I learned is that this job will never make me rich. So I work a job at nights and I invest the money from my second job into real estate."

"That's great," I replied. "How have you done so far?"

"I've bought six properties in a year and a half."

"Great," I said. "I'm proud of you. Have you made any money?"

"No, not yet," the handsome young man said. "But I have learned something very important."

"What is that?" I asked.

"It gets easier. Once I got over my initial doubt, fear, and lack of money, I find it's getting easier to be an investor. The more deals I look at and the more investments I buy, the easier investing becomes. My financial IQ would never have gone up if I had let my doubt and fear keep me paralyzed. Instead of feeling fear today, I feel excitement, even though I still have not made much money . . . in fact I lost money on two of my six investments. As you say in your books, mistakes are learning experiences. They are priceless if you learn from them. So now I can see myself being a full-time property investor someday soon. In a few years, I will never need a job or a paycheck ever again."

"Do you have a goal, a specific date you will be out of the rat race and financially free?" I asked.

"Definitely," said the young man with a smile. "I have three other friends about the same age. We all are doing this together. We don't waste our time like other guys our age do. We study together, go to seminars together, and we help each other invest. We don't plan on following in our parents' footsteps. We don't want to make the same mistakes they did, working for forty-five years, afraid of losing our jobs, hoping for a pay raise, and waiting till sixty-five to retire. My parents worked so hard climbing the corporate ladder they had no time for the kids or for the things they really loved. They're now getting ready to retire but they're old. I don't want to be like them. I don't want to be old when I stop working. All four of us are under twenty-four and we all have goals of being financially free by the age of thirty."

"Congratulations," I said and shook his hand. As he finished processing my bags for the flight, I thanked him for reading my book and making me feel like a proud dad.

As I left the counter the young man smiled and shouted, "The biggest thing is that it's getting easier," said the young man. "The more I focus on building my assets, the easier it's getting."

I waved goodbye and rushed for my flight.

Check Our Web Site for New Ideas

In the coming years, we at richdad.com will be adding more and more information to our Web site. Our Web site is dedicated to helping anyone gain the ideas, education, and experience through which to retire young and retire rich. Check the Web site on a regular basis and make retiring young and rich your reality.

In my reality, the better you are at acquiring assets, the easier it becomes to become richer faster and faster. If you keep your humility, even though rich, being grateful rather than arrogant about your wealth, I believe you have a better chance of keeping that money forever.

So continue to check our Web site for the latest information and ideas. In the near future, we will have our CASHFLOW 101 and 202 games online on the World Wide Web so you can have fun playing and learning from people just like you . . . people who want to retire young and retire rich.

Specifically from Sharon

Most of the time, I intertwine my financial philosophies with Robert's when we co-author the Rich Dad books. I remain relatively invisible. But every once in a while I feel so strongly about an issue that we decide to highlight it for you. This is one of those times!

Most of my fellow accountants, financial planners, and bankers just don't get it! The path to financial freedom is simply to:

BUY ASSETS

"Buy assets that generate cash flow—NOW, not sometime in the future!"

Remember how rich dad defines assets: "Assets put money in your pocket, liabilities take money from your pocket." It is just that simple. The more assets you can buy, the more your money will be working for you.

Many accountants, financial planners, and bankers are stuck on net worth calculations. They just don't understand cash flow. They have been trained that you put money away until you need it sometime in the future—a saver's mentality. If they would work with their clients on generating cash flow from assets NOW, their clients would be much better off financially, now and in the future.

The problem is that they calculate your net worth, including your home, your car, your golf clubs, and all your other personal property, as assets. We call these doodads. This is NOT how an investor looks at net worth. Review your financial statement and remove all entries in your asset column that do not generate cash flow for you currently.

When you have assets that generate enough monthly cash flow to cover your monthly expenses, you are financially free!

BUY ASSETS, not liabilities!

—Sharon Lechter

HOT TIP #3

Hot tip #3 may sound strange, so please read carefully. Hot tip #3 is to tell lies about your future.

The young baggage handler could see his future and he was excited about it. Not everyone can see such a bright future, which is why hot tip #3 might sound strange, yet it is an important part of the process in retiring young and retiring rich.

A few months ago, I was teaching an investment course, and several of the participants could not stop saying such things as:

1. "I can't do that."
2. "I'll never be rich."
3. "I'm not a good investor."
4. "I'm not smart enough."
5. "Investing is risky."
6. "I'll never get the money to do what I want."

There was a very successful psychotherapist in the class who raised her hand to help out. She said, "Anything said about the future is a lie."

"The future is a lie?" I asked. "Why do you say that?"

"First of all," she said, "I want to be clear that I am not encouraging anyone to lie for the purpose of deception. Is that clear?"

I nodded my head. "I understand, but my question is, Why do you say that the future is a lie?"

"Good question," she said. "I'm glad to hear that you keep an open mind. What I mean by the future is a lie is that anything said about the future is not yet a fact, so anything you say about anything in the future is technically a lie."

"So how is that useful for these participants who cannot seem to shake some of their negative perceptions about themselves or their abilities?"

"When the person who said, 'I'll never be rich,' made that statement he was making a statement about something that was supposedly true in the future . . . in this case the idea that he'll never be rich," said the therapist. "Well that statement is technically a lie. I'm not calling the individual a liar, I am just saying that the statement is a lie, since the future has not yet happened."

"So what does that mean?" I asked.

"It means exactly what you have been trying to get this class to realize. They need to understand that what they say and what they think has the power to become real and become their reality. So many people tell lies about their future and those lies become their future."

"You mean when someone says, 'I'll never be rich,' they are telling a lie because they are referring to an event projected sometime into the future. Is that what you mean?"

"Exactly," said the therapist. "And the problem is, a lie becomes true."

"So when someone says, 'Investing is risky,' they are in some ways telling a lie if they are speaking about the future?"

"Yes . . . and then a lie becomes truth, if they do not change the lie. Always remember that anything in reference to the future is technically a lie simply because nothing in the future is yet a fact or truth."

"So how is this bit of information useful?" I asked again.

"Well, as a therapist, I have found that most unsuccessful, unhappy, unfulfilled people tell the most horrible lies about themselves. They say what you have been trying to stop people from saying. They say, 'I'll never be rich.' 'I could never do that.' 'That will never work.' All lies . . . but lies that have the power to become truths."

"And if they don't say those lies, they spend time with other people that will tell them those same lies," I added.

"That is true," said the therapist. "Birds of a feather do spend time together."

"And so do liars," I said.

The therapist chuckled and nodded in agreement.

"So I ask you once more, how is this bit of enlightened information useful?" I asked.

"Well, since anything you say about the future is technically a lie, why not tell lies about the kind of future you want rather than the kind of future you do not want?" replied the therapist.

I thought about what she had said in silence, as did the rest of the class. Finally I said, "Lie about the future on purpose?"

"Sure, we all do it, some of us do it unconsciously or automatically. Let me ask you this: When it came to money, did your rich dad speak of the future positively?"

"Yes," I said.

"And did much of what he said come true?" she asked.

Again I said, "Yes."

"And when it came to money and the future, did your poor dad speak negatively?"

"Yes," I said.

"And did what he said come true?"

I nodded my head.

"So both sets of lies came true," said the therapist.

I just nodded, realizing that both men were lying about their future and yet their lies came true. "So are you saying that I should lie about the future I want rather than the future I don't want?"

"Yes," she said. "That is exactly what I am saying. In fact I'll bet you do it already. I'll bet that when you were down and out you kept telling your wife and close friends about how good the future was going to be and how much money you were going to make. You kept saying that even though you had not a penny to your name."

Chuckling I said, "Yes I did. But I only told my lies to friends who loved and supported me. I never told my positive lies about my future to people who would put down my lies about the future."

"Very wise of you," said the therapist. "So what lies did you say to your wife during your darkest of financial hours?"

"You want me to tell the class?" I asked, becoming somewhat embarrassed.

"Yes. Tell the class what you really said when times were at their worst."

I thought for a while and remembered a moment when Kim and I were at our lowest point financially. Slowly I said to the class, "I remember holding Kim tightly and saying, 'Someday all of this will be behind us. Someday we'll be rich beyond our wildest dreams. Today our problem is not enough money, but someday soon, our problem will be too much money.'"

"And has that come true?" asked the therapist.

"Yes it has," I replied. "More than we could have dreamed. I'm kind of embarrassed to say that today we have a big problem of too much money. I realize how poor a background I came from because today, Kim and I have a hard time trying to think of things we can buy. Much of our money goes to charity, but there is still plenty left and we need to stretch our reality on what to buy since we can afford almost anything we can think of. Trying to find things to buy beyond what we can afford is a very interesting process."

"Why do you think your lies came true?" she asked.

20 Percent of All People Are Hard-core Liars

"Because both dads insisted that I never make a promise I could not keep. And if I could not keep the promise, I should be the first one to inform the person I broke the promise with that the agreement could not be kept. Both dads stressed that we are only as good as our word and both men were good to their word."

"Very good," said the therapist. "You see 80 percent of all people are basically honest. About 20 percent are hard-core liars and no matter what they do, they have to lie. So even if they lie positively about their financial future, it becomes a negative lie anyway, since hard-core liars have no integrity in their soul. But I have found that most people are honest, so even when they lie, their lies come true." The therapist paused for a moment and then said, "Enough talking about lying. Let's start learning how to lie positively about our futures. And remember, the purpose of this exercise is not to deceive but to help each of us move to a new and better reality about ourselves."

I agreed and the therapist had the class get into pairs. "Now," she said, "I want you to tell your partner the biggest and best lie about how rich you will be in the future. Tell them about the millions of dollars you receive each month from your real estate investments, your revenue from your oil company, and how big the mansion you live in is."

Some people had a difficult time telling exaggerated lies about their future financial success. Others were quite well rehearsed at the process. Nonetheless, in a matter of minutes, the energy in the room was up 100 percent and the noise was deafening. There were outbreaks of hysterical laughter as people told gigantic and exaggerated fibs about their future. Most people really loved being granted permission to tell exaggerated stories about their future financial success. Many reported that their lives and their futures changed at that moment.

So the hot tip #3 is, whenever you find yourself feeling down and telling negative lies about yourself and your financial future, find a trusted friend and ask them if you can tell them a big fat lie about how financially successful you will be in the near future. I think you will find it great therapy and, who knows, the lie you tell about your financial future might someday come true.

If you are brave enough, do not wait till you feel down before you begin lying positively. As soon as possible, find a trusted friend or loved one and ask them permission to allow you to tell them your great big lies about how fantastic your financial future will someday be. As I said, it can be great fun and the lie you tell today might come true tomorrow.

The Home Run King

The point is that your future is yet to be made. You may as well make it up today and make it up the way you want it to be, rather than what you're afraid it might not be. Too many people go to the *worst-case scenario,* rather than the *best-case scenario,* when they think about changing their financial future. Worst or best, the future scenario is a lie anyway, at least according to the therapist. The great Babe Ruth had a habit of taking his bat and pointing it to the home run fence. It was his way of saying, "I'm going for the wall." He did this continually although he struck out more times than most people. Although he struck out the most, he never stopped pointing his bat at the far wall and today he is known as the home run king, not the strikeout king.

The Boogeyman

When we were kids, many of us imagined a boogeyman hiding under our bed or in our closet. Some of us stayed up shaking and worrying about this character that existed only in our minds, late at night, when all the lights were out. After we grow up, many of us replace the boogeyman with the bill collector or some horrible financial disaster that has not yet happened. Regardless if it is the boogeyman or the bill collector, the results are the same . . . we lie awake at night worrying about things we really should not worry about. We also depress our future telling lies to ourselves about some financial disaster or calamity that has not occurred and may never occur.

So instead of waking up in the morning and acting like Babe Ruth pointing our home run bat to the fence, we trundle off to a job, selling our precious lives for a few dollars, living with a false sense of financial security from some imaginary boogeyman, saying, "What if this happens?" "What if that happens?" "What happens if . . . ?" The person may be older but the boogeyman still exists and he continues to rob people of the wonderful possibilities of life. That is why this process of lying about your future can be a valuable one for honest people who want to move forward boldly, pointing their baseball bat to the far, far fence.

Rich dad said, "We all have good luck and bad luck. Unsuccessful people live lives doing nothing, avoiding bad luck and also good luck. It's hard to have any kind of luck if you're doing nothing, paralyzed by fear. A successful person is one who takes action and takes the good with the bad, knowing that he or she can turn bad luck into good luck."

One day a reporter was asking me how I overcame my fear of failure and some tips on the secret to my success. I thought for a moment and said, "My rich dad taught me to turn bad luck into good luck." So for good luck, start with baby steps, and go for the life you dream of rather than live in fear of some imaginary nightmare. Don't let the boogeyman steal your dreams. Be like Babe Ruth . . . tell big lies about your future and boldly swing for the fence.

An important note: Please remember that this tip is not a license to lie with the intent to deceive or cover up the truth. I would never endorse such a practice. The above recommendation is for honest people only, *not* habitual liars. If you are a habitual liar, please seek professional help and begin learning to tell the truth rather than lying.

12 More Tips for You

Summary of Previous Tips from This Book with a Few Additional Tips Thrown In

In the introduction, I promised that I would provide a list of things that anyone could do to improve their chance of retiring young and retiring rich. Most of them have already been discussed, but a simple, condensed review list may be helpful.

These are things I do on a regular basis. These are things that have assisted me greatly in retiring young and retiring rich. I trust they can also be of use to you. Always remember that the process of retiring young and retiring rich is primarily a mental and emotional process . . . more than a physical process. Once you begin that journey in your mind and in your heart, the rest of you should soon follow.

*1. **Decide.*** Every day I get up and I choose who and what I want to be. I ask myself, Do I want to live today as a person with a poor context, a middle-class context, or a rich context?

Remember that a person with a poor context will say something like, "I'll never be rich." A person with a middle-class context might say, "Job security is important." A person with a rich context might say, "I need to increase my financial IQ so I can work less and make more money."

2. Find a friend or loved one who wants to go on the journey with you. I know that I would not have made it without my wife, Kim, and my friends like Larry Clark. Be sure to have friends who demand more of you rather than tell you why you cannot do what you want to do.

Choosing the right friends or life partners is very important to a successful life. If you have friends or family who are not committed to improving their financial IQ, life can be a long financial struggle, regardless of how much money you earn.

3. Seek competent advice and begin building your own team of financial and legal advisors. Always remember what rich dad said, "Your most expensive advice is the free advice you receive from your financially struggling friends and relatives." Rich dad later expanded his statement to include financial advisors who did not practice what they preached or did not buy the investment products they sold you. Again, choosing the right people is a very important skill. People can be either assets or liabilities.

One day rich dad said to me, "If your car is broken, you take it to a trained mechanic to fix. The moment you pick up the car, you know whether or not the mechanic was a good mechanic or not. The problem with these so-called professional financial advisors is that you will not know if they gave you good advice or bad advice until years later. What happens if you begin taking a financial advisor's advice at twenty-five and at age sixty-five you find out your financial advisor was giving you bad advice? You can't take your ruined financial life back to the financial advisor like you can take your broken car back to the mechanic. I trust auto mechanics and used car salesmen more than I do most financial advisors simply because I can see the results of their work faster. The reason most people end up poor or middle-class is because they spend more time selecting a used car than they spend time looking for good financial advice."

The point is, be very careful about the advice you place in your head. Take your time to find good financial advisors. They are out there and the fee you may pay them could be the best investment you make.

4. ***Set a retirement date. Sit down with your loved ones, your advisors, and set a date for your early retirement.*** This is like Babe Ruth pointing his bat at the far wall. If you will actually do this process and discuss an actual date with these people, your present context will begin to argue with your future context. It is a great and fun process to go through. You will definitely hear many different realities and different contexts.

Hold quarterly meetings with this group and continue to discuss your early retirement date.

5. ***Write down a plan on a piece of paper once you have set the date for your early retirement.*** Put that plan on your refrigerator so you have to look at it every day. Update the plan as you progress and learn more and more.

When Kim, Larry, and I spent that week up on Whistler Mountain, frozen in the snow, the plan we came up with changed the direction of our lives. That is the power of a plan. The point is, just because you may be poor today does not mean you have to be poor tomorrow. Becoming rich and staying rich requires a plan and the determination to follow it, one day at a time. Kim and I followed our plan one day at a time for nearly ten years. As I said, today our problem is that we have too much money and we struggle to find ways of spending it wisely. It may be a struggle but it's the kind of struggle I like and want you to have also.

6. ***Plan your early retirement party.*** Be excessive and be lavish. Once you can retire early, money will no longer be a problem. Even if you do not achieve your goal, you will have great fun going through this process. And who knows, you might even have to throw that *early* retirement party *early*.

7. ***Look at a deal a day. Remember it costs you nothing to go shopping.*** The point is to do something every day to improve your financial intelligence for at least ten minutes a day. It may be something as simple as read-

ing one article from the money or business section of your newspaper . . . even if you are not interested in it. It will begin to improve your vocabulary. Listen to financial or business information tapes or CDs while you drive or work out at the gym. Attend a financial seminar at least once a year. If you do not want to pay for a seminar, just look in the financial section of your local newspaper and you will find many free investment seminars. Even if you do not learn anything, you are bound to meet other people just like you.

8. Remember that all markets follow three main trends. They are up, down, and sideways. Some markets go up, down, and sideways over years and sometimes markets can trend up, down, and sideways in less than a minute. That is why when someone advises you to "Invest for the long term" ask them what they mean. Ask them for a more detailed explanation. Most financial advisors are simply parroting what they have been taught by their sales manager so they may have difficulty explaining what they say.

If you want to get rich quickly, one of the best ways to get rich is at the point where a trend changes. There is a lot of truth to that old saying "Being at the right place at the right time." If you will look at deals daily, you will better sense changes and improve your chances of being at the right place at the right time. For example, if you had entered the stock market in 1991 and invested a lot of money in technology stocks you would be rich today. But when the trend changed down, in March of 2000, if you did not change your strategy, you would have lost all that you had gained. If you had changed strategy in March of 2000, you would have made money faster on the way down . . . only increasing your wealth instead of losing it. That is why, if you want to get rich quickly and stay rich forever, you must be aware of trends and have three different strategies for three different trends. I have met many people who made money on one trend and went bankrupt when the trend changed.

Buy High, Sell Low

The June 2001 issue of *Forbes* magazine ran an interesting article. The headline read:

> "Buy High, Sell Low. What you always knew: Analysts are great advisors if you do the opposite."

Quoting the article:

> New research by four California professors shows that not only would you have lost money buying stocks that analysts pushed last year, but you would have made money if you bought those they recommended selling. And not just a small return. You would have made 38 percent on your money, better than the S&P 500 has done since 1958.

In another article, titled "Is Wall Street Serious About Reform?," in the July 16, 2001, edition of *Fortune,* the writer Shawn Tully seems to agree. That article reads: "On a humid morning in June, Representative Richard Baker, a homespun Republican from Louisiana, opened a dramatic congressional hearing by hammering a theme that stirs everyone from bartenders to soccer moms—call it 'How Wall Street Screws the Little Guy.' In a molasses drawl, Baker voiced his outrage at how the Street's new aristocrats—securities analysts—fleece small shareholders."

In my opinion, most analysts and financial advisors are not professional investors. They do not know what a professional investor must know. So most advice about investing is good advice for the average investor, but the same advice is bad advice for the professional investor . . . especially if you want to get rich quickly and stay rich forever.

A professional investor knows that the trend is your friend. A professional investor is someone who knows that no one is strong enough to go against the trend. As kids surfing, we always had tremendous respect for the changes in the trends or mood of the ocean. It was the tourist, who came only knowing what swimming in a lake or pool was like, that got into trouble in the ocean, some even drowning. You must respect the trends just as a surfer respects the power of the ocean. If you want to keep up-to-date with trends and changes, you definitely want to take tip #9 to heart.

9. ***Go to our Web site regularly.*** It is our commitment to you to keep it refreshed and interesting. Think of our Web site as the place for people who are going to retire young and retire rich.

In the near future, we will have our CASHFLOW games online so you can have fun, learn quickly, and meet people who think just like you. In the near future, you will play our games and learn how to trade an up trend, a down trend, and a sideways trend, and make money in any direction.

When someone says to you, "Invest for the long term," ask them what they mean by long term. *Long term* means one thing to the *average investor* and something else to a *professional investor*. If you want to get rich quickly and stay rich forever, you cannot be an average long-term investor. You must be a professional investor who is far better educated than the average investor. That is why I recommend you check our Web site, richdad.com, regularly. It is our job to keep you up-to-date with the most *fun and profitable financial education in the world.*

If you do not plan on following your parents' footsteps and working hard all your life, then start by checking in regularly with richdad.com. One of the problems with following your parents' advice on money is that technology and financial IQ are changing faster than most people can change. Today, it is possible to get rich quickly and stay rich forever if you stay abreast of the changes in technology and financial intelligence. For example, in the world of options, there are new options coming out today that are called "knockout options." They are far faster than the standard puts and calls that most day traders are using today. The reason most people do not know about "knockout options" is because they were invented by foreign exchange or foreign currency traders. In a few years, these new "exotic options," as they are called, will begin to filter into the stock market. Without going into much detail, simply put, a knockout option means you can make more money, faster, and safer than with standard options. Just remember this, as we make advances in technology, so will humans make advances in financial intelligence. That means it's getting easier and easier to become rich quicker with more safety. The catch? You need to keep up and keep learning and get good advisors. That is why you want to stay up-to-date, checking in regularly on our Web site.

Old Dogs Learn New Tricks

As you may have guessed, I love *Forbes* magazine. In the May 2001 issue of *Forbes Global,* their magazine for international businesspeople and investors, there was an interesting article about Sir John Templeton. Sir John Templeton is known as a value investor, investing in undervalued stocks globally and watching them grow. The *Forbes* article, entitled, "Old Dog,

New Tricks," describes how even Templeton, a hard-core bull and fundamental investor, can learn to be a technical trader, investing into a bear market. The article talks about how in the year 2000, instead of investing for the long term, which he used to advise, he went short for the first time. It was a new way of investing for him. In one year he made over $86 million learning a new way of investing. As rich dad said, "Money is just an idea." In this day and age, you do need to keep coming up with new ideas. If Sir John Templeton can change his context at eighty-eight years of age, so can you.

While the average investor was listening to their financial advisors about investing for the long term, the real investors were changing strategy and going short. Millions of investors going long listening to such advice ultimately lost trillions of dollars. Can this happen again? Most certainly. That is why if you want to get rich quickly and stay rich forever, you need to be careful about who is giving you your financial advice.

10. Always remember that words are free. If you want to get rich quickly, you need a rich vocabulary. Always remember that there are three basic classes of assets. They are businesses, paper assets, and real estate. Each of these assets uses different words. Each of these assets is like a foreign country with a foreign language. If you are interested in real estate, begin to learn the vocabulary or the jargon. Once you learn the words, you will be better able to communicate to yourself and others in that asset class.

Words are the most powerful tools we have as human beings. So choose your words carefully. Always remember there are two basic types of words:

1. One type is words for content. For example, *internal rate of return* is an important group of words especially for real estate investors who use a lot of leverage to invest with. Internal rates of return are content words.
2. The second type of words is context words. For example, when someone says, "I'll never understand internal rates of return," this person is describing their mental context about the content words, in this case internal rates of return.

Be aware of constantly improving your content vocabulary and watching your context vocabulary . . . because words are the tools that power one of your most powerful assets . . . your brain. That is why I suggest you forbid yourself from ever saying, "I can't afford it." Or "I can't do it." Or "I could never learn that." Ask yourself instead, "How can I afford it?" or "How can I do it?" or "How can I learn it?"

Remember that a big difference between a rich person and a poor person is simply the quality of their words. Your financial IQ begins with your financial vocabulary. So watch your words because words do become flesh and do become your future. If you want to get rich quickly and stay rich forever so you can retire young and retire rich, your words hold the key . . . and words are free.

11. Talk about money. When I was in China and Japan recently, many people came up to me and said, "In Oriental culture, it is not polite to talk about money . . . so we never talk about it." When I am in America or Australia or Europe, many people say a similar thing. They say, "In our family we did not discuss money."

So the hot tip is talk about money. If your friends don't want to talk about it, you may want to find a new group of friends. In my group of friends, we talk about money, business, investing, successes, and problems. Most of my friends are also very rich and do not have the context that talking about money is evil or dirty. My wife, Kim, and I talk about money constantly. To us making money, getting rich, and having an abundant lifestyle is fun . . . and we enjoy the game of money so we talk about money. We enjoy the game of money just as people enjoy other sports. Because we have money as a game in common, our marriage is closer, educational, exciting, and fun. Money is a subject all people all over the world have in common . . . so why not talk about it?

12. Make a million dollars starting with nothing. One of the reasons I do not need a job or a paycheck is because rich dad trained me to make money from nothing.

One of the saddest things I see today is people not knowing how to make money out of nothing. The other day, a young woman applied for a job in one of my companies. She came from a large multinational corporation where she was a senior vice president of marketing. She had been downsized and wanted to try her hand as vice president of marketing in my small entrepreneurial company. So, as a test, I asked her to prepare a media budget for this company. She came back three days later with a budget of $1.6 million for the year.

"$1.6 million," I gasped. "That is a lot of money."

"I realize that," she said in her most big corporate tone. "But if you want to achieve the result you want, that is what it will cost."

"I am willing to pay that," I replied. "But before I agree to this budget, tell me how we could achieve the same result for $160,000 or even nothing."

"Oh you can't do that," she said in her haughty corporate tone. "You have to spend money to make money."

Needless to say, she did not get the job. We obviously come from a different reality or context. As an entrepreneur, I have built companies spending absolutely nothing on formal advertising. We do spend on PR or public relations, but we do not spend on what is known as formal advertising. When you look at the success of richdad.com, you are looking at worldwide success, hundreds of millions in sales, and not one dollar spent on formal advertising . . . and maybe someday how we did that will be the subject of another book. But that success is because rich dad taught his son and me how to make millions out of nothing or virtually nothing.

The point is, it saddens me to see grown, highly paid executives of major corporations know how to spend a lot of money, but not really know how to make a lot of money on their own. I sit on boards of a few public companies and I watch these executives churn through investors' money, as the dot-coms did in the late 1990s, but not be able to turn a profit.

Rich dad often said, "There are big differences between entrepreneurs and bureaucrats. Most people are bureaucrats because our schools train people to become bureaucrats. An entrepreneur must know how to be both. Many bureaucrats dream of becoming entrepreneurs, but most never will." Rich dad said, "A bureaucrat only knows how to make money if it is given to him. An entrepreneur can make money out of nothing."

A few months ago, I was sitting with an executive of a large international publishing house. He had just come from one of my talks on entrepreneurship and how to grow a business. He looked me straight in the eye and said, "I will never be rich because it takes a lot of money to make money. I have a $20 million advertising budget and I need every dollar of it to produce the sales volume I want." At that moment I knew why he was a bureaucrat of a large corporation and not an entrepreneur. His reality will forever keep him there.

It also saddens me to see small companies not able to grow because the entrepreneur does not know how to make money out of nothing or next to nothing. Rich dad said, "There is a big difference between a baby-business and a small business. A baby-business has the potential to grow into a big business in the B quadrant. A small business may be profitable but it has no potential of growing into a B quadrant business." Rich dad went on to explain that the difference was not found in the business but in the mind-set of the entrepreneur behind the business. A classic example is the story of the McDonald brothers and Ray Kroc. Ray Kroc took a small hamburger stand run by two brothers and turned it into the very, very, very big worldwide business we know as McDonald's.

In summary, Ray Kroc was an E quadrant employee selling milk shake mixers who bought an S quadrant business and turned it into a big B quadrant business. That is the power of this simple process I will share with you now . . . a process you can do on a regular basis and it will cost you nothing . . . but it could make you rich beyond your wildest dreams.

So the last tip is, with your loved one or friends who are on the journey with you, spend time together brainstorming how you can take an idea and turn that idea into millions of dollars, starting with no money or very little money. This process is like going to the gym for your muscles. This regular exercise strengthens you brain and gets it ready for the moment you make your move.

Before I met Kim, Larry and I would sit in a coffee shop on the ground floor of the office building where the Xerox office was located. We would spend hours over many cups of coffee coming up with ideas on how to make millions of dollars out of nothing. We came up with some really good ideas, some bad ideas, and many, many stupid ideas. We came up with T-shirt ideas, puzzles made out of wood, a tourist product involving sugar packets from Hawaii, a financial newsletter. Most of those ideas never got off the ground, yet they gave us great mental exercise. Even though most of the ideas did not work, we did come up with the nylon and Velcro surfer wallet idea and took that idea and turned it into millions of dollars. Unfortunately, we didn't take the steps to protect the idea and ended up losing it to competition.

Earlier, I mentioned that I had read that the capitalization of the Coca-Cola company was over $8 billion, but the value of the Coca-Cola brand is closer to $80 billion, almost ten times the capitalization of the entire company. How is that possible? Coca-Cola has aggressively protected its intellectual property internationally and as a result the Coca-Cola brand has become incredibly valuable.

"Rich Dad" Is Just 2 Words!

Let's review the success of the words "Rich Dad." Rich Dad is just two words.

When Kim and I met Sharon Lechter and we started CASHFLOW® Technologies, Inc. in 1997, the words "rich dad" were just two meaningless words and worth nothing.

Today the words "Rich Dad" are worth tens of millions of dollars. How did that happen? We took the advice of Michael Lechter, Sharon's husband and our intellectual property attorney (who, as some of you know, actually introduced us to Sharon). We took the time to sit down with him and create a strategy to intentionally *build* intellectual property assets. With his guidance, we have carefully followed that strategy, and created and protected our intellectual property. We made sure that we protected our inventions with patents. We have created and protected strong "Rich Dad" and "CASHFLOW" brands and a strong trade dress (purple, black, and gold) that is recognizable all over the world. The initial trademark cost us less than $1,000 to file. Next year when we launch the online version of the CASHFLOW game, the value of the brands could reach billions of dollars. Our experience proves that you can make money with little to no money.

For further information on how you can create money with little to no money, you can read Michael's book, *Protecting Your #1 Asset: Creating Fortunes from Your Ideas—An Intellectual Property Handbook,* published by Warner Books. Michael is an internationally recognized intellectual property attorney who has helped countless people create fortunes from their ideas. As he puts it, he "builds forts and fights pirates" to protect intellectual property. Michael often says, "Each one of us has had a million-dollar idea! Unfortunately, very few of us take the steps to protect that idea—and if you don't protect it, it won't be you that makes the million dollars from that idea." The $20 investment in Michael's book could help you see how to make a fortune from your own idea.

In Conclusion

You and I know that your brain is still your most underused asset. It has plenty of horsepower yet to be used. Rich dad used to say, "Lazy people want to get rich quickly, and successful people want to get financially smart quickly and keep getting smarter." The point is, if you want to retire young and retire rich, and you don't have much money, education, or experience, begin using your brain. In my reality, it does not take money to become rich. In my reality it does take mental and emotional power. All the hot tips listed are there for you to consider and practice if you want.

The final point of all these tips is that none of the above exercises require much time or money. All of the above exercises will help you retire young and retire rich if you do them regularly and faithfully. Always remember that your future is determined by what you do *today,* not tomorrow.

If you will faithfully make some of these simple exercises a part of your everyday life, you may find yourself going through the looking glass and into a completely different world. And that is the subject of the next section.

A Final Thought on Section 3: You Are Already An Expert

As you may already realize, it is not so much what you *do* that makes you rich or poor. It is more the context surrounding what you do that makes you rich or poor. That is why when people ask me what I do or what I invest in I reply, "Please don't ask me what I do. Ask me what I think about what I do." For example, many people invest in stocks but only a few people become rich investing in stocks. The same is true for real estate or building a business. What is the difference? I say it is the context surrounding the actions or content. I have met people who say to me, "Real estate is a lousy investment. I have not made any money in it." Well in my opinion, it is not real estate that is the lousy investment, it is the person who is a lousy investor. A person with a rich investor's context can take a bad investment and turn it into a rich investment. In fact, that is what most rich investors do.

"All Debt Is Good"

The same is true with the subject of debt. Most people know how to get into debt. Most people are experts at getting into debt. The problem is, they get into debt and get poorer. Most people take good debt and make it bad. As rich dad said to me, "All debt is good debt. But not all people know how to use debt, so they turn good debt into bad debt."

If you want to be rich, you first need to work on your context, more than on what you do. As rich dad said, "Most people already know how to get into debt. The problem is, they do not know how to use debt in their favor. If someone wants to get rich using debt, they first need to change their context and then they can use debt to become very rich." If you cannot change your poor or middle-class person's context regarding the subject of debt, it is best you cut up your credit cards, pay off your house as quickly as possible, and just try and save money.

If you want to retire young and retire rich, you must first change your context. That is why I recommend you occasionally review these hot tips and continually work on upgrading your context. If you have a rich person's context, no matter what you do you will become richer and richer. If you have a poor person's context, no matter what you study or what you do, the results will be the same, a poor person's results. Remember it is your context or what you think is real that becomes your reality, regardless of what you do. As rich dad said, "Debt does not necessarily make you poor. But a poor or middle-class person's context will."

Free Offer

If you want to listen to me personally discussing these hot tips, please go to our Web site at richdad.com and listen to the audio presentation I have made just for people like you . . . people who want to retire young and retire rich. If you are committed to retiring young and retiring rich, our Web site is for you. If you want to work hard all your life for job security, or invest with high risk and low returns, there are better Web sites than ours.

Chapter 20

The Final Exam

The following is an optional exercise that you can do, if you are brave enough. These questions are to be asked at your next dinner party, or over lunch with co-workers, or with friends and family. The reason I say that it is optional is because the following questions will bring up different realities about money from the people you ask.

If you give the person time to fully answer each question you will hear many different realities, reasons, excuses, lies, assumptions, and other psychobabble that people have about money and their lives. You may hear such responses as, "What a stupid question." "Who does this guy think he is?" "You can't do that." "That's impossible." "I love my work. I'll never stop working." Rather than agreeing or disagreeing with the answers or comments to the questions, simply listen and see if you can more clearly pick up the person's reality about money and his or her financial life. If you have the courage to ask these questions of your loved ones, friends, or co-workers, I wish you luck. If you do the exercise with other people, I think you will learn a tremendous amount about the power of one's reality over those people's financial condition in life.

The following are the questions or groups of questions to ask:

What Kind of Life Do You Want to Live?

A Comparison of Realities

1. If you had all the money in the world and never had to work again, what would you do with your free time?

2. If you (and your spouse if married) stopped working today, what would happen to your life? How long could you survive and still maintain your standard of living and lifestyle?

3. At what age will you be able to retire if you are not already retired? Would you like to retire earlier? When you retire, will you be making more money than you are today or less?

4. Would you rather live a life where you no longer need a paycheck or would you rather live a life where you're always working at or looking for a higher paying job? Would you rather be unemployable or more employable? Which life are you leading today?

5. Do you want to live a life where you work hard trying to spend more money because you have too much money or live a life working hard trying to save money? Which life are you leading?

6. Would you rather live a life where you do not have to work hard to earn more or would you rather live a life where you have to work harder to earn more? Which life are you living?

7. Do you think investing is risky? Do you think it takes money to make money? Would you like to be able to invest without any money and without much risk for very high returns? If you could invest with someone else's money would you?

8. Who are the six people other than your family that you spend the most time around? What is their attitude toward money? Is it rich, poor, or middle-class? Of those six people, how many will be able to retire young and retire rich? Is it time for you to make new friends?

9. Would you rather live a life where you work to become rich building or buying assets, or would you rather live a life working for job security and a steady paycheck? Which life are you living?

10. If you were offered a billion dollars to quit your job, would you? If a billion dollars is more important than your job, why not go for the billion

dollars? What specifically holds you back? If you would not quit your job for a billion dollars . . . then why? Could you not use the billion dollars to do more good than you are doing now?

11. Do you live a life where you make money regardless if the market goes up or down or do you live a life where you live in fear of market crashes and losing money? Which life do you live? Why?

12. Regarding the subject of money, if you could do things differently, what would you do differently? If there is something you would do differently, why aren't you doing it?

The reason I suggest this exercise only if you are brave enough is because after the discussion, you may wind up without any friends, and need to make new ones. If you find your family, friends, and co-workers are not coming from the context you want to come from, then go to our Web site at richdad.com to meet people who are. At least you will have fun discussing the responses you get from this twelve-question final exam. The most important thing is that you will see the different realities and different worlds different people come from when it comes to the subject of money. As rich dad said, "Money is just an idea." When you ask these questions, you will find out many different ideas and different realities.

The most important thing from this exercise is to listen to different thoughts and realities, and decide what kind of reality or financial world you want to see. Having two dads allowed me to see both worlds, and I made my choice which world I wanted to see. So the choice is up to you. If you ask these questions of your family and friends, you will hear their ideas. After listening to their ideas, then you can begin to better choose the ideas you want and what kind of life you want to live.

Share Your Results

Go to our Web site at richdad.com and share the answers you receive from this test. In our discussion forum share the more humorous, cynical, entertaining, or surprising responses you get from these questions. In these forums you may meet your future business partners and go on to become richer than your friends or maybe even richer than Bill Gates. You may even retire young and retire very rich.

Section IV

The Leverage of the First Step

Rich dad said, "The first step is to decide what kind of world you want to live in. Do you want to live in the world of the poor, the middle class, or the rich?"

"Wouldn't most people choose to live in the world of the rich?" I asked.

"No," said rich dad. "Most people dream of living in the world of the rich . . . but they do not take that first step and that is to decide. Once you decide, and if you have truly decided, there is no coming back. The moment you decide, everything in your world will change."

Chapter 21

How to Keep Going

I am frequently asked, "After you made the decision to retire young, what kept Kim and you going? How did you handle the adversity and not turn back when times got tough?" Most of the time, I answer with clichés such as determination, strong will, and vision. I use such overused clichés because I rarely have the time to explain much of what I have already explained in this book. Since you have read this far and hopefully understood most of what has been written to this point, I will share with you in greater depth a more honest explanation of what kept us going.

Two of the more profound fairy tale type of stories rich dad had me read were the classics by Lewis Carroll, *Alice's Adventures in Wonderland* and *Through the Looking-Glass*. Both stories share the journey into different realities. In *Alice's Adventures in Wonderland,* Alice follows the White Rabbit down its burrow and into a different world, a world that reminds me of the financial services industry. In *Through the Looking-Glass,* Alice again journeys to another reality behind the looking glass. Behind the looking glass Alice finds looking glass books that cannot be read unless held up to a mirror, much like a personal financial statement. Nonetheless, to rich dad, the value of both stories was the idea of traveling from one reality to another. Rich dad said, "The problem is most people live only one reality and tend to think that *their* reality is the *only* reality."

Answering a Frequently Asked Question

Most of the time, when asked such a question as, "What kept you and Kim going? How did you keep going when you were out of money, out of a job, and on a financial losing streak?" I answer with tried and true simple clichés. I reply with "It took determination." Or "We knew we were never going back." But those clichés do not tell the real story. I hesitate beginning the true explanation because the answer is out of the reality of most people, so I just say very little.

A few weeks ago in a seminar, I had the time to more fully explain the reason Kim and I kept going. Since you have read this far, I will tell you the answer I shared with the class. I do not think it fully answers the question, the question of how we kept going, but I think the answer will give you a little extra food for thought.

As the seminar drew to a close, a student raised his hand and asked, "When it seemed the darkest, what kept you and Kim going? I want to hear the real reason . . . not the ones you have given us so far."

The Answer

I considered his request for a while and finally decided to disclose our driving motivation to keep going, once Kim and I had made our decision to retire young and retire rich. The explanation began:

"In my late twenties, rich dad imparted a lesson that began with this question. The lesson and dialogue lasted for years . . . and even though he is gone, I continue to review the lesson and seek further answers."

A World of No Risk That Requires No Money

"What would you do if there was no risk and it required no money to become rich?" asked rich dad.

"No risk and no money?" I repeated, not certain where rich dad was going with this question. "Why ask the question?" I finally asked. "Such a world does not exist."

Rich dad let me sit with my answer for a moment. His silence was my cue that I had best listen to my answer and take the time to rethink it. Once he knew I had rethought my answer he finally said, "Are you sure such a world does not exist?"

"A world of no risk and no money required?" I asked, seeking to make sure we were discussing the same points. All I could hear was my own dad saying, "Investing is risky" and "It takes money to make money."

Rich dad nodded his head. "Yes. What would you do if such a world existed?"

"Well, I would go find it," I said. "But only if it existed."

"And why would it not exist?" asked rich dad.

"Because it's impossible," I replied. "How could there be a world where there was no monetary risk or money required to become rich?"

"Well if you have already decided that it is impossible for such a world to exist, then it cannot exist," rich dad said softly.

"Are you saying it does exist?" I asked.

"It does not matter what *I* think. What is important is what *you* think," said rich dad. "If you say it does not exist . . . it does not exist. What I think is inconsequential."

"But such a world is impossible," I repeated. "I know it is impossible. There has to be risk."

"Then it does not exist," shrugged rich dad. "If you think it is impossible, then it's impossible." Rich dad was now answering me with a little more energy and a hint of frustration in the tone of his voice. "The reason such a world does not exist is because you still have your dad's reality and his beliefs. You cling to those beliefs because that is the reality you were raised in. I cannot teach you much more unless you are willing to change that reality. I can give you more and more answers about how to become rich, but my answers are no good if you cling to your family's reality on money and how life is."

"But no money and no risk? Come on," I said. "Be real. No one believes there is a world of no money and no risk."

"I know," said rich dad. "That is why so many people cling to job security and often assume investing is risky or that it takes money to make money. They do not question their assumptions. They do not challenge their assumptions. Instead they believe their assumptions are real, never asking if there might be another reality or maybe a different assumption. You cannot become richer if you do not first question the assumptions under your beliefs. That is why so few people become rich or ever become truly financially free. But you're still not answering the question."

"So repeat the question," I replied, feeling very frustrated and wondering what he meant by not questioning my assumptions.

"The question was, 'What would you do if there was no risk and it required no money to become rich?'" rich dad said, repeating himself slowly and deliberately, doing his best to get through my reaction to the question, so I could hear the question.

"I still think it is a ridiculous question but I'll answer anyway," I replied.

"Why do you say it's ridiculous?" asked rich dad.

"Because such a world does not exist," I snapped back. "It's a silly question and a waste of time. Why should I even answer or think about such a question?"

"Okay," said rich dad. "I got my answer. I also hear your underlying assumption. To you it's a waste of time to even think about such a world so you would not bother to think about the question. You already assume such a world does not exist so you think questioning that idea is a waste of time. You don't want to question your assumption. So because you don't think such a world exists you don't want to think about it. You only want to think the way you have always thought. You want to become rich but live in fear of losing money or live with the idea that you don't have enough money. To me that is a strange reality, but I can accept your answer. I understand your assumptions, because they are very common assumptions."

"No, no, no," I said. "I'll answer your question. I'm just asking you if you are saying that such a world exists?" I said, raising my voice, becoming angry and defensive.

Rich dad sat quietly, again not answering my question and letting me listen to myself. He was letting me listen to my reality.

"Do you want me to believe that world exists?" I asked heatedly.

"Let me repeat myself. It does not matter what I believe," said rich dad. "It's what you believe."

"Okay, okay, okay," I said. "If such a world existed, a world without financial risk and a world that did not require me to use any money to become rich, then I would be richer beyond my wildest dreams. I would not be afraid. I would not make the excuse that I don't have any money or that I might fail. I would live in a world of infinite abundance . . . a world where I could have anything I wanted. I would live in a completely different world . . . definitely not a world I was brought up in."

"So if such a world existed, would it be worth the journey?" asked rich dad.

"Of course," I replied sharply. "Who wouldn't make the journey?"

Rich dad just shrugged his shoulders in silence, again letting me listen to my own words.

"Are you saying such a world exists?" I asked again.

"That is for you to decide. You can decide what kind of world exists. I can't do that for you," said rich dad. "I made my decision years ago as to what kind of world I wanted to have exist."

"Did you find your world?" I asked.

Rich dad never answered the question. His only reply was, "Do you remember the story of Alice and *Through the Looking-Glass*?"

I nodded my head.

"Years ago, I went through the looking glass. If you believe such a world exists, then you may decide to make the journey through the looking glass. But you will only make the journey if you believe the possibility of such a world existing. If you don't believe it exists, then you will only see a mirror and you will stay on this side of the mirror, looking at you looking at you, looking at you looking at you."

My Answer to the Class

When I had shared this story with the class, it was silent. I do not know if my answer was making any sense. Regardless if it made sense or not, I had given them the story behind the story. Beginning to wrap up the answer I said, "So that is when my journey began. After that conversation with rich dad I became very curious. I thought about what he said for several years. The more I thought about it, the more what he said became a possibility. When I was in my early thirties I knew I had to push my reality. I knew my school days with rich dad were over. I knew rich dad could not teach me much more or give me any more answers until I decided to change my reality and begin my journey. More answers were not going to help. I needed a new expanded reality. I knew it was time to leave the nest, as they say. I did not know if such a world existed, but I wanted it to exist. So my journey had begun once I made the decision that such a world was possible. With that decision, I went looking for that world, a world where there is no risk and a world that does not take money to make money. I was tired of looking in the mirror and not liking what I saw. That is when I went looking for a world through the looking glass."

The class remained silent. I could sense that some of them were open to the idea and some were fighting it. A student raised his hand and said, "So you believed such a world existed? Is that what you're telling us?"

I did not answer his question. Instead I just continued on with the story. "Soon after making the decision that such a world might be possible, I met Kim and told her of the journey I was embarking on. For some reason she wanted to come along. She said, 'Well, what you talk about beats the reality

I have right now . . . the reality of working at a job all my life. I don't like my current reality so I'm willing to find a new reality.'"

The student who was trying to get me to answer his question finally put his hand down and just listened. "Kim was the first woman I met who was willing to entertain such a crazy thought. I was hesitant about telling her, yet she did not fight my ideas. Instead she listened for days as I told her of the world I thought might be possible. That was when our journey began. It was not about money but more about a search for a different world. So I faithfully say to you all, that more than anything else, it was the search for that world that kept Kim and me going.

"Once we made the decision, we began our journey through the looking glass. We knew that once we started the journey we needed to be brave, be humble, study, keep learning, learn quickly as lessons appeared, and most importantly, we kept pushing our reality, for we knew the journey was a journey only in our hearts and in our minds. We knew the journey had little to do with the world outside of us, and everything to do with the realities inside of us. When times got really bad, it was this search of a different reality, a different world, that ultimately kept us going. Once the journey began, we knew we were never turning back. That search for a different world is what kept us going."

There was a long silence in the seminar room. Suddenly, a student shot her hand up in the air and asked, "So did you find it? Tell me if you found it. If it does exist, I want to go there. I don't want to spend fifty years of my life working for money. I don't want to spend a life taking orders from money, living in fear of not having enough money. Tell me if another type of world exists."

I paused for a moment, doing to them as rich dad had done with me years and years ago, allowing them the time to listen to their own realities. "That is for you to decide," I finally responded after an extended silence. "It is not what *I* believe, it is what *you* believe exists. If you think such a world exists for you, then you'll go through the looking glass. If not, then you'll stay on this side of the looking glass, looking at you looking at you. When it comes to money, you have the power to decide what is real and what kind of reality you want to live in." The class was over. Most of the class was in deep thought. As I finished packing my briefcase, I turned to them and said, "Thank you for your attention. Thank you for listening. Class is dismissed."

In Closing

In the fall of 1994, Kim and I took an extended break in Fiji. A friend had recommended this small exclusive resort, on a small private island. Before the sun came up one morning, a staff member from the hotel greeted us at our luxurious grass hut. "Your horses are ready," he said with a smile and in a whisper.

We had been on the island for five days at this point. I was finally relaxing, winding down, and becoming more in sync with the slow gentle pace of this beautiful island paradise, surrounded by the crystal blue waters of the Pacific Ocean. It had been nine years since Larry, Kim, and I had sat on Whistler Mountain, north of Vancouver, British Columbia, covered in snow, freezing, and creating our plans for financial freedom. As I climbed up on my horse, I reflected back to that time on the cold freezing mountain. Settling in the saddle, I thought about how different things now were in our lives. We were not shivering with cold anymore and we were not poor, with no money anymore. More important than just having a lot of money, we were now free. We never had to work again for the rest of our lives.

The horses slowly wandered along the trail that paralleled the beautiful white sand beach that surrounded the island. Although I could not see anything since it was still dark, I could hear the ocean just a few feet away, and feel the ocean's breeze as the horse gently navigated the narrow beach trail. The smell of the island soil and the tropical plants, combined with the salt air, took me back to my childhood in Hawaii, to a time when Hawaii was still Hawaii. Although the horse ride was a short one, the memories that came back spanned a lifetime.

After a half-hour ride, the staff member from the hotel stopped the horses and assisted us to the ground. In the near distance I could see several candles dancing in the wind. The guide took our hands and gently walked us toward the candles. The candles were sitting on a table with a white tablecloth, in the sand, just a few feet from the gently lapping waves. The staff member sat Kim and me at the only table in the most beautiful restaurant in the world. As soon as we were seated, another staff member appeared with a bottle of my wife's favorite champagne. Through the candlelight, Kim and I toasted ourselves and our journey. Never in my life had I felt more love for my beautiful wife. She had stuck by me through some of the most trying times of my life. We did not say anything. We silently reached across the tiny table and held each other's hand, held our champagne glasses in the other hand, and said, "Thank you and I love you" with our eyes. We had made it.

As if on cue, the glow of the sun peaked over the ocean's horizon and we began to see nature's masterpiece surrounding us. On one side we could see the lush green island rising from the sea. In front of us was pristine white sand, and behind us were tall green trees with birds beginning to call out. Across the sand, seeming to bring all things together, was a calm blue ocean stretching away from the beach and greeting the sun.

The waiter brought our breakfast of fresh tropical fruits as we sat silently watching the sun rise out of the water, slowly illuminating the beauty that surrounded us. Except for the waiter, we were the only people there. There was perfect silence, except for the sounds of nature. There were no neighbors, no cars, no beachgoers, no loud music, no cell phones. Best of all, there was no business to go back to. No meetings. No deadlines. No budgets. The business was gone. It had done its job and we had sold it. We had nothing to go home to except our freedom. All there was at that moment was Kim and me and the overwhelming beauty of nature . . . God's magnificent creation.

Just as the sun finally broke free of the water, something snapped inside my head. My vision did not blur, it just seemed to vibrate and then the rest of me shook very briefly. It was a tiny earthquake, a tremor had suddenly moved through my body and my soul. Something was changing deep inside of me. The experience caused me to loosen up even more. As the warmth of the sun began to reach us from across the water, a feeling of immense gratitude started in my chest and spread throughout my body. Without realizing it, my context had completely shifted—I had stepped through the looking glass and now could clearly see a new way of life. I began to cry, not with sadness, but with profound wonder at the perfection, bounty, and abundance that surrounded not just Kim and me . . . but all of us.

Slowly, I realized that too much of the time my fear of not being enough or not having enough prevented me from allowing the abundance that life here on earth offers. I realized that my personal struggle to become rich was primarily my personal struggle against my fear of being poor. I also realized why my rich dad always said, "It is your fear that makes you your own prisoner. It is your fear that locks you in your own cell, a prison that does not let the abundance of God in." My mind drifted back to my youth and I could hear him saying, "Too often we think we are alone and we have to survive on our own. Too often we believe that in order to survive, we need to do our job on our own. We are often taught that it is the survival of the fittest and if we are not fit we do not survive. That is the way a prisoner thinks. Many people are financial prisoners of their fears. That is why they cling to threads of security, become greedy and fight for scraps of money like starving dogs fighting over a meatless bone, rather than seek financial freedom.

"Finding your own freedom is easy. All you have to do is first look and see what God wants done, and then do what God wants done with the gifts that God has given you. If you will faithfully do that, the abundance of God will pour into your life. Life is not about earning a living. Just look at the birds, the plants, and all of nature's creations around you. Birds don't earn a living. Birds and God's other creatures simply do what they were sent here to do. If you will simply trust in God and do what you were sent here to do, God's abundance will be with you forever." Rich dad also said, "You don't have to do the bird's job . . . the bird's already doing it." He said that because he saw too many humans competing for jobs rather than looking to see what needs to be done. He said, "If you will look to see what needs to be done, and do what needs to be done, you will tap into God's abundance."

Kim and I sat at our little table on the beach for another hour. For the first time in my life, I understood what rich dad was saying. I did not fully understand him before this. I still had my personal context or reality in the way of letting his words in. But sitting on that beach I finally stepped through the looking glass, and fully understood my rich dad.

As the wind off the ocean began to pick up, I could hear the horses in the background becoming restless. It was time for them to go home and so it was for Kim and me. A year later, I was sitting silently in my cabin on my mountaintop asking myself the questions, "What needs to be done?" and "What can I do?"

When people ask me today why I keep working even though I do not need the money, the answer is my rich dad's answer. I say, "I keep working because there are things that need to be done." Today, all Kim and I do is leverage what we have learned to do more of what needs to be done. Ironically, the more Kim and I apply leverage in order to do what needs to be done, the happier and richer we become.

The good news is that you do not have to quit your job to do what needs to be done. You do not have to retire to do what needs to be done. Just look around you and you will see what needs to be done. All you have to do is do what needs to be done with the gifts you have been given. If you will do that, you will tap into the abundance . . . the abundance that has always been here for all of us . . . not just some of us.

My last day on that beautiful private island in Fiji was spent sitting on the beach doing absolutely nothing. I had nothing to go home to except a whole new way of living . . . living as a free person. I squeezed Kim's hand, letting her know how much I loved her, respected her, and thanked her for sticking with me through this journey. I could not have made it without her. Just before we picked up our beach mat and headed back for dinner, I could hear rich dad saying, "Many small people spend their lives attacking giants. They criticize, gossip, spread rumors, and lie about them, doing their best to tear them down. They see what is wrong with the giant rather than what is right. That is why they remain small. David may have been young, and he did not have much, only a simple slingshot, and he may have been physically smaller than Goliath, but David was not a small person." The point of this book is that each of us has a small person, a David, and a Goliath inside of us. David could have stayed a small person by taking on the context of a small person, saying, "He's bigger than me. How can I take on a giant with only a slingshot?" Instead, David became a giant by choosing to take on the context of a giant. That is how he beat Goliath and became a giant himself. You can do the same.

In closing, leverage is everywhere. Leverage is power. Leverage is found inside of us, all around us, and invented by us. With each new invention, inventions such as the automobile, airplane, telephone, television, and World

Wide Web, a new form of leverage is invented. With each new form of leverage, new millionaires and billionaires are created because they used the leverage, not ruined or abused the new leverage. So always remember that the power of leverage can be used, abused, or feared. How you choose to use the power of leverage in your life is up to you and only you.

Thank you for reading this book and remember to keep an open context. The future is very bright and the future will bring freedom for more and more people.

About the Authors

Robert T. Kiyosaki

Born and raised in Hawaii, Robert Kiyosaki is a fourth-generation Japanese-American. After graduating from college in New York, Robert joined the Marine Corps and went to Vietnam as an officer and helicopter gunship pilot.

Returning from war, Robert went to work for the Xerox Corporation and in 1977 started a company that brought the first nylon Velcro surfer wallets to market. In 1985 he founded an international education company that taught business and investing to tens of thousands of students throughout the world.

In 1994 Robert sold his business and retired at the age of 47. During his short-lived retirement, Robert wrote *Rich Dad Poor Dad.* Soon afterward he wrote *Rich Dad's Cashflow Quadrant, Rich Dad's Guide to Investing,* and *Rich Kid Smart Kid.* All the books have been on the best-seller lists of the *Wall Street Journal, Business Week, New York Times, E-Trade.com,* and other distinguished lists. Robert also created his educational board game CASHFLOW to teach individuals the same financial strategies his rich dad spent years teaching him . . . the same financial strategies that allowed Robert to retire at the age of 47.

Robert is often heard saying, "We go to school to learn to work hard for money. I write books and create products that teach people how to have money work hard for them . . . so they can enjoy the luxuries of this great world we live in."

Sharon L. Lechter

C.P.A., co-author of the Rich Dad series of books and CEO and co-founder of CASHFLOW® Technologies, Inc. Sharon Lechter has dedicated her professional efforts to the field of education. She graduated with honors from Florida State University with a degree in accounting, then joined the ranks of what was then one of the big eight accounting firms and went on to hold management positions with companies in the computer, insurance, and publishing industries, all while maintaining her professional credentials as a C.P.A.

Sharon has been happily married to Michael Lechter for over 20 years and has three children, Phillip, Shelly, and William. As her children grew, she became keenly involved in their education and always served in leadership positions in their schools. She became a vocal activist in the areas of mathematics, computers, reading, and writing education. So in 1989 she was delighted to join forces with the inventor of the first electronic "talking book," and helped him expand the electronic book industry to a multimillion-dollar international market. Today she remains a pioneer in developing new technologies to bring education back into children's lives. As co-author of the Rich Dad books and CEO of CASHFLOW® Technologies, Inc. she now focuses her efforts in the field of financial education. "Our current educational system has not been able to keep pace with the global and technological changes in the world today. We must teach our young people the skills, both scholastic and financial, that they will need to not only survive but to flourish in the world they face."

An avid philanthropist, Sharon "gives back" as both a volunteer and a donor. She runs the Foundation for Financial Literacy, and is a director on the Arizona board of Childhelp USA, a national organization formed to eradicate child abuse in the U.S. As an active member of the Womens Presidents Organization, she enjoys networking with other professional women across the country.

Robert Kiyosaki, author of the Rich Dad books and her partner says of her: "Sharon is one of the few natural entrepreneurs I have ever met. My respect for her continues to grow every day we work together." You can contact Sharon at sharon@richdad.com.

EBSI RichDad.com

CASHFLOW® TECHNOLOGIES, INC.

CASHFLOW® Technologies, Inc. and richdad.com, the collaborative efforts of Robert and Kim Kiyosaki, and Sharon Lechter produce innovative financial education products.

The Company's mission statement is:

"To elevate the financial well-being of humanity."

CASHFLOW® Technologies, Inc. presents Robert's teaching through books; *Rich Dad Poor Dad™*, *Rich Dad's CASHFLOW® Quadrant™*, *Rich Dad's Guide to Investing™*, *Rich Kid Smart Kid™*, and *Retire Young Retire Rich*, board games; *CASHFLOW® 101*, *CASHFLOW® 202*, and *CASHFLOW for Kids®*, and tape sets. Additional products are available and under development for people searching for financial education to guide them on their path to financial freedom. For updated information see rich dad.com or contact info@richdad.com.

Rich Dad's *ADVISORS™*

Rich Dad's Advisors is a collection of books and educational products, reflecting the expertise of the professional advisors that *CASHFLOW®* Technologies, Inc. and its principals, Robert and Kim Kiyosaki, and Sharon Lechter, use to build their financial freedom. Each advisor is a specialist in their respective areas of the B-I Triangle, the business foundation taught by *CASHFLOW®* Technologies, Inc.

Robert Kiyosaki's Edumercial
An Educational Commercial

The Three Incomes

In the world of accounting, there are three different types of income, earned, passive, and portfolio. When my real dad said to me, "Go to school, get good grades and find a safe secure job." He was recommending I work for earned income. When my rich dad said, "The rich don't work for money, they have their money work for them," he was talking about passive income and portfolio income. Passive income, in most cases is derived from real estate investments. Portfolio income is income derived from paper assets, such as stocks, bonds, and mutual funds.

Rich dad used to say, "The key to becoming wealthy is the ability to convert earned income into passive income and/or portfolio income as quickly as possible." He would say, "The taxes are highest on earned income. The least taxed income is passive income. That is another reason why you want your money working hard for you. The government taxes the income you work hard for more than the income your money works hard for."

The Key to Financial Freedom

The key to financial freedom and great wealth is a person's ability or skill to convert earned income into passive income and/or portfolio income. That is the skill that my rich dad spent a lot of time teaching Mike and me. Having that skill is the reason my wife Kim and I are financially free, never needing to work again. We continue to work because we choose to. Today we own a real estate investment company for passive income and participate in private placements and initial public offerings of stock for portfolio income.

Investing to become rich requires a different set of personal skills, skills essential for financial success as well as low-risk and high-investment returns. In other words, knowing how to create assets that buy other assets. The problem is that gaining the basic education and experience required is often time consuming, frightening, and expensive, especially when you make mistakes with your own money. That is why I created my patented education board games trademarked as CASHFLOW.

Three Different Games

CASHFLOW, Investing 101®:

CASHFLOW® *101* teaches you the basics of Fundamental Investing, but it also does much more. *CASHFLOW*® *101* teaches you how to take control of your personal finances, build a business through proper cash flow management, and learn how to invest with greater confidence in real estate and other businesses.

This educational product is for you if you want to improve your business and investing skills by learning how to take your ideas and turn them into assets such as your own business. Many small businesses fail because the owner lacks capital, real-life experience, and basic accounting skills. Many investors think investing is risky simply because they cannot read financial statements. *CASHFLOW*® *101* teaches the fundamental skills of financial literacy and investing. This educational product includes the board game, a video, and audiotapes. It takes approximately two complete times playing the game to understand it. Then, we recommend that you play the game at least six times to begin to master the fundamentals of cash flow management and investing.
Price $195 US

***CASHFLOW, Investing 202®*:**

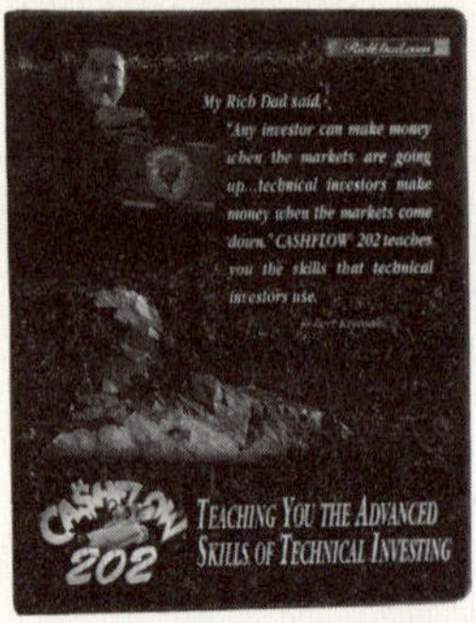

CASHFLOW® 202 teaches you the advanced skills of technical investing. After you are comfortable with the fundamentals of *CASHFLOW® 101*, the next educational challenge is learning how to manage the ups and downs of the markets, often called volatility. *CASHFLOW® 202* uses the same board game as *101*, but it comes with a completely different set of cards and score sheets and more advanced audiotapes. *CASHFLOW® 202* teaches you to use the investment techniques of qualified investors—techniques such as short selling, call options, put options, and straddles, techniques that can be very expensive to learn in the real market. Most investors are afraid of a market crash. A qualified investor uses the tools taught in *CASHFLOW® 202* to make money, when the markets go up and when the markets come down.

After you have mastered *101*, *CASHFLOW® 202* becomes very exciting because you learn to react to the highs and lows of the markets, and you make a lot of paper money. Again, it is a lot less expensive to learn these advanced trading techniques on a board game using paper money than trading in the market with real money. While these games cannot guarantee your investment success, they will improve your financial vocabulary and knowledge of these advanced investing techniques.

Price $95 US

***CASHFLOW, Investing for Kids*®**:

Could your child be the next Bill Gates, Anita Roddick of the Body Shop, Warren Buffet, or Donald Trump? If so, then *CASHFLOW for Kids*® could be the family's educational and fun game that gives your child the same educational head start my rich dad gave me. Few people know that Warren Buffet's father was a stockbroker and Donald Trump's father was a real estate developer. A parent's influence at an early age can have long-term financial results. *CASHFLOW for Kids*® includes the board game, book, and audiotape.

Price $59.95

FREE!

AUDIO DOWNLOAD

In each of our books we like to provide an audio interview as a bonus with additional insights. As a thank-you to you for reading this book, you may go to the Web site www.richdad.com/retireyoung to download the *Secret to Retiring Young* with Robert Kiyosaki and Dolf de Roos, Ph.D.

Thank you for your interest in your financial education.

Rich Dad's
GAME™

Play CASHFLOW® Around the World

In 1996, when I created the game, one of my dreams was to make available to people around the world, the same financial education my rich dad taught me. Now, with the Internet and the electronic version of the CASHFLOW board game, this dream becomes more possible.

All of us at CASHFLOW® Technologies, Inc. are excited to announce the release of the electronic version of CASHFLOW 101 and 202.

Would you like to meet people from around the world who think like you? Soon you will be able to do just that when you play CASHFLOW® internationally. If things go as planned, the electronic version of the life-changing educational game, CASHFLOW® 101 will be available to be played all over the world online by June of 2002. CASHFLOW® 202 will soon follow, again if things go as planned.

When I was a kid, my rich dad could only teach his son and me. It was a full-time job that took years. Now with the game and the Internet, rich dad's priceless lessons can be taught worldwide. Soon players in North America, South America, Japan, China, and the rest of the world, can play CASHFLOW® worldwide, simultaneously, and in their own languages. That is a realization of our dreams.

The Web and this electronic game helps us at CASHFLOW® Technologies, Inc. fulfill our mission which is to "Elevate the financial well-being of humanity." Electronic games to this point have been primarily for entertainment, have been competitive and many are incredibly violent. This new electronic game is the exact opposite. The electronic version of CASHFLOW® will promote education, cooperation, and living lives of prosperity. If you would like to participate in the launch of this world elevating event, assisting in teaching rich dad's lessons to the rest of the world, and meeting other people who think like you worldwide, visit our Web site, richdad.com and stay abreast of our progress.